Rick Steves' Europe Through the Back Door

Best of Europe
Tour Members' Handbook

Second Edition

Rick Steves' Europe Through the Back Door

Best of Europe
Tour Members' Handbook

Second Edition

©1996 Rick Steves' Europe Through the Back Door, Inc.

Written and researched by Rick Steves
Edited by Risa Laib and Rich Sorensen
Layout and design by Colleen Murphy
Maps by Dave Hoerlein

Published by Rick Steves' Europe Through the Back Door, Inc.
Printed in the USA by McNaughton & Gunn

Special thanks to Kendra Roth, Steve Smith and Dave Hoerlein for their help in
making this handbook possible.

John Muir Publications has generously allowed us to excerpt text and maps
from *Rick Steves' Europe* to make this book. For a copy of *Rick Steves' Europe*
($17.95, 544 pages, 1996, ISBN 1-56261-261-1), contact your local bookstore,
ETBD, or JMP (800/888-7504).

For a complete listing of Rick's guidebooks, see his Europe Through the Back
Door newsletter/catalog. To receive a free copy, write to:

Rick Steves' Europe Through the Back Door, Inc.
120 Fourth Avenue North, Box 2009
Edmonds, WA 98020 USA.
Tel. 206/771-8303, fax 206/771-0833

While every effort has been made to provide accurate and up-to-date information, the
author and publisher accept no responsibility for loss, injury, loose stools or inconve-
nience sustained by any person adventurous enough to use this book.

Contents

Dear Back Door Traveler,

Thank you for joining our Best of Europe tour program. For more than 15 years Europe Through the Back Door has organized and led this tour of Europe's most exciting and diverse 21 days and 3,000 miles. To help you enjoy maximum travel thrills per mile, minute and dollar, we've published this comprehensive tour handbook. Our goal is to give you the best of both worlds, mixing the efficiency and economy of group travel with the sense of adventure and discovery of doing Europe on your own.

This handbook is designed for members of our fully-guided tours as well as our less structured Bus, Bed & Breakfast tours. If you take full advantage of this handbook, your trip will be smoother, you'll learn more, and you'll expand your comfort zone, venturing out on your own to not only feel the pulse of today's Europe — but to rock with it.

A few years ago, I knew every traveler who took an ETBD tour. Now, with over 1,700 people a year joining our tours, that isn't possible. But I know you'll be in very good hands with your guide and assistant guide, or BB&B escort. And judging from all the happy tour surveys we get each year, I'm sure you're on your way to a great European adventure.

Thanks for touring with us.

Happy travels,

Rick Steves and the ETBD Team

How to use your Tour Handbook

Please bring this Tour Handbook with you to Europe!

Your comprehensive Tour Handbook is actually a Rick Steves guidebook tailored to fit your tour itinerary. It is divided into two sections:
- Pre-Trip Guide
- Sightseeing Guide

The Pre-Trip Guide: Please read the Pre-Trip Guide several weeks before your tour begins. It answers nearly every question you'll have before you leave for Europe. This section contains important, practical information on:
- Your daily schedule
- What your tour includes
- Items you'll get when your balance is paid
- Answers to common pre-trip questions
- Recommended reading and viewing
- What to pack
- Reserving your pre- and post-tour hotels
- Using telephones in Europe (including calling from the USA)

The Sightseeing Guide: While we also encourage you to read the much longer Sightseeing Guide before you leave for Europe, you'll mainly want to read it a chapter or two at a time as your tour progresses. You'll find the sightseeing information and maps especially valuable if you're on a less-structured Bus, Bed & Breakfast tour.

Sights are rated to help you prioritize:
▲▲▲ — Don't miss
▲▲ — Try hard to see
▲ — Worthwhile if you can make it
no rating — Worth knowing about

Why it's so detailed: For members of fully-guided tours, some of the day-by-day sightseeing information may seem too detailed, but BB&B tour members will appreciate the inclusion of optional sights, museum hours, tourist information sources, and other nitty-gritty. No matter which tour you're on, you'll enjoy taking advantage of the restaurant listings for the meals you'll have on your own.

Another reason for including so much in this book is that your sightseeing options will often be affected by weather, the day of the week, and the interests of your particular tour group. As a result, you

— and your tour guide/escort — will need to stay flexible. Having information covering all your possible options will help you get the most out of every day of your tour.

Reserving hotels: See page 29 of this handbook for important information regarding making pre- and post-tour hotel reservations.

Other questions? Chances are, most of your tour questions are answered in this book. After reading it, if you still have some questions, please feel free to give our Tour Desk a call at 206/771-8303 ext. 17. If you have more detailed questions such as those regarding your post-tour travel plans, please jot them down and send them (PO Box 2009, Edmonds, WA 98020) or fax them (206/771-0833) to our Tour Desk.

Rough Exchange Rates
(As of December 1995)

Country—Currency	Units per U.S. dollar	Approximate U.S. dollar value
Netherlands—guilder	1.7	.70
Germany—mark	1.4	.70
Austria—shilling	10	.10
Italy—lire	1600	1000 = .65
Switzerland—franc	1.2	.85
France—franc	5	.20

These rates are rough and rounded off. But they should be close enough for you to use as a guide while you travel in 1996.

Part 1: Pre-Trip Guide

Daily schedule for fully-guided tours

This schedule will help you plan for each day of your tour. It lists your likely activities for each day, how much time you'll be on the bus, and where you'll be sleeping. You'll find more detailed information in each day's chapter of this handbook. Please note that your actual sightseeing schedule will change according to your guide plans, the weather, your group's mood, and the fact that a few tours may spend a couple of nights in different locations. Each evening your guide will announce or post the next day's schedule and meal plan. (Bus, Bed & Breakfast tour members: please see the BB&B tour schedule on p. 13.)

Your tour schedule will look a lot like this:

Day 1: Arrive in Holland. By mid-day, you will find your room assignment already made at the Hotel Amadeus on the main square in Haarlem (30 minutes by train, bus or taxi from the Amsterdam airport or 20 minutes by train from downtown Amsterdam — see page 32). We'll do no organized sightseeing in Haarlem so do what you like on your own (several interesting sights are listed in this handbook). Plan on attending an informal group meeting at the hotel at 5:00 p.m. For specifics, your guide will post a note by the hotel desk by the afternoon of this day. Sleep in Haarlem.

Day 2: Amsterdam. We'll meet the bus after breakfast for the short drive into Amsterdam. Likely group activities include: Anne Frank's House, Beguinhof, canal boat orientation tour, Rijksmuseum. You may also have free time to see the Van Gogh Museum on your own. We'll return to Haarlem for an Indonesian dinner (included), sleep in Haarlem.

Day 3: To the Rhine. We'll work our way down to the Rhineland with a two-hour drive to Arnhem's folksy Dutch Open Air Museum and a five-hour drive to Germany's Rhineland. After dinner (included), we'll have a group orientation meeting. Sleep in Bacharach on the Rhine.

Day 4: The Rhineland. The mighty Rheinfels castle overlooking St. Goar will be our hiking destination today. We'll tour the castle, cruise the Rhine, and have free time to shop and browse or do some exploring on your own by foot or rental bike. Eat dinner (included) and sleep in Bacharach on the Rhine.

Day 5: To Rothenburg and Munich. After an early start and a four-hour drive, we'll have the afternoon free in Rothenburg, Germany's cutest medieval walled town. You may want to see Riemenschneider's altarpiece (the best wood-carving in Germany), walk the medieval wall, tour the medieval crime and punishment museum, or just shop 'til you drop. After a three-hour drive, we'll arrive in Munich in time for a late dinner (included) in a beerhall. Sleep in Munich, close to the pedestrian-friendly center.

Day 6: Munich. After a morning walking tour through the heart of Munich, you'll be on your own to explore the wonderful museums, streetlife, parks and markets of Germany's most entertaining and livable city. Sleep in Munich.

Day 7: To Austria. We'll leave Munich early for the short drive to tour the Dachau concentration camp. After this powerful pilgrimage, we'll drive three hours south, stopping at the Rococo Wies Church before heading into Austria and Reutte, our small-town Tirolean homebase. Eat dinner (included) and sleep in Reutte.

Day 8: Castle Day. We'll take a 30-minute drive to "Mad King" Ludwig's Neuschwanstein Castle. We'll tour the fairy tale castle, ride the luge (if open and if dry) and hike to the Ehrenburg ruins above our hometown of Reutte. Eat dinner (included) and sleep in Reutte.

Day 9: To Venice. A two-hour drive will take us to Innsbruck or Hall-in-Tirol for a short stop, then we'll drive five hours south to Venice. We'll leave the bus and ride a boat to our favorite medieval hotel near the historic Rialto bridge. After settling in, we'll take an evening orientation walk. Sleep in Venice.

Day 10: Venice. After a brief morning orientation and possible glass-blowing demo, you'll be free all day to tour St. Mark's, the Doges Palace, the great Accademia art gallery — or shop, explore the alleys, cruise the canals, and "crawl" the pubs. Sleep in Venice.

Day 11: All-day drive to Rome. After an eight-hour drive south, we'll check in to our Rome hotel, and get oriented with a hike across the eternal city with its floodlit ambiance. Sleep in Rome.

Day 12: Rome. Today we'll do the "Caesar Shuffle," visiting the essential ancient sights — Colosseum, Forum, and Pantheon. After a siesta, we'll visit St. Peter's, the greatest church in Christendom. We'll have plenty of time to climb to the top of Michelangelo's dome for a memorable view of the Vatican grounds and all of Rome at our feet. Sleep in Rome.

Day 13: Rome, Città, Florence. After a morning tour of the Vatican museum and the newly restored Sistine Chapel, we'll drive two hours north for a hike to Città di Bagnoregio (Italy's quintessential Back Door hill town), then drive another three hours to Florence. Sleep in Florence.

Day 14: Florence and the Cinque Terre. We'll spend much of today discovering Italy's treasure chest of art in Florence. An exciting "Renaissance Walk" will wind us through the historic core of town, taking us to the Uffizi Gallery and Michelangelo's David at the Accademia. Sample Italy's best gelato. In the afternoon, we'll drive four hours to the beaches of Italy's hidden Cinque Terre — five perfectly preserved fishing villages, surrounded by vineyards and the Mediterranean. To get there, we'll leave the bus in Levanto and take a 15-minute train ride to Vernazza. Sleep in Vernazza.

Day 15: The Cinque Terre. Ahh, today will be our vacation from our vacation. We couldn't see a museum here even if we wanted to! This is simply hard-core traditional Italy with nothing to do but hike through the vineyards that connect the five villages, hang out on the beaches, swim, or lounge around the town as if we lived here. Sleep in Vernazza.

Day 16: To the Alps. Today we'll catch an early train to Levanto, then drive nine hours into the heart of the Swiss Alps. After a stop in Interlaken, we'll ride the gondola into traffic-free Gimmelwald in time for dinner. Eat dinner (included) and sleep in Walter's creaky old chalet in Gimmelwald.

Day 17: The Alps. Pray for sunshine. If the weather is good, you may want to ride the gondola up to the Schilthorn for breakfast at 10,000 feet (not included, about $50), loiter around in the thin air, hike all or part way down, or just lay low and play Heidi. For more Alpine thrills, ride mountain trains and lifts and hike at the foot of the majestic Eiger and Jungfrau. Back at the chalet, Walter will have fondue waiting for the pre-dinner happy hour. Bad weather options include the Ballenberg open air museum, Trümmelbach falls, valley hikes, or just relaxing in Gimmelwald. Fondue and dinner are included. Sleep in Gimmelwald.

Day 18: To Beaune, France. Today we'll say, "Auf Wiedersehen" to the Alps and "Bonjour" to France. After breakfast, we'll ride the gondola back down into valley-floor reality, re-acquaint ourselves with our bus, and drive five hours to Beaune in Burgundy for a look at small-town France. There will be time for touring Beaune's medieval charity hospital, strolling the pedestrian streets in Beaune's medieval core, and dining on local specialties. Sleep in Beaune.

Day 19: To Paris. After breakfast, we'll make the four-hour drive into Paris. Our driver will give us a quick city orientation tour, drop us at our hotel and bid us "adieu" as he heads home for Belgium. Our hotel is in the characteristic Marais district, Paris' old Jewish quarter which is now quite chic. After check-in and a short rest, we'll have a Paris orientation and a hands-on lesson with Paris' great subway system, the Metro. Sleep in Paris.

Day 20: Paris. This day is a fitting finale for our tour. We'll visit Notre Dame and Ste-Chapelle, and get the most out of the newly renovated Louvre museum. Sleep in Paris.

Day 21: Tour over after breakfast. Paris has much more to offer and you'll be fully oriented to enjoy a few more days here if your travel plans allow. "Bonne chance!"

Note: These itinerary specifics are subject to change during your trip.

Fully-guided tour basics

Your fully-guided Best of Europe tour price includes:

◆ **An experienced Back Door guide and assistant,** trained by Rick Steves to make the art, history and culture of Europe come alive for you.

◆ **All group sightseeing tours and admissions,** with guided tours in most major stops: Amsterdam canal tour, Rijksmuseum, Anne Frank's house, Arnhem Open Air Museum, Rhine cruise, Rheinfels Castle, a local guided tour of Munich, visit to Dachau, a mountain luge ride (weather permitting), tour of Mad Ludwig's Neuschwanstein Castle, tour of the Uffizi Gallery and Michelangelo's David in Florence, Rome's Colosseum, Forum, Pantheon, St. Peter's Basilica and Vatican Museum, Paris' Louvre, Ste-Chapelle, and Notre Dame (specifics are, of course, subject to change).

◆ **20 nights of accommodations** in small, quaint, centrally-located hotels. While hotel rooms will nearly always be doubles, you may spend a few nights with more than one roommate. Your guide will work to make room assignments as fair as possible, but please understand that squeezing group travel through Europe's magical "back doors" has its limits, and memorable and characteristic hotels are, by definition, small.

◆ **All breakfasts and half your lunches and dinners.** This does not mean exactly two meals a day. On some days all three meals are included, and on some days only breakfast is included. Your guide will usually tell you a day in advance which meals you will be responsible for. You will always pay for your drinks with dinner, and any breakfast supplements you may order (breakfasts usually include coffee or tea with bread, butter and jam, and sometimes a little meat or cheese).

◆ **Bus connections** from the beginning of the tour in Haarlem to your arrival in Paris three weeks later.

◆ **All tips.** Your driver is well tipped by ETBD, with an additional bonus from ETBD based on your post-tour survey comments (we'll mail you a survey right after your tour). Likewise, your guide and assistant guide are fully paid by ETBD. Please do not tip beyond this. It is not necessary to tip the hotel staff.

◆ **Books.** *Mona Winks,* Rick Steves' *'3-in-1' French/Italian/German Phrase Book,* and this comprehensive *Tour Handbook.*

◆ **Cancellation coverage.** $2900 worth of tour interruption and cancellation coverage.

Daily schedule for Bus, Bed & Breakfast tours

This will give you a rough idea of how your days will be scheduled, and when you'll have blocks of free time for sightseeing. It is just an outline, and is subject to change. You'll find driving distances estimated in hours at the beginning of each "Day" chapter of the Sightseeing Guide. Each evening your BB&B escort will post a more specific schedule for the next day.

Day 1: Arrive in Holland. Meet at Hotel Amadeus in Haarlem (30 minutes by train, bus or taxi from the Amsterdam airport or 20 minutes by train from downtown Amsterdam — see page 32). Check in any time after 2:00 p.m. and plan on an informal group meeting with your escort in the hotel at 5:00 p.m. No bus today. Sleep in Haarlem.

Day 2: Amsterdam. No bus. See Amsterdam, an easy 20-minute train ride from Haarlem. Sleep in Haarlem.

Day 3: To the Rhine. Depart after breakfast on tour bus, see Arnhem Open Air Folk Museum (guided tour included, lunch on your own), depart mid-afternoon, arrive at hotel on the Rhine in time for dinner (included). Sleep in Bacharach on the Rhine.

Day 4: The Rhineland. No bus. Free day to explore by boat (included), bike or train. Included dinner, sleep in Bacharach on the Rhine.

Day 5: To Rothenburg and Munich. Bus departs after breakfast, early afternoon free in Rothenburg, late afternoon drive to Munich, check into hotel in town center. Sleep in Munich.

Day 6: Munich. No bus, free day. Sleep in Munich.

Day 7: To Austria. Depart after breakfast, late morning free to visit Dachau, drive to Wies Church on way to Austria, check into hotel in Austrian village of Reutte in time for dinner (included). Sleep in Reutte.

Day 8: Castle Day. Depart after breakfast, early morning tour of Neuschwanstein castle (included), late morning free, spend the afternoon with a ride on the luge (if open and dry), hiking to the ruined Ehrenberg castle, or strolling through Reutte, finish in time for dinner (included). Sleep in Reutte.

Day 9: To Venice. Depart after breakfast, drive all day to Venice with a break in Innsbruck or Hall, check into pension in Venice before dinner. Sleep in Venice.

Day 10: Venice. No bus, free day. Sleep in Venice.

Day 11: All-day drive to Rome. Depart after breakfast, drive all day to Rome, check into Rome hotel before dinner. Free evening in Rome. Sleep in Rome.

Day 12: Rome. No bus, free day. Sleep in Rome.

Day 13: Rome, Cività, Florence. Depart after breakfast, spend part of the afternoon exploring Cività and Bagnoregio, drive to Florence, evening free. Sleep in Florence.

Day 14: Florence and the Cinque Terre. Much of the day free in Florence. Then depart for Vernazza on the Cinque Terre. Sleep in Vernazza.

Day 15: The Cinque Terre. No bus, free day for fun in the sun on the Cinque Terre. Sleep in Vernazza.

Day 16: To the Alps. Depart before breakfast, drive north into, over and under the Alps, have a late afternoon stop in Interlaken, then check into Gimmelwald's Hotel Mittaghorn, where Walter will have your included dinner ready. Sleep in Gimmelwald.

Day 17: The Alps. No bus, free day in Alps. Included dinner. Sleep in Gimmelwald.

Day 18: To Beaune, France. Depart for France after breakfast, late afternoon check into Beaune hotel. Free time to tour Hotel Dieu (medieval hospital). Sleep in Beaune.

Day 19: To Paris. Depart after breakfast, spend bus time going over post-tour plans and questions with your escort, mid-afternoon check into hotel in Paris' Marais district, say "Au revoir" to bus. Reconfirm post-tour hotel plans upon arrival. Sleep in Paris.

Day 20: Paris: No bus, free day. Sleep in Paris.

Day 21: Tour over after breakfast. Check out of hotel (unless you've extended your reservation).
  Note: These itinerary specifics are subject to change during your trip.

Bus, Bed & Breakfast tour basics

Your 'BB&B' tour price includes:

◆ **An experienced BB&B escort,** able and eager to help you get the most out of your time in Europe.

◆ **20 nights of accommodations** in the same hotels as the fully-guided tours. Keep in mind that quaint hotels in central locations that can handle groups our size are rare indeed. While hotel rooms will nearly always be doubles, you may spend a few nights with more than one room-mate. Your escort will work to make room assignments as fair as possible, but please understand that squeezing group travel through Europe's magical "back doors" has its limits, and memorable and characteristic hotels are, by definition, small.

◆ **All breakfasts** (provided by hotels), and six dinners (dinners for two nights each in the Rhine, Reutte and Gimmelwald hotels). You will always pay for your drinks with dinner, and any breakfast supplements you may order (breakfasts usually include coffee or tea with bread, butter and jam, and sometimes a little meat or cheese).

◆ **Bus connections** for the schedule designed by your escort (a general outline appears on page 13). You'll be free to work your own sightseeing into the daily blocks of unstructured time that this schedule provides.

◆ **Bus driver/escort tips.** Your driver is well tipped by ETBD, with an additional bonus based on your post-tour survey comments (we'll mail you a survey right after your tour). Likewise, your BB&B escort is fully paid by ETBD. Please do not tip beyond this. It is not necessary to tip the hotel staff.

◆ **Books.** *Mona Winks,* Rick Steves' *'3-in-1' French/Italian/German Phrase Book,* and this comprehensive *Tour Handbook.* These books make your BB&B tour self-sufficient and efficient. Your *Tour Handbook* is your vital tour-guide-in-your-pocket for help on sightseeing options, using your time wisely, smart eating and shopping, public transportation tips, telephoning, and so on. *Mona Winks* is your museum tour guide. Mona lets Rick Steves and Gene Openshaw take you on easy and fun-to-follow tours of the essential cultural stops on this tour: Amsterdam (Rijks and Van Gogh museums), Venice (St. Mark's, Doges Palace, Accademia), Florence (Renaissance Walk, Uffizi, Bargello, David), Rome (Caesar shuffle, Colosseum, Forum, Pantheon, Vatican Museum, St. Peter's Basilica), and Paris (Louvre, Orsay, Pompidou Gallery of Modern Art, Versailles). And your *Phrase Book* will help you eat, drink and be merry in French, Italian and German.

◆ **The fruits of your kitty.** Your BB&B tour escort comes equipped with roughly $100 per person (included in your tour cost) to be used entirely as your escort feels is appropriate for the greater good. This works out to an average of about $5 a day per tour participant for things that nearly everybody will do, which are cheaper, easier, and faster if paid for as a group. Possible uses for your group kitty include: bus munchies, orange juice, a few picnics, tour parties, transportation connections to hotels inaccessible by bus (vaporetto to Venice hotel, train to Riviera hotel, and the Alpine lift to your Swiss chalet), sightseeing (such as the Dutch open air folk museum at Arnhem, Rhine cruise, Munich guided tour, and Neuschwanstein Castle), music for dinner at Walter's hotel, and the mountain luge ride in Austria. Your escort is free to use the group kitty in any way she/he thinks best serves the needs of the group (not individuals).

Items you'll get 60 days in advance

For fully-guided and BB&B tours:

Your tour balance is due 60 days before departure. To make sure you are properly equipped for your tour, we are including these items for free (sorry, but we cannot exchange any of these if you already have one or don't need yours). You will receive these items about 60 days before your tour departs.

Moneybelt: Every participant receives a moneybelt, and you are expected to wear it throughout the tour. In Europe, tourists rarely get mugged — but they often get their pockets picked and their purses snatched. We move fast and walk through some places teeming with highly-skilled pickpockets. Because our tour members always wear moneybelts, we've rarely had anyone lose a passport or plane ticket. If you do lose your trip documents, the tour cannot stop while you work on a replacement. As you can imagine, losing your valuables can turn into a major, time-consuming, expensive hassle. Each tour member (including each husband and each wife) needs to wear their own moneybelt containing their own passport and hotel list at all times.

French/Italian/German Phrase Book: This little book is your passport to connecting with the real Europe — its people. Although many of the locals you meet will know a little English, making an effort to communicate in their language is an important courtesy that often gets you a warmer reception. And in those cases when no one around speaks your language, your phrase book will be your hero, turning an awkward situation into a positive, memorable experience. Practice your phrase book's "survival phrases" for each language. Most Europeans think that American accents are cute.

Mona Winks: With 26 people in each group, with some museums prohibiting guided tours, and considering the way people's interest in art varies, we find that it's best for each participant to have the chapters from *Mona* that cover the great museums of our tour (the Van Gogh and Rijks museums in Amsterdam; the Accademia, St. Mark's and Doges Palace in Venice; the Renaissance Walk, Michelangelo's David, and Uffizi in Florence; Ancient Rome, the Vatican and St. Peter's in Rome; and the Louvre, Orsay, and Versailles in Paris). Grisly as it may sound, we recommend ripping *Mona* apart and taking along only the chapters (stapled into a small individual booklet) that apply to these places. This way you can read up on the museums before each visit, and in cases when your guide won't be leading you through personally, you'll have just as much information on your do-it-yourself tour, thanks to *Mona*.

Earplugs: We choose hotels in colorful older neighborhoods where night noises abound. Bring your earplugs along (included with your tour packet) for the rare night when you're more interested in sleep than nocturnal culture. They come in handy for bus naps and your guide's lectures on German economics, too.

Additional information:

Your tour roster and flight information: This may change a bit between now and your departure, but it should be fairly accurate. If any information on this roster is incorrect, please let us know.

Hotel list: Leave the larger version with your friends/family, and carry the smaller version with you inside your moneybelt. Remember, our buses have and will leave late tour members behind. If that happens to you, it is **your** responsibility to find your way to the next hotel, so this list may come in very handy.

Answers to common pre-trip questions...

How should I prepare for my trip? Your tour will be an intensive learning experience, as well as a physically active one. Those who prepare get much more out of their tour and their guide. Get in shape. You should be comfortable walking five miles per day, and climbing long, steep stairways. Do some reading between now and your departure (we suggest some good books and movies on page 23). Rick's all-day "History and Art for Travelers" class (taught several times a year and available on video through ETBD's newsletter) and his *Europe 101* book are both worthwhile. To use your time more efficiently on a BB&B tour, read all the sightseeing information in this handbook (and make many of your sightseeing decisions) well in advance of arriving in each city.

Will I need a passport, visas and shots? You must travel with a valid passport, so check to see that your passport will not expire before the end of your trip. There are no shots or visas required for your tour at this time.

How much luggage can I bring? You are limited to one carry-on sized bag (9"x22"x14"), which just happens to be the size of our recommended Back Door Bag convertible suitcase/rucksack ($75 from ETBD, including shipping). For packing tips, see page 25. What you haul home from Europe is up to you. (You can store souvenirs under the bus as you accumulate them during the tour.) Bring a small day bag to use while your big bag is stowed underneath the bus or back at your hotel. (ETBD's Civita Day Bag is ideal for this.)

What will the weather be like? It's tough to predict, but plan on some rain and cool nights. For any tour, Rome by day will be hot, and the Alps by night will be nippy. It gets dark and cool quite early in October. Pack as you would for a trip from Seattle to southern California in the month you're traveling.

Europe is a bit more colorful and festive in the summer, more relaxed and less touristy in the spring and fall. The climate chart on the following page should be helpful for packing decisions. This table lists average temperatures and days of no rain for each region we'll be visiting.

Climate Chart

	J	F	M	A	M	J	J	A	S	O	N	D
GERMANY	29	31	35	41	48	53	56	55	51	43	36	31
Frankfurt	37	42	49	58	67	72	75	74	67	56	45	39
	22	19	22	21	22	21	21	21	21	22	21	20
ITALY	39	39	42	46	55	60	64	64	61	53	46	41
Rome	54	56	62	68	74	82	88	88	83	73	63	56
	23	17	26	24	25	28	29	28	24	22	22	22
SWITZ.	29	30	35	41	48	55	58	57	52	44	37	31
Geneva	39	43	51	58	66	73	77	76	69	58	47	40
	20	19	21	19	19	19	22	21	20	20	19	21
FRANCE	32	34	36	41	47	52	55	55	50	44	38	33
Paris	42	45	52	60	67	73	76	75	69	59	49	43
	16	15	16	16	18	19	19	19	19	17	15	14

(All temperatures listed are in Fahrenheit. 1st line: average daily low. 2nd line: average daily high. 3rd line: rainless days per month)

When should I book my flights? It's up to you to arrange your flights to and from Europe 2 or 3 months before your departure. If you need a good travel agent, we can recommend one. Remember to reconfirm your flight three days before departure and to call to confirm the take-off time before leaving for the airport.

How will I meet the tour in Europe? This handbook includes a map and instructions on getting to our first hotel on the main square of Haarlem (see page 32). At 5:00 p.m. on the day that your tour starts, you'll meet your group at our hotel for an informal meeting. Look by the hotel desk for a posted update on your guide/escort's plans. Breakfast on the following morning is the first real scheduled group event.

How much spending money should I bring? During the course of your fully-guided tour, you will need to pay for about half your lunches and dinners, public transportation costs and entrance fees during your free time, alpine lift tickets during your free day in Switzerland ($20 to $100 depending upon how much exploring you do), and beverages at meal-times. Plan to bring $800 to $1,000 for your extra expenses during the tour.

If yours is a 'BB&B' tour (which provides fewer meals and less sightseeing), your extra expenses will be much higher. Figure on spending at least $1000 to cover $15 dinners, $5 lunches and roughly $20 per day in not-included sightseeing, drinks and shopping.

Traveler's checks vs. credit cards: which should I bring?: Traveler's checks in U.S. dollars are still the most dependable way to carry spending money (you'll change them into local cash along the way). Some European cash machines accept American banks's ATM cards, but by far the most reliable cards for these machines are Visa and MasterCard or Visa Debit cards (make sure you get a four-digit PIN number before you leave!). Every year more and more restaurants and shops in Europe accept credit cards for payment, but to be on the safe side, you should carry nearly all the extra funds you'll need in traveler's checks. (Also bring a couple of $20 bills.)

Why should I buy a cash pack? When you pay your tour balance, we recommend that you add $100 to the total to buy a foreign currency cash pack from us. Your cash pack gives you $100 worth of local starter money, spread between four or five countries. This is a time and money saver, since your group won't need to wait at each border while you stand in line to change money at a lousy rate. With your cash pack, you'll function easily until you can change money at a fair rate at a bank in the city the next day.

Dutch money is not included in your cash pack, but the Amsterdam airport's exchange desks (smack dab in the baggage claim area) have reasonable rates. When you get off the plane, change only what you'll need for Holland. Your fully-guided tour price includes most of your meals and sightseeing in the Netherlands, but there's plenty to buy, drink and snack on, so change about $50 per person to cover your 2 days with the tour here (more if you arrive a day or two early).

How can I keep in touch with the folks back home? If you want to receive mail during the tour, Walter's Hotel Mittaghorn in Switzerland is your most reliable address. Allow about ten days for letters from the USA to reach you at Walter's hotel. The handiest way for you to keep in touch with loved ones by phone is for you to call them, using your ATT, MCI, or SPRINT international calling card number from Europe. To get a card, just call your long-distance provider. This is easy and reasonably-priced (international access numbers for each country are listed on page 28 of this handbook). If you think someone from home will want to phone you during the tour, give them a copy of your hotel list — it includes dialing instructions and phone numbers for each tour hotel. On most days it will be best for you to get calls during breakfast, at about 7:30 a.m. European time. During most months our tours are nine hours ahead of Pacific time, so a person in Seattle calling at 10:30 p.m. Saturday will reach you at 7:30 a.m. Sunday in Europe. See the "Telephoning" section of this book for more details.

Can I mail gifts home? On ETBD tours we try to minimize the shopping focus that dominates other tours at the expense of sightseeing. But even with our tight security, shoppers do manage to infiltrate our groups. You can "deep store" purchases under the bus until the end of your tour or until your tour reaches the best places from which to mail items home. Surface mail takes a month, and a big box generally costs around $50 to ship.

What kind of camera should I bring? Your camera is the most likely thing to get lost, broken or stolen. A basic point-and-shoot model with a built-in flash is best for most people. Buy all the film you'll need and a new battery before you leave. A snapshot collection with post cards works fine for those doing scrapbooks. Bring an expensive camera only if you're a serious photographer. If you want to bring a video camera (which we do not encourage), please make it one of the smaller models. Our "Travels in Europe with Rick Steves" PBS-TV series videos include over six hours of prime-time-quality video covering your entire tour route and most of the sightseeing you'll do.

Will there be a bathroom on the bus? Yes.

Will there be music on the bus? Each bus has a good sound system, and your guide/escort will have some tapes to play. Feel free to bring a favorite tape to share with your group.

When should I make my pre- and post-tour plans? It can be difficult to find a room in Paris on short notice. **If you plan to stay in Paris longer than the two nights provided by the tour, you should book your post-tour Paris accommodations on your own a couple of months in advance** (this is especially important for groups that are followed immediately by another ETBD tour). We recommend you try the hotels listed in this handbook under the Day 21 chapter. For a change of scene, you may want to stay in the Rue Cler area — a great neighborhood near the Eiffel Tower (we prefer the Hotel Leveque). You can make a phone call or send a fax from the USA to reserve a room in Paris for less than $2 per minute (see "Telephoning" on page 27, and "Reserving...hotels" on page 29 of this handbook). Many hotels have someone who speaks English, and will take your credit card number for a deposit to cover your first night. **See p. 38-39 for a list of pre-tour Haarlem hotels.**

Recommended reading & viewing

Recommended readings from Rick Steves and Gene Openshaw's *Europe 101* and *Mona Winks:*

◆ **Netherlands: Europe 101** chapters on the Northern Renaissance and Reformation, Art patronage, and Symbols in Art. **Mona Winks** chapters on the Rijksmuseum and Van Gogh museum.

◆ **Italy: Europe 101** chapters on Ancient Rome, Italian Renaissance, and the Age of Nationalism (Italian Unification). **Mona Winks** chapters on Venice, Florence and Rome.

◆ **Germany: Europe 101** chapters on medieval lifestyles, castles, feudalism, Romanticism, the unification of Germany, and our turbulent 20th century.

◆ **Switzerland and France: Europe 101** chapters on the Enlightenment, Revolution, Napoleon, Neo-Classicism. **Mona Winks** chapters on Paris.

Other books and films we recommend (* = both book and movie):
◆ **Netherlands: Lust for Life*** (Stone) takes you into the artistic but troubled world of Van Gogh. An understanding of how chapters of his tumultuous life shaped his art will make your trip to Amsterdam's Van Gogh Museum even more interesting. **Vincent and Theo,** a Robert Altman film which focuses on the emotional relationship between the two Van Gogh brothers, is also worthwhile. **Anne Frank, the Diary of a Young Girl*** (you'll be touring her house in Amsterdam on fully-guided tours) and **The Hiding Place*** (you can tour this house above a clock shop in Haarlem, two blocks from our first hotel) are each inspirational books and films of Jewish families hiding out during the Nazi occupation. **Soldier of Orange** (film) offers a thrilling look at the Dutch resistance in WWII.

◆ **Germany: Inside the Third Reich*** is the most intimate account of the Third Reich by Hitler's close friend and architect, Albert Speer. It's great reading. The TV mini-series is also good.

◆ **Italy:** Mary McCarthy studies Venice and Florence in two travel writing classics: **Venice Observed** and **Stones of Florence**. Irving Stone's **The Agony and the Ecstasy*** (offering a great look at Michelangelo, the Medici family, Savonarola and Florence during the Renaissance) is a must for any art and history buff heading for Florence. The movie features Charlton Heston and Rex Harrison. **Lives of the Artists** (Vasari) is a collection of stories by a Florentine architect/painter/sculptor/author who was a contemporary of many of the great Renaissance artists. This oft-quoted book forms the basis of much of what we know about the period. **The Italians** (Barzini) is full of opinionated insights into work-a-day Italy by this famous journalist. **That Fine Italian Hand** (Hoffman) is a good read offering a look at contemporary Italian life.

   The Name of the Rose* (Umberto Eco), a Sherlock Holmes-style murder mystery, gives a great look at monastic life, theological/political corruption in 14th-century Italy, and how the church effectively kept secular knowledge locked up and literally in the attic. The film version starring Sean Connery is quite gritty.

♦ **France: Les Miserables*** (Hugo) a classic novel, a powerful film, and a stirring play, hurls you mercilessly into the Parisian barricades of 1848 and has you shouting "Vive la revolution!" **Is Paris Burning?*** is a gripping account of the events surrounding the German evacuation of Paris in 1944, and Hitler's order that the city be destroyed. The film version is a thriller. For a friendly, warm look at small-town France, read Peter Mayle's **A Year in Provence** and **Toujours Provence**. Victor Hugo's **Hunchback of Notre Dame** gives an endearing look at one of Paris' most enduring monuments. **A Distant Mirror** (Tuchman) is a long but readable account of French life and the exploits of the nobility during the Middle Ages.

♦ **General Europe:** In his two books **The Winds of War** and **War and Remembrance**, Herman Wouk makes history palatable to non-history buffs as he intertwines the 2,500-page saga of the fictionalized Henry family with the very real events of WWII. **Innocents Abroad** is Mark Twain's entertaining story of an American group's "Grand Tour" through Europe and the Holy Land. **Civilisation** (Clarke) is a BBC-TV series and a book that teaches European art and civilization like nothing else. It's great. **Connections** (Burke) is a fascinating book and TV series that links historical events and scientific discoveries across the centuries. If the Normans didn't have better stirrups, we'd be speaking French. Warning: "Connections" turns plumbers into history buffs.

   Travels in Europe (Rick Steves) - The first 13-part PBS-TV series traces your tour route, and gives you an insightful look at what you'll see. By buying the tapes of this 6.5 hour PBS series (available from ETBD on 5 videotapes for $25 ea. — or tape the reruns with your VCR at home for free), you can have a prime-time-quality video version of your tour.

Packing

Each tour member is allowed to take only one carry-on size bag (9"x 22" x 14"). To many, packing this light is a radical concept. But every year several hundred travelers manage wonderfully on our tours with one carry-on size bag — usually our $75 Back Door Bag convertible suitcase/rucksack. European stairways, alleys, and paths are not like airport corridors. If you bring a bag with wheels, you may love it half the time, but you'll find it a nuisance the other half. We don't recommend them.

Give your travel bag a short workout before you leave. Carry it (packed) on a walk through your neighborhood to see how you'll get along overseas. . . then lay out the items again and see what you can live without.

Our tour members learn in Europe that they manage better with less stuff. No one has ever told us, "Oh, I wish I'd brought more with me." We travel very casually. While you'll want to avoid looking too scruffy, there's no need to go out and buy new clothing and shoes (in fact, relying on shoes that aren't well-broken-in can ruin a trip). Bring **comfortable clothes** that you can wash in a sink and dry overnight indoors (give them a test "wring and dry" before leaving home).

You should also bring a small day bag for your Tour Handbook, sweater, camera, and other daily needs ($20 from ETBD). This type of bag is more practical and safer from theft than a purse or fanny pack. Pickpockets love fanny packs.

Suggested take-alongs:

- ♦ **2 long-sleeve blouses/shirts**.
- ♦ **2 short-sleeve shirts/T-shirts**.
- ♦ **Wool sweater/sweatshirt** (lighter cotton is fine for mid-summer).
- ♦ **2 pairs of long pants**, 1 very lightweight (summer tours), 1 medium.
- ♦ **1 pair of shorts**.
- ♦ **1 skirt** or culottes (better than a dress for access to your moneybelt).
- ♦ **Bathing suit**.
- ♦ **Jacket**. Should be lightweight and water-repellent (Gore-Tex is perfect, can be layered with sweater for warmth).
- ♦ **5 pairs of socks**, made of light, quick-drying material.
- ♦ **5 pairs of underwear**.
- ♦ **Walking shoes** that are sturdy, comfortable and well-broken-in (quality running shoes or Vibram soles are great). If you bring a second pair, make them lightweight, like sandals.
- ♦ **Day bag**, small/lightweight (ETBD's $20 Civita Day Bag works well).
- ♦ **Traveler's checks** in US dollars (a mix of $50 and $100 checks), one

credit card, plus a few $20 US bills in cash (due to counterfeiting problems, some banks and change offices won't accept $100 US bills).

◆ **Moneybelt**. Required, free with tour.

◆ **Small flashlight**.

◆ **Travel alarm clock, wristwatch** (the bus waits for no one...).

◆ **Camera and film**. It's easier and cheaper to bring film from home. Ten rolls of 36 shots is normally plenty for a one-month trip. Airport x-ray machines really are "film safe." Lead-lined x-ray bags are not necessary. Put in a new battery before leaving.

◆ **Small sewing kit**.

◆ **Toiletries kit. ETBD's $26 Tirolean Toiletries Kit** includes a sewing kit, tiny scissors, five empty squeeze bottles, toothbrush case, pill bottles, dipey wipes, and a mirror.

◆ **Soap** for your body, your hair, and your clothes (you can buy in small tubes), best kept in small, sturdy squeeze bottles (inside a ziplock baggie for the flight).

◆ **Small towel** (some hotels run short, others provide teeny-tiny towels), wash cloth.

◆ **Address list** (on gummy labels saves time).

◆ **2nd pair of glasses + prescription.** If you wear contacts, also bring glasses and your lens prescription.

◆ **Medicine** in original bottle, or with label. For important medication, bring a **written prescription** from your doctor in case you lose it.

◆ **Cold remedies** (colds spread quickly on tours).

◆ **Ear plugs**, free with tour.

◆ **Ziplock bags**, handy for lots of uses.

◆ **Books:** This **Tour Handbook**, your **Phrase Book**, and appropriate chapters from **Mona Winks.**

Optional bring-alongs:

◆ **Compact umbrella.**

◆ **Swiss Army knife** (w/corkscrew will make you popular at picnics).

◆ **Journal notebook, pens.**

◆ **Trashy novel, small travel game**, or **Walkman**.

◆ **Tapes** of your favorite music (we'll have other tapes on the bus).

◆ **Postcards** and pictures of home to show your European friends.

◆ **Hair dryer.**

Suggested leave-at-homes:

◆ **Expensive jewelry.**

◆ **Strong perfume or aftershave** (bad on bus).

◆ **Electrical appliances** (curling irons, shavers, etc).

◆ **Fanny/waist packs** (can cause pickpocket feeding frenzies).

Telephoning

The key to using phones is understanding the various access codes and area codes, plus having the right coins, local phone card, or international calling card from AT&T, MCI or SPRINT. European hotel room phones are reasonable for local calls, but a terrible rip-off for long-distance calls. Never call home from your hotel room (unless you are using an international calling card).

Calling Direct: To call beyond the borders of any country, you first must dial the "international access code" of the country you are in (011 from the USA, 00 from the Netherlands, Germany, Italy, Switzerland, or Austria, 19 from France). Once you hear the new dial tone, you should then dial the "country code" of the country you are trying to reach (1 to the USA, 31 to the Netherlands, 49 to Germany, 39 to Italy, 41 to Switzerland, 43 to Austria, 33 to France). Then dial the local area code (if it starts with a zero, don't dial the zero), and finally the local phone number. For example, to call the Haarlem's Hotel Amadeus from the USA, you would dial 011 (USA int'l access code), 31 (Netherlands country code), 23 (Haarlem area code without the zero), 532-2328 (local number). To call the Hotel Leveque in Paris from the USA, you would dial 011 (USA int'l access code), 33 (France country code), 1 (Paris area code), 47-05-49-15 (local number).

When dialing long distance within a country, start with the area code (including its zero), then the local number. In Europe it's typical for each town to have its own area code.

Phone cards, metered phones, or coins: Some pay phones in Europe still accept coins, but most require phone cards. Each country has its own local phone card you buy for a set price (usually at a post office, newsstand, or street kiosk). You then slide it into a pay phone, and it keeps working until you've used up that amount in charges (to keep track of this, each card contains either a magnetic strip or a wee computer chip). When you hang up, push a button on the phone to spit out your card so you can use it for future calls. These cards are handy for calls within Europe, but for calls to the USA they get used up fast. As an alternative, some post offices have metered long distance phone booths. The person at the counter assigns you a booth, you do your own dialing, and then pay the person at the counter when you're finished. If you're calling from a coin-operated phone, be prepared to feed coins quickly, and don't be surprised if you get cut off without warning.

International calling cards: These offer a great, affordable way to call home. You simply dial the local AT&T, MCI or SPRINT number for the country you're calling from, give the English-speaking operator your calling card number and the phone number in the USA you want to reach, and voilà, you're in. (To get a dial tone you may need to insert a coin or local phone card, but you should get it back at the end of your call. Do not stick your American calling card into the phone.) Even though a $3 hook-up fee will appear on your next long-distance bill, the cheaper minute-to-minute rate makes any call over 3 minutes a good deal. Just be sure you get an international calling card from your long distance carrier before you leave home. (Getting an answering machine is a $5 mistake. To avoid this, first make a quick call with a coin or phone card to see if someone is home.)

An even cheaper way to communicate is to have a friend call you from home (especially since they're paying). Although your tour schedule will vary from day to day, you are most likely to be reached at your hotel during breakfast, at around 7:30 a.m. European time.

USA international calling card numbers

Country	ATT	MCI	SPRINT
Netherlands	06-022-9111	06-022-9122	06-022-9119
Germany	0130-0010	0130-0012	0130-0013
Austria	022-903-011	022-903-012	022-903-014
Italy	172-1011	172-1022	172-1877
Switzerland	155-00-11	155-02-22	155-97-77
France	19 (tone) 00-11	19 (tone) 00-19	19 (tone) 00-87

For Direct Dialing

International access codes (dial first when calling from...):

USA:	011	Canada:	011	France:	19
Belgium:	00	Germany:	00	Italy:	00
Netherlands:	00	Switzerland:	00	Austria:	00
Great Britain:	00				

Country codes (dial next when calling to...):

USA:	1	Canada:	1	France:	33
Belgium:	32	Germany:	49	Italy:	39
Netherlands:	31	Switzerland:	41	Austria:	43
Great Britain:	44				

Reserving pre- and post-tour hotels

Most people who take our tours either arrive in Holland a few days early, or remain in Paris for a few days after the tour ends. If you plan to do either, or both, please read the information on Haarlem hotels (pgs. 33 & 38) and Paris hotels (p. 190) right away, and **make your hotel reservations a couple of months before your tour begins**. You'll find instructions for faxing hotels on the following page, and for telephoning in the "Telephoning" section.

Probable tour hotel list

Please note that you will get a complete and accurate hotel listing with your tour packet. For your convenience, we have included the probable listing of the hotels you'll have during your tour. Tours often vary slightly from this list. (SE = speaks English, NSE = no speaka da Engleesh.)

Nights 1 and 2: Holland
Hotel Amadeus
(Dave and Mike - SE)
Grote Markt 10
2011 RD Haarlem
Netherlands
tel. 31/23/532-4530
fax 31/23/532-2328

Nights 3 and 4: Rhineland
Hotel Kranenturm
(Kurt, Fatima - SE)
Langstrasse 30
55422 Bacharach, Germany
tel. 49/6743/1021

Nights 5 and 6: Munich
Hotel Munchner Kindl
(Staff - NSE)
Damenstiftstrasse 16
8000 Munich 2, Germany
tel. 49/89/26/4349
fax: 49/89/26/4526

Nights 7 and 8: Tirol
Hotel Schluxenhof
(Herbert - SE)
A-6600 Pinswang-Reutte, Austria
tel. 43/5677/8903

Nights 9 and 10: Venice
Albergo Guerrato
(Piero, Roberto - SE)
Calle Drio la Scimia 240a, Rialto
30100 Venice, Italy
tel. and fax 39/41/528-5927

Nights 11 and 12: Rome
Pension Alimandi
(Paolo, Rico - SE)
Via Tunisi 8
00192 Roma, Italy
tel. 39/6/397-23941, 26300, or 23948
fax 39/6/397-23943

Night 13: Florence
Hotel Universo
(Staff - SE)
20 Piazza S.M. Novella
50123 Florence
tel. 39/55/211-484 or 281-951
fax 39/55/292-335

Nights 14 and 15: Cinque Terre
Trattoria Gianni Franzi
(Franzi family - NSE)
19018 Vernazza, Italy
tel. 39/187/812228

Nights 16 and 17: Alps
Hotel Mittaghorn
(Walter - SE)
CH-3826 Gimmelwald (Bern), Switzerland
tel. 41/36/551658

Night 18: Burgundy
Hotel Grand St. Jean
(Mr. Neaux, son - SE
Mr. Neaux, father - NSE)
18 Place Madeleine
21200 Beaune, France
tel. 33/80 24 12 22,
fax 33/80 24 15 43

Nights 19 and 20: Paris
Castex Hotel
(the son, Blaize - SE)
5 rue Castex
75004 Paris, France
tel. 33/1/42 72 31 52
fax 33/1/42 72 57 91

Faxing your hotel reservation

Most hotel managers know basic "hotel English." Faxing is the preferred method for reserving a room. It's more accurate and cheaper than telephoning and much faster than writing a letter. Use this handy form for your fax. Photocopy and fax away.

One page fax

To: _____ @ _____
                          hotel   **fax**

From: _____ @ _____
                          name   **fax**

Today's date: _____ / _____ / _____
                          day   month   year

Dear Hotel _____,
Please make this reservation for me:

Name: _____

Total # of people: _____ # of rooms: _____ # of nights: _____

Arriving: _____ / _____ / _____   My time of arrival (24-hr clock): _____
                   day   month   year   (I will telephone if later)

Departing:_____ / _____ / _____
                   day   month   year

Room(s): Single_____ Double_____ Twin_____ Triple_____ Quad_____
With: Toilet_____ Shower_____ Bath_____ Sink only_____
Special needs: View_____   Quiet_____   Cheapest room_____

Credit card: Visa_____ Mastercard_____ Amex_____

Card #: _____ Exp. date: _____

Name on card: _____

You may charge me for the first night as a deposit. Please fax me confirmation of my reservation, along with the type of room reserved, the price, and whether the price includes breakfast. Thank you.

Signature: _____

Name:_____

Address:_____

City:_____ State:_____ Zip code:_____

Country:_____

Part 2: Sightseeing Guide

Day 1: Arrive in Holland

You'll find your room assignment already made at the Hotel Amadeus on the main square in Haarlem. Your tour will do no organized sightseeing in Haarlem, so do what you like on your own (several interesting sights are listed below). Your guide/escort will host an informal group meeting at the hotel at 5:00 p.m. Look for a note posted near the hotel desk for any updates.

Likely activities today...
Hotel check-in*
Informal group meeting at 5:00 p.m.*

---

*Note: Throughout this book, an activity listed with a * indicates that it is included as an activity on BB&B tours, too.*

Today you may walk about half a mile from the station to the hotel with your bag (unless you take a taxi), and sleep in Haarlem.

Getting to Haarlem
Your tour will start at the Hotel Amadeus on Haarlem's main square (Grote Markt). Haarlem is a short 30-minute bus or train ride from Amsterdam's Schiphol Airport. Change $50 per person into Dutch guilders at the bank window right in the baggage area (open daily 6:00-24:00). Then go through customs and enter the main lobby of the airport, where you'll see signs directing you to trains, taxis, and tourist information. Most Dutch people speak English and will gladly point you in the right direction.

The **express buses 236, 302,** and **362** are fast (20 min.), run twice hourly, and cost f9. Head straight outside the lobby 20 yards until you see several bus stops, and look for one of these buses or ask someone for the "express bus" to Haarlem. **Taxi** rides to Haarlem take about 20 minutes and cost f70.

Trains run twice hourly from the airport to Haarlem, with one change, either in Amsterdam's CS (central station) or the more direct suburban station of Sloterdijk. Either route takes about 30 minutes and costs f10 ($7). From the airport lobby, follow the signs that say "To Trains." Buy a one-way ticket to Haarlem and follow signs to the proper track.

Buses and trains all arrive at the Haarlem Station, about a 15-minute walk or short taxi ride (f10) to the hotel on Grote Markt.

Your room will be assigned and ready for you at the Hotel Amadeus by around 2:00 p.m. If you arrive earlier than 2:00 p.m., leave your luggage at the reception desk, do some sightseeing, and check in later.

Your guide/escort will schedule an informal group meeting for 5:00 p.m. — look for an update posted near the hotel desk.

Reserving a room: If you'd like to stay at the Hotel Amadeus for a night or two before the tour begins, plan on calling or faxing them a couple of months in advance. We schedule our tours to run back-to-back, so the Amadeus may be filled with another ETBD tour group. If you can't get into the Amadeus early, relax. We've included information on other Haarlem hotels and B&Bs below, under "Sleeping in Haarlem."

THE NETHERLANDS

■ 13,000 square miles (the size of Maryland).
■ 15 million people (1,150 per square mile, 15 times the population density of the U.S.).
■ 1 guilder = about 70 cents.

The Netherlands, Europe's most densely populated country, is also one of its wealthiest and best organized. Efficiency is a local custom. The average income is higher than America's. Though only eight percent of the labor force are farmers, they cultivate seventy percent of the land, and you'll travel through vast fields of barley, wheat, sugar beets, potatoes, and flowers.

Holland is the largest of 12 states that make up the Netherlands. A generation ago, Belgium, the Netherlands, and Luxembourg formed the nucleus of a united Europe when they joined economically to form Benelux.

The word "Netherlands" means "low lands." Half the country is below sea-level, reclaimed from the sea (or rivers). That's why the locals say, "God made the Earth, but the Dutch made Holland." Modern technology and plenty of Dutch elbow grease are turning more and more of the sea into fertile farmland. In fact, a new 12th state—Flevoland, near Amsterdam—has recently been drained, dried, and peopled.

The Dutch generally speak English, pride themselves on their frankness, and like to split the bill. Traditionally, Dutch cities have been open-minded, loose, and liberal (to attract sailors in the days of Henry Hudson), but they are now paying the price of this easygoing style. Amsterdam has become a bit seedy for many travelers' tastes, so we enjoy more sedate Dutch evenings by sleeping in a smaller town nearby and day-tripping into the big city.

The Dutch guilder (written as "f" for its older name, florin) is divided into 100 cents (c). There are about f1.50 in a U.S. dollar (f1.50 = $1). To find prices in dollars, simply cut the price in guilders by a third (e.g., f60 = $40). The colorful Dutch money has Braille markings and classy watermarks.

Benelux: Belgium, Netherlands, Luxembourg

The country is so small, level, and well covered by trains and buses that transportation is a snap. Major cities are connected by speedy trains that come and go every 10 or 15 minutes. Connections are excellent, and you'll rarely wait more than a few minutes. Round-trip tickets are discounted. Buses take you where trains don't, and bicycles take you where buses don't. Bus stations and bike rental places cluster around train stations. The national bus system (both within and between cities) runs on a uniform "strip card" system. You can buy various strip cards on the bus or more cheaply (15-strip cards, f11) at train stations, post offices, and some tobacco shops. If you're caught riding without a card, you have to take off your clothes.

The Netherlands is a biker's dream. The Dutch, who average four bikes per family, have put small bike roads (with their own traffic lights) beside every big auto route. You can rent bikes at most train stations and drop them off at most other stations. (You can take bikes on trains, outside of rush hour, for f9.)

Shops are open weekdays from 9:00 to 18:00 (21:00 on Thursdays), but are generally closed from mid-afternoon Saturday through Monday noon. Sundays are very quiet in Holland.

The best "Dutch" food is Indonesian (from the former colony). Find any Indisch restaurant and experience a *rijsttafel* (rice table). With as many as thirty spicy dishes, a rijsttafel can be split and still fill two hungry tourists. *Nasi rames* is a cheaper mini-version of a rijsttafel. Local taste treats are cheese, pancakes (*pannekoeken*), Dutch gin (jenever, pronounced: "ya nayver" know what hit you), light Pilsner beer, and "syrup waffles" (*stroopwafel*). Yogurt in Holland (and throughout Northern Europe) is delicious and drinkable right out of its plastic container. Broodjes are sandwiches of fresh bread and delicious cheese—cheap at snack bars, delis, and broodje restaurants. For cheap fast food, try a Middle Eastern shwarma, roasted lamb in pita bread. Breakfasts are big by continental standards. Lunch and dinner are served at American times.

Experiences you owe your tongue in Holland: a raw herring (outdoor herring stands are all over), a slow coffee in a cozy "brown café," or a smooth, old jenever with a new friend, and a hearty rijsttafel dinner (planned for Day 2 of your tour).

Netherlands nitty-gritty

Country code (to dial the Netherlands from another country): 31
International access (to dial another country from Netherlands): 00
MCI: 06-022-9122
ATT: 06-022-9111
SPRINT: 06-022-9119
Emergency: 0611
Assistance calling USA: 06 04 10
Public telephones are green. Some only take Dutch phone cards, some only take coins (f1 or 25-cent coins). Telephone cards are for sale at tourist information and post offices, train stations, and tobacco shops for f5, f10 or f20.
Senior/youth discount age: 65+
Bank hours: 9:00-17:00, M-F. Visa cash advance at train station banks. Later-hour banks at train station and PTT (post office).

Haarlem

Cute, cozy yet real, handy to the airport, and just 20 minutes by train from downtown Amsterdam, Haarlem is a fine home base, giving you small-town, overnight warmth with easy access to wild and crazy Amsterdam.

Haarlem is a busy Dutch market town buzzing with shoppers biking home with fresh bouquets. Enjoy Saturday and Monday market days when the square bustles like a Breughel painting with cheese, fish, flowers, and families. You'll feel comfortable here. Buy some flowers to brighten your hotel room.

The following information will be especially valuable if you plan to arrive in Haarlem a day or two before the tour begins.

Tourist Information: Haarlem's VVV (tourist info) just outside the train station, is friendlier, more helpful and less crowded than Amsterdam's. Ask your Haarlem and Amsterdam questions here.

Trains: Direct to Amsterdam (20 minutes, 6/hour, f10 return); Delft; Schiphol Airport (one easy change at Sloterdijk).

Biking: The train station rents bikes cheap and easy (f5 for 4 hours, f8 per day, f100 or other cash equivalent deposit, open daily 6:00-24:00).

Sights—Haarlem

▲▲**Frans Hals Museum**—Haarlem is the hometown of Frans Hals, and this excellent museum displays several of his greatest paintings in a glorious old building (f7.50, Monday-Saturday 11:00-17:00, Sunday 13:00-17:00). The museum across the street features the architecture of old Haarlem.

Corrie Ten Boom House—As many Americans, but few Dutch, know, Haarlem is also home to Corrie Ten Boom (popularized by The Hiding Place, an inspirational book and movie about the Ten Boom family's experience hiding Jews from the Nazis). The Ten Boom House, at 19 Barteljorisstraat, is open for English tours (Tuesday-Saturday 10:00-16:00, donation requested).

Grote Kerk (church)—You'll see (and maybe hear) Holland's greatest pipe organ (regular free concerts, summer Tuesdays at 20:15, some Thursdays at 15:00, TI office has schedule). The church is open and worth a look if only to see its Oz-like organ (Monday-Saturday 10:00-16:00).

▲**Teylers Museum**, famous as the oldest museum in Holland, is interesting as a look at a 200-year-old museum. The dusty exhibits are diverse but nothing earth-shaking (f7.50, Tuesday-Saturday 10:00-17:00, Sunday 13:00-17:00).

Red Lights—For a little red-light district cute as a Barbie shop, wander around the church in Haarlem's cutest Begijnhof (two blocks northeast of the church, off Lange Begijnestraat, f50, no senior or student dis-

Haarlem

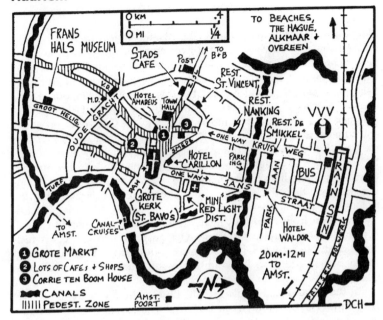

counts). Don't miss the mall marked by the red neon sign, t'Steegje. The nearby t'Poortje, "office park," costs f7.50.

Nightlife in Haarlem

Haarlem's evening scene is great. The bars around the Grote Kerk (church) and along Lange Veerstraat are colorful, lively, and full of music. The **Studio** (next to the Hotel Carillon), jammed with Haarlem's thirty-something crowd, has a pleasant ambience. **Café Brinkman**, on the square, is a good people-watching perch. **Café 1900** (across from the Corrie Ten Boom House) is classy by day and draws a young crowd with live music on Sunday nights. Lange Veerstraat behind the church is probably the best bar street in town. The **Crack** (32 Lange Veerstraat) is the wild place to go to find leather-clad bikers, loud music and smoking. Pot is legally served across the street at **High Times**. The **Imperial Café and Bar** (next to the Crack) has live jazz on Sundays and Thursdays. For live jazz on Thursdays, Fridays, Saturdays, and Sundays, visit the **Haarlem Jazz Club** near the Frans Hals Museum.

Don't be shocked if locals drop into a bar, plunk down f25 for a baggie of marijuana, and casually roll a joint. (If you don't like the smell of pot, avoid "coffee shops" sporting Rastafarian yellow, red and green colors, wildly painted walls, or plants in the windows.) Holland is an easygoing, love-yourself-as-you-love-jenever kind of place.

Sleeping in Haarlem (f1 = about 70 cents, tel. code: 023)

Let's assume you'll arrive a night or two before the tour begins, so you'll need to find a room on your own. No problem, provided you reserve a couple of months in advance. Haarlem is most crowded in April, on Easter weekend, May, and August, but if you phone ahead, our recommended hotels will happily hold a room without a deposit (though they may ask for a credit card number). Nearly every Dutch person you'll encounter speaks English. We've listed our favorite places below. From the USA, first dial 011 (international access code) , then 31 (Dutch country code), then 23 (Haarlem area code), then the phone or fax number listed. If you're calling from Amsterdam or Schiphol Airport, start dialing with 023, then the number listed. From within Haarlem, skip the 023 and dial the number directly.

Prices are from 1995. They include breakfast unless otherwise noted. **S** = single, **D** = double, **T** = triple, **Q** = quad, **B** = bath, **CC** = which credit cards are accepted. (If CC doesn't appear in a listing, you'll need to pay cash in guilders.) To avoid this town's louder than normal street noises, forego views for a room in the back.

If the places listed below are filled by the time you try to reserve, the helpful Haarlem tourist office ("VVV" at the train station, Monday-Saturday, 9:00-17:30, f1/minute, tel. 06/320-24-043) can nearly always find you a f30 bed in a nearby private home (for a f9 per person fee plus a cut of the hotel's money).

Hotel Amadeus is where you'll stay once the tour begins. It has 15 small, bright rooms, all with simple modern furnishings, TV, private shower, and toilet. Some rooms have views of the square. This hotel, ideally located above an Italian restaurant in a characteristic building on the market square, is relatively quiet and has an elevator. The lush old lobby is on the second floor in a "pianola bar" (SB-f85, DB-f110, TB-f150, nicer rooms cost a little more, CC:VMA, seconds-on-everything-welcome buffet breakfast, kid-friendly, a 12-minute walk from train station, brothers Dave and Mike run the place for their family, Grote Markt 10, 2011 RD Haarlem, tel. 532 4530, fax 532 2328, e-mail: amadeus@euronet.nl, use credit card to secure reservations).

Hotel Carillon, also right on the town square, has ste-e-e-p stairs. Its location is ideal, many of its well-worn rooms small, and front rooms come with great town square views and lots of street noise (22 rooms, tiny loft singles-f52.50, DB-f115, TB-f160, CC:VMA, no elevator, 12-minute walk from train station, Grote Markt 27, 2011-RC Haarlem, tel. 531 0591, fax 531 4909).

The rollicking **Stads Café** has big, bright, and cheery rooms, most

Day 1: Arrive in Holland

with TV and solid modern wood furniture. Its restaurant hops at night (see Eating below), but most of its rooms are in the back and quiet (13 rooms, S-f50, D-f75, DB-f100, TB-f130, QB-f160, plus f2 per day per person tax, breakfast f9, CC:VMA, Zijlstraat 56-58, 2012-TP Haarlem, two blocks off the marketplace, tel. 532 5202, fax 532 0504).

Hotel Joops is an innovative concept. A well-organized central office just behind the church in the town center administers a corral of apartments and rooms (all within two blocks of the church). They have bright and spacious rooms (S-f37.50, D-f75, T-f110) and elegant full-furnished apartments with kitchen facilities and the lived-in works (D-f125, Q-f165 to f190, 6-bed apartments-f235, rates are 30% cheaper mid-September to March, tel. 532 2008, fax 532 9549, office at Oude Groenmarkt 12).

Bed and Breakfast Hans de Kiefte, your cozy, get-into-a-local home budget option, epitomizes the goodness of B&Bs. Marjet (mar-yet) and Hans, a young couple who speak fluent American, rent 4 bright and cheery no-smoking rooms (with a hearty breakfast and plenty of travel advice) in their 100-year-old home on a quiet neighborhood street (5-minute walk from the center, minimum 2 nights, S-f40, SB-f65, DB-f80, TB-f115, QB-f150, 5B-f175, family loft sleeps up to 5, very steep stairs, kid-friendly, easy parking, 15-minute walk or f10 taxi from train station, from Market Square walk straight out Zijlstraat, past Stads Café, over bridge, fourth street on left, Coornhertstraat 3, 2013 Ev Haarlem, tel. 532 2980).

Family Dekker B&B (small D-f50, D-f60, T-f90, Q-f120, two blocks from the station at Ripperdastraat 9, 2011 KG Haarlem, tel. 532 0554) is in a fine, quiet neighborhood near the station. For 25 years Mrs. Dekker has given her guests a cheery welcome in her clean but well-worn and borderline ramshackle place.

Hotel Lion D'Or (DB-f230, extra beds-f50, weekend discounts, across the street from the station at Kruisweg 34, 2011 LC Haarlem, tel. 532-1750, fax 532-9543) is a classy business hotel with all the professional comforts and a very handy location.

Hotel Waldor, a creaky, musty old building, has sleepable rooms (D-f75, DB-f120, CC:VMA, 2-minute walk from train station and a big cheap car park, Jansweg 40 Hoek Parklaan, tel. 531 2622, fax 532 2279).

The 300-room, very American **Motel Haarlem Zuid** is sterile, but a good value for those interested only in sleeping and eating (DB-f90 to f115, TB-f120, f13 for breakfast, CC:VMA, elevator, easy parking, inexpensive hotel restaurant, in an industrial zone a 20-minute walk from the center on the road to the airport at Toekenweg 2, 2035 LC Haarlem, tel. 536 7500, fax 536 7980). Buses easily connect it to the train station and Market Square.

Sleeping near Haarlem

The **Hotel Fehres** offers 8 rooms in a quiet, kid-friendly, garden-filled, residential setting (bus #7 from Haarlem station or Market Square, or a 5-minute walk from the Overveen station, one stop west of Haarlem with twice hourly train connections to Amsterdam). Friendly Mrs. Fehres pampers her guests (DB-f90, TB-f120, QB-f140, 299 Zijlweg, tel. 527 7368). **Pension Koning**, a 10-minute walk north of the station or quick hop on bus #71, has 5 simple rooms in a row house in a residential area (S-f35, D-f70, T-f105 with breakfast, Kleverlaan 179, tel. 526 1456).

Youth Hostel Jan Gijzen, on Jan Gijzenpad 3, is two miles from the Haarlem station (bus #2) or a 5-minute walk from the Samtpoort Zuid train station
9beds-f23, includes breakfast, plus f5 for non-members, 20-bed dorms, 7:00-24:00, tel. 537 3793, fax 537 1176, closed November-February).

Eating in Haarlem

All restaurants listed are a few blocks of the Market Square. Enjoy a memorable Indonesian rijsttafel feast at the **Nanking Chinese-Indonesian Restaurant** (Kruisstraat 16, tel. 532 0706, daily until 22:00). Couples eat plenty, hearty, and more cheaply by splitting a f22 Indonesian rice table for one. (Each eater should order a drink.) Say "hi" to gracious Ai Ping and her daughter, Fan. Don't let them railroad you into a Chinese (their heritage) dinner. They also do cheap and tasty take-out.

On the second night of the tour, fully-guided tour groups will likely dive into a hearty Indonesian rijstaffel ("rice table") feast at the **Nanking**, so you may want to skip doing the rijstaffel shuffle on your own.

For more expensive and impressive meals, try **Mooi Java** (they don't mind diners splitting a f33 *rijsttafel*, across from the station, tel. 532 3121, daily 17:00-22:00) or **De Lachende Javaan** ("The Laughing Javanese") at Frankestraat 25.

Going Dutch? How about pancakes for dinner at **Pannekoekhuis "De Smikkel"** (tel. 532 0631, Kruisweg 57, two blocks in front of station, open until 20:00). Dinner and dessert pancakes cost f10 each (f2.50 per person cover charge, so splitting pancakes is okay).

For a "bread line" experience with basic/bland food, well-worn company, and the cheapest price in town (f9), eat at **Eethuis St. Vincent** (22 Nieuwe Groenmarkt, Monday-Friday 12:00-13:30, 17:00-19:00).

For good food, classy atmosphere, and f30 dinners, try the **Bastiaan** (Lange Veerstrasse 8). **La Plume** is a less expensive steak house on Lange Veerstrasse near the church. For a candle-lit dinner of cheese and wine, consider **In't Goede Uur** (Korte Houtstraat 1), or eat well and reasonably, surrounded by trains, in a classy Old World restaurant between tracks 5 and 6 in the Netherlands' oldest train station. **Jacobus Pieck** is a classy hole in the wall with no menu and a f12 dinner special (until

20:00, 18:00 on weekends, Warmoesstraat 18, tel. 532 6144).

Eko Eet Café (f18 menu, Zijlstraat 39, near the Nieuwe Greenmarket, daily 17:30-21:30) is great for a cheery, tasty vegetarian meal in Haarlem.

The **Stads Café** (daily until midnight, Zijlstraat 56-58, tel. 532 5202), a three-ring circus of reasonable food (f10 dinner special, f21 cheese or meat fondue buffets, salad bar, or "meat on a hot rock sizzling at your table"), with stained glass, candle-lit, honky-tonk atmosphere, and piano music (Friday-Sunday), has fun being a restaurant.

For a healthy budget lunch with Haarlem's best view, eat on the top floor or roof garden of the **Vroom Dreesman** department store (9:30-18:00; Thursday until 21:00, closed Sunday, on Grote Houtstraat). For a f2 cone of old-fashioned local French fries, drop by the **Vlaams Friethuis** on Warmoesstraat just behind the church.

Transportation Connections

Haarlem and Schiphol Airport: Connected by **train**, twice hourly, in both directions (f10, 30-40 minutes, transfer at suburban Amsterdam-Sloterdijk or at Amsterdam CS — central station). Express buses 236, 302 and 362 are faster (20 minutes, 2 rides/hour, f9). By **taxi,** it's a f70 ride.

Haarlem and Amsterdam: The train is easiest (departures every ten minutes, 20-minute ride, f10 round-trip). Major trains depart to all points from Amsterdam.

Day trips from Haarlem

Any of the sights listed below is an easy day trip by bus or train from Haarlem. Match your interest with the village's specialty: choose from flower auctions, folk museums, cheese markets, Delft porcelain, resort beaches, and riding bikes on the dikes.

▲▲▲**Keukenhof**—The greatest bulb flower garden on earth, each spring 6 million flowers conspire to make even a total garden-hater enjoy them. This 70-acre park is packed with tour groups daily (8:00-19:30, last tickets sold at 18:00, about March 23 through May 23, f15, bus from Haarlem via Lisse, tel. 02521/19144). Go early or very late in the day for the best light and least groups.

▲▲**Aalsmeer Flower Auction**—This stop is included on most tours on Day 3. But if your tour starts on a Friday, you'll miss Aalsmeer (because it's closed weekends). We include this info. for those who arrive early for their Friday tour and want to do Aalsmeer on their own. Aalsmeer is your best look at the huge Dutch flower industry. About half of all the flowers exported from Holland are auctioned off here in six huge auditoriums. Visitors are welcome to wander on elevated walkways (through what is claimed to be the biggest building on earth), over literally trainloads of fresh-cut flowers. (f5, Monday-Friday 7:30-11:00, it's pretty dead after 9:30 and on Thursday, bus #172 from Amsterdam's station, from Haarlem, take bus #191 at 7:02 or 13:40, tel. 02977-32185.)

Zandvoort—For a quick and easy look at a dike and a shell-lover's Shangri-la, visit the beach resort of Zandvoort, a breezy bike ride or 10 minutes by car or train west of Haarlem (from Haarlem, follow signs to Bloomendal). Caution: between posts 68 and 70, beach bathers work on all-around tans.

Volendam, Marken, and Monnikendam—These famous towns are as quaint as can be (although Volendam is too touristy).

▲**Hoorn**—This is an elegant, quiet, and typical seventeenth-century Dutch town north of Amsterdam. Its TI (tourist information) can rent you a bike or give you a walking tour brochure. Any TI has a brochure describing the "Historic Triangle" which connects Hoorn, Medemblik, and Enkhuizen by steam train and boat (f20, tel. 02290/14862).

▲**Alkmaar**—This town is Holland's cheese capital, especially fun (and touristy) during its weekly cheese market, Fridays from 10:00 to noon.

▲**Delft**—Peaceful as a Vermeer painting (he was born there) and lovely as its porcelain, Delft is a typically Dutch town with a special soul. Enjoy it best just wandering around, watching people, munching local syrup-waffles, or daydreaming from the canal bridges. The town bustles during its Saturday antique market. Its colorful Thursday food and flower market (9:00-17:00) attracts many traditional villagers. (TI on main square, 9:00-18:00, Saturdays 9:00-17:00, Sundays 10:00-15:00, tel. 015/12 61 00.) The town is a museum in itself, but if you need a turnstile, it has an impressive army museum, and you can tour the Royal Porcelain Works (daily 9:00-17:00, Sundays 10:00-16:00, tel. 015/56 92 14) to watch the famous 17th-century blue Delftware turn from clay to art.

▲▲**Edam**—For the ultimate in cuteness and peace, sample tiny Edam. It's very sweet, but palatable, and 30 minutes by bus from Amsterdam (2/hour). Don't miss the Edam Museum, a small, quirky house offering a fun peek into a 400-year-old home and a floating cellar. Wednesday is the town's market day. In July and August, from 10:00 to 12:30, market day includes a traditional cheese market.

▲**Rotterdam**, the world's largest port, bounced back after being bombed flat in World War II. See its towering Euro-mast, take a harbor tour, and stroll its great pedestrian zone. (TI tel. 06-34034065, f1 per 2 minutes.) It's an easy train connection from Haarlem.

▲▲**The Hague** is the capital of the Netherlands. Locals say the money is made in Rotterdam, divided in the Hague, and spent in Amsterdam. Catch tram 7 to the Peace Palace, 7 to the beach resort of Scheveningen, and 1 or 9 to the mini-Holland amusement park of Madurodam. (TI tel. 06-34035051, f1 per 2 minutes.)

Day 2: Amsterdam

Likely activities today...
35-minute drive into Amsterdam
Anne Frank's House
Neighborhood walk
Beguinhof
Canal boat tour
Rijksmuseum
Free time (Van Gogh Museum is recommended)
Indonesian Rijstaffel dinner in Haarlem

You'll walk about 5 miles today, and sleep in Haarlem.

---

*Note: Throughout this book, an activity listed with a * indicates that it is included as an activity on BB&B tours, too.*

BB&B tours: No bus today. Hop a train into Amsterdam for a day of sightseeing on your own. Lots of suggestions are included below.

Amsterdam
Amsterdam is a progressive way of life housed in Europe's most seventeenth-century city. It's a city built on good living, cozy cafés, great art, street-corner jazz, stately history, and a spirit of live and let live. It has 800,000 people and as many bikes, with more canals than Venice—and as many tourists. While Amsterdam may box your puritan ears, this great and historic city is an experiment in freedom.

Planning Your Time
Amsterdam is worth a full day of sightseeing on even the busiest itinerary. While the city has a couple of must-see museums, its best sight is its own breezy ambiance. If the weather is good and you're on a BB&B tour, Amsterdam is best experienced Dutch-style: on two wheels.

Orientation (tel. code: 020)
The central train station is your starting point (tourist information, bike rental, and trolleys and buses fanning out to all points). Damrak is the main street axis connecting the station with Dam Square (people-watching and hangout center) and the Royal Palace. From this spine, the city spreads out like a fan, with ninety islands, hundreds of bridges, and a

Amsterdam

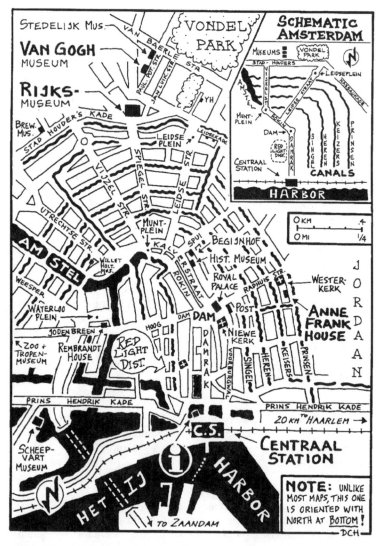

series of concentric canals laid out in the seventeenth century, Holland's Golden Age. The city's major sights are within walking distance of Dam Square. Tourists are considered green and rich and the city has more than its share of hungry thieves.

Tourist Information (TI)

Try to avoid Amsterdam's inefficient VVV office across from the train station. (VVV is Dutch for tourist information office, daily 9:00-17:00, or later). Most people wait 30 minutes just to pick up the information brochures and get a room. Avoid this line by going straight to the cash window (where everyone ends up anyway since any information of substance will cost you). Consider buying: a city map, the f4 historic downtown walking tour brochure, and *What's On* (f3.50, bimonthly entertainment calendar listing all the museum hours and much more). *Use It*, Amsterdam's yearly youth tourist magazine (f2.50), has a map and lists museum hours. It's more helpful than the f6 Amsterdam brochure that the TI would rather sell.

The TI on Leidsestraat is much less crowded. But for 50 cents a minute, you can save yourself a trip by calling the tourist information toll line at 06-3403-4066 (Monday-Saturday, 9:00-17:00). The Haarlem TI (see Haarlem) can answer all your questions and provide you with the brochures.

Getting Around Amsterdam

Amsterdam swings and the hinge that connects it to the world is its perfectly central Central Station. The crowded-in-summer but helpful transit information office (GVB) is next to the TI (in front of the train station). Its free multilingual *Tourist Guide to Public Transport* includes a transit map and explains ticket options and tram connections to all the sights.

By Bus and Tram: Individual tickets cost f3 (pay as you board) and give you an hour on the system. "Strip cards" are cheaper. Any downtown ride costs two strips (good for an hour of transfers). A card with 15 strips costs f11 at the GVB, train stations, post offices, or tobacco shops throughout the country. These strips are good on buses all over Holland (e.g., 6 strips for Haarlem to the airport), and you can share them with your partner. For f12, a Day Card gives you unlimited transportation for a 24-hour period from 06:00 to 06:00. If you get lost, ten of the city's 17 trams take you back to the central train station.

By Foot: The longest walk a tourist would take is 45 minutes from the station to the Rijksmuseum. Watch out for silent, but potentially painful, bikes and trams.

By Bike: One-speed bikes with brrringing bells and two locks rent for f8 per day at the central train station (deposit of f200, $150, or your credit card required, 8:00-22:00 daily, entrance to the left down the ramp as you leave the station, tel. 624 8391). The f1 flier shows a fun countryside bike ride starting with the free shuttle ferry behind the station. To take advantage of their (unadvertised) 4 hours for f5 rate, have the time of your checkout noted on the receipt. For a good Amsterdam biking itinerary, look under "sights" below.

By Boat: While the city is great on foot or bike, there is a "Canal Bus" and a similar Museum Boat with an all-day ticket that shuttles tourists from sight to sight (every 30 minutes). Tickets cost f22 (with discounts that'll save you about f5 on admissions). A sales booth is in front of the central train station, offering handy free brochures with museum times and admission prices. The narrated ride takes 80 minutes if you don't get off.

Helpful Hints

On Monday many shops are open only in the afternoon. Handy telephone cards (f5, f10, or f25) are sold at the TI, GVB, tobacco shops, post office, and train stations. Beware of the bogus telephone offices dressed up like government outlets but ready to rip you off. A *plein* is a square, *gracht* means canal, and most canals are lined by streets with the same name.

Sights—Amsterdam

▲▲▲**Rent a Bike**—Spending a day enjoying the bridges, bike lanes, and sleepy off-the-beaten-path canals on your own one-speed is the essential Amsterdam experience. The real joys of Europe's best preserved seventeenth-century city are the countless intimate glimpses it offers: the laid-back locals sunning on their porches under elegant gables, rusted bikes that look as if they've been lashed to the same lamp post since the '60s, and wasted hedonists planted on canalside benches.

Head west down Haarlemmerstraat, working your wide-eyed way through the Prinsengracht (along the canal) and gentrified Jordan area to Westerkerk, with the tallest spire in the city. Tour Anne Frank's House.

Pedal past the palace, through the Dam Square, down Kalverstraat (the city's bustling pedestrian mall), poke into the sleepy Begijnhof. Roll down tacky Leidsestraat. Lunch at the Atrium (Spui) or a salad bar in the American Hotel (Leidseplein).

Tour the Rijksmuseum and the Van Gogh museum. Bike Spiegelstraat to Muntplein. Catch the hour-long canal boat tour at Spui.

Pedal back down Damrak to the station. For a detour through seedy, sexy, pot-smoking Amsterdam, roll down Damstraat then down Oudezijds Voorburgwal through the land of Rastafarian "coffee shops," red lights over black tights, and sailors lost without the sea.

To escape to the countryside, hop on the free ferry that departs from behind the Amsterdam station across the canal. In 5 minutes, Amsterdam will be gone, and you'll be rolling through your very own Dutch painting. Train back to Haarlem for an Indonesian feast.

Note: Those arriving early for fully guided-tours will enjoy the bike ride, but should skip the sights covered by the tour (Anne Frank's House, Rijksmuseum, Van Gogh museum, canal cruise, Indonesian dinner).

▲▲▲**Rijksmuseum**—Focus on the Dutch masters: Rembrandt, Hals, Vermeer, and Steen. Pick up the museum map listing its top 20 (f1) and plan your attack (or follow the self-guided tour, one of twenty, in my *Mona Winks* guidebook).

Follow the museum's chronological layout to see painting evolve from narrative religious art, to religious art starring the Dutch love of good living and eating, to the Golden Age when secular art dominates. With no local church or royalty to commission big canvases in the post-1648 Protestant Dutch republic, artists specialized in portraits of the wealthy city class (Hals), pretty still lifes (Claesz), and non-preachy slice-of-life art (Steen). The museum has four quietly wonderful Vermeers. And, of course, a thoughtful brown soup of Rembrandt. Study the Night Watch history room before you see the real thing. Other works by Rembrandt show his excellence as a portraitist for hire (De Staalmeesters) and offer some powerful psychological studies (St. Peter's Denial—with Jesus in the murky background).

The bookshop has good posters, prints, slides, and handy theme charts to the museum—like if you always wondered about the role of cats in Dutch art (f12.50, daily 10:00-17:00, decent cafeteria, tram 2 or 5 from the station, tel. 673 2121).

▲▲▲**Van Gogh Museum**—Next to the Rijksmuseum, this outstanding and user-friendly museum is a stroll through a beautifully displayed garden of van Gogh's work and life. (f12.50, daily 10:00-17:00. Poster collectors, buy your cardboard tube here, or get one free with a poster purchase at the Rijksmuseum, tel. 570 5200.)

Stedelijk Modern Art Museum—Next to the Van Gogh Museum, this place is fun, far-out, and refreshing, with mostly post-1945 art, but a permanent collection of Monet, van Gogh, Cezanne, Picasso and Chagall (f8, daily 11:00-17:00, tel. 573-2911).

Vondelpark—Amsterdam's huge and lively city park gives the best look at today's Dutch youth, especially on a sunny summer weekend.

▲▲**Anne Frank House**—A fascinating look at the hideaway where young Anne hid when the Nazis occupied the Netherlands. Pick up the English pamphlet at the door, and don't miss the thought-provoking neo-Nazi exhibit in the last room. Fascism smolders on. (f8, Monday-Saturday 9:00-17:00, Sundays 10:00-17:00, summer until 19:00, tel. 556 7100, 263 Prinsengracht.) For an entertaining glimpse of Holland under the Nazis, rent the powerful movie Soldier of Orange before you leave home.

Westerkerk—Near Anne Frank's house, this landmark church, with a barren interior and Amsterdam's tallest steeple, is worth climbing for the view. (f3, ascend with a guide only, departures on the hour, April-September, 10:00-16:00, closed Sundays.)

Royal Palace Interior—It's right on Dam Square, built when Amsterdam was feeling its global oats, and worth a look (f5, open some weekdays 12:30-16:00).

▲▲Canal Boat Tour—These long, low, tourist-laden boats leave constantly from several docks around the town for a 60-minute quadra-lingual introduction to the city (f12). The only one with a live guide is very central at the corner of Spui and Rokin, about 5 minutes from Dam Square. No fishing, but bring your camera for this relaxing orientation. If you get seasick, consider a bike or walking tour by the Yellow Bike Tour company (daily April - November by bike: 3 hours, f29, on foot: 2 hours, f15, tel. 620 6940).

▲Begijnhof—Step into this tiny, idyllic courtyard in the city center to escape the crazy 1990s and feel the charm of old Amsterdam. Notice house 34, a 500-year-old wooden structure (rare since repeated fires taught city fathers a trick called brick). Peek into the hidden Catholic church opposite the English Reformed church where the pilgrims worshiped while waiting for their voyage to the New World (marked by plaque near door). Be considerate of the people who live here (free, on Begijnensteeg Lane, just off Kalverstraat between 130 and 132, pick up English info flier at office near entrance).

Amsterdam History Museum—The fine Amsterdam historical museum (with a good-value restaurant) offers the town's best look into the age of the Dutch masters. It's next to the Begijnhof at 92 Kalverstraat (f8, weekdays 10:00-17:00, Saturdays and Sundays 11:00-17:00). Its free pedestrian corridor is a powerful teaser.

Rembrandt's House—Interesting only to his fans, with 250 etchings. (f8, 15 minute English A-V presentation upon request, Jodenbreestraat 4; Monday-Saturday 10:00-17:00, Sundays 13:00-17:00.)

▲Tropenmuseum (Tropical Museum)—As close to the Third World as you'll get without lots of vaccinations, this imaginative museum offers wonderful re-creations of tropical life scenes and explanations of Third World problems. (f10, Monday-Friday 10:00-17:00, Saturday and Sunday 12:00-17:00; 2 Linnaeusstrasse, tram 9.)

Netherlands Maritime (Scheepvaart) Museum—This is fascinating if you're into Henry Hudson or scheepvaarts. (f14, Monday - Saturday 10:00-17:00, Sunday 12:00-17:00, closed Mondays off season, English explanations; 1 Kattenburgerplein, bus 22 or 28.)

▲Herrengracht Canal Mansion, the Willet Holthuysen Museum—This 1687 patrician house offers a fine look at the old rich of Amsterdam, with a good 15-minute English introduction film and a seventeenth-century garden in back. (f5, weekdays 10:00-17:00, Saturday and Sunday 11:00-17:00; Herrengracht 605, tram 4 or 9.)

Our Lord in the Attic—Near the station, in the red-light district, you'll find a seventeenth-century merchant's house-turned-museum (Amstelkring museum) with a fascinating hidden church. This dates from 1661, when post-Reformation Dutch Catholics were not allowed to worship in public. The church fills the attics of several homes (f5, weekdays 10:00-17:00, Saturday and Sunday 13:00-17:00, O.Z. Voorburgwal 40).

▲**Red-Light District**—Europe's most high-profile ladies of the night shiver and shimmy in display case windows between the station and the Oudekerk along Voorburgwal. It's dangerous late at night, but a fascinating walk any other time after noon.

According to CNN, over 60 percent of Amsterdam's prostitutes are HIV positive (but a naive tourist might just see them as just hard-working girls from Latin America or Africa trying their best to build up a bank account—f35 at a time). Only Amsterdam has two sex museums—one in the red-light district (lousy) and one on Damrak (at #17, is cheaper and better). Both are open late, graphic, with something to offend almost everyone, but heck, it's historic (and safe), and there are descriptions in English (erotic hours).

Shopping—Amsterdam brings out the browser even in those who were not born to shop. Ten general markets, open 6 days a week, keep those who brake for garage sales pulling U-ies. Shopping highlights include Waterlooplein (flea market), the huge Albert Cuyp street market, various flower markets (along Singel Canal near the mint tower, or Munttoren), diamond dealers (free cutting and polishing demos at shops behind the Rijksmuseum and on Dam Square), and Kalverstraat, Amsterdam's teeming walking/shopping street (parallel to Damrak).

Eating in Amsterdam
Dutch food is basic and hearty. Picnics are cheap and easy. Eetcafes are local cafés serving cheap broodjes (sandwiches), soup, eggs, and so on. Cafeterias, sandwich shops, and automatic food shops are also good bets for budget eaters.

In the train station: A surprisingly classy budget self-service cafeteria is on platform 1.

Near Spui in the center: The city university's **Atrium** is a great and cheery budget cafeteria (f8 meals Monday-Friday, 12:00-14:00, 17:00-19:00, from Spui, walk west down Grimburgwal past the canalside Cafe Gasthuys three blocks to Spui Oude Zijds Achterburgwal 237, tel. 525-3999). **Keuken van 1870** has been cooking very simple meals in a simple setting since 1870 (cheap self-service, 4 Spuistraat, tel. 624 8965).

Near Anne Frank's: For pancakes in a smoky but family atmosphere, try the **Pancake Bakery** (f15 pancakes, splitting is okay, even an Indonesian pancake for those who want two experiences in one, Prinsengracht 191, tel. 625 1333). Across the canal, **DeBolhoed** serves great vegetarian food (Prinsengracht 60).

Near the Rijksmuseum, on Leidseplein: The art deco **American Hotel** dining room serves an elegant f9 salad bar (small plate with bread, fruit, and nobody caring if you get refills, weekdays 12:00 - 22:00, where Leidesplein hits Singel Canal). The **Theater Cafe** (next to Hotel Maas, 50 meters down Singel canal from the American Hotel) offers classy and tasty f20 meals.

At any bar: Try a jenever (Dutch gin), the closest thing to an atomic bomb in a shot glass. While cheese gets harder and sharper with age, jenever grows smooth and soft. Old jenever is best.

Drugs: Amsterdam is Europe's counterculture mecca. While hard drugs are definitely out, marijuana causes about as much excitement as a bottle of beer. A "pot man" with a worldly menu of f25 baggies is a fixture in many bars (walk east from Dam Square on Damstraat for a few blocks, then down to Nieumarket). While several touristy **Bulldog** cafés are very popular with tourists, less glitzy smaller places farther from the tourists offer a better value and a more comfortable atmosphere. For a complete rundown on this side of the town, buy a copy of the "Mellow Pages."

Day 3: To the Rhine

We'll stop and smell the roses on the way to Arnhem's Open-Air Dutch Folk Museum, share a Dutch pancake lunch, then drive deep into Germany's Rhineland for a hearty dinner.

Likely activities today...
Aalsmeer Flower Auction (if open)*
Two-hour drive to Arnhem*
Arnhem's Open-Air Dutch Folk Museum*
Five-hour drive to Germany's Rhineland*
Dinner at hotel in Bacharach*
Group meeting after dinner*

You'll walk about 2 or 3 miles today, and sleep in Bacharach.

Included as an activity on BB&B tours.

▲▲**Aalsmeer Flower Auction**—This is your best look at the huge Dutch flower industry. About half of all the flowers exported from Holland are auctioned off here in six huge auditoriums. Visitors are welcome to wander on elevated walkways, through what is claimed to be the biggest building on Earth, over literally trainloads of fresh-cut flowers. (Monday-Friday, 7:30-11:00, it's pretty dead after 9:30 and on Thursdays, f5, tel. 02977-32185.)

▲▲**Arnhem's Open-Air Dutch Folk Museum**—An hour east of Amsterdam in Arnhem is a home show in a time tunnel: Holland's first, biggest, and best folk museum. You'll enjoy a huge park of windmills, old farms, traditional crafts in action, and a pleasant education-by-immersion in Dutch culture. The f15 English guidebook explains each historic building. (f16, daily April-October, 9:30-17:00, Saturdays and Sundays from 10:00.) The park has several good budget restaurants and covered picnic areas. Its rustic Pancake House serves hearty (split-able) Dutch flapjacks.

Hotel Kranenturm gives you the feeling of a castle without the coldness or the climb. It's hard to beat its combination of comfort and hotel privacy with Zimmer warmth, central location, and medieval atmosphere. Run by hardworking Kurt Engel and his intense but friendly wife Fatima, this hotel is actually part of the medieval fortification. Its former *Kranen* (crane) towers are now round rooms. When the riverbank was higher, cranes on this tower loaded barrels of wine onto Rhine boats.

Hotel Kranenturm is 5 yards from the train tracks (just under the medieval gate at the Frankfurt end of town), but a combination of medieval sturdiness, triple-pane windows, and included ear plugs make the riverside rooms sleepable. The Kranenturm really stretches it to get toilets and showers in each room. Kurt, a great cook, serves fine dinners. His big-enough-for-three Kranenturm ice cream special may ruin you (9 DM). Want to dance, and take a fun trip to the South Pacific in a medieval German cellar all at the same time? Check out Kurt's bar downstairs, known by our dance-till-you-drop staff as the Tacky Teutonic Tiki Disco Bar.

Germany (Deutschland)
■ United Germany is 136,000 square miles (the size of Montana).
■ Population is 77 million (about 650 per square mile, declining slowly).
■ The West was 95,000 square miles (like Wyoming) with 61 million people.
■ The East was 41,000 square miles (like Virginia) with 16 million people.
■ 1 Deutsche Mark (DM) is about 70 cents; $1 is about 1.4 DM.

Deutschland is energetic, efficient, and organized, and Europe's muscleman—economically and wherever people are lining up. Eighty-five percent of its people live in cities; and average earnings are among the highest on earth. Ninety-seven percent of the workers get a one-month paid vacation, and during the other eleven months they create a gross national product of about one-third that of the United States, and growing. Germany has risen from the ashes of World War II to become the world's fifth-biggest industrial power, ranking fourth in steel output and nuclear power and third in automobile production. Its bustling new cities are designed to make people feel like they belong. It shines culturally, beating out all but two countries in production of books, Nobel laureates, and professors.

While its East-West division lasted about forty years, historically Germany has been and continues to be divided north and south. While northern Germany was barbarian, is Protestant, and assaults life aggressively, southern Germany was Roman, is Catholic, and enjoys a more relaxed tempo of life. The southern German, or Bavarian, dialect is to High (northern) German what the dialect of Alabama or Georgia is to the speech of the northern United States. The American image of Germany is Bavaria (probably because that was "our" sector immediately after the war) where the countryside is most traditional. This historic north-south division is less pronounced these days as Germany becomes a more mobile society. Of course, the big chore facing Germany today is integrating the rotten and wilted economy of what was East Germany into the powerhouse economy of the West. This monumental task has given the West higher taxes (and second thoughts).

Germany's most interesting tourist route today—Rhine, Romantic Road, Bavaria—was yesterday's most important trade route, along which its most prosperous and important medieval cities were located. Germany as a nation is just 120 years old. In 1850, there were 35 independent countries in what is now one Germany. In medieval times, there were over 300, each with its own weights, measures, coinage, king, and lotto. Many were surrounded by what we would call iron curtains. This helps explain Germany's many diverse customs.

Germany

Germans eat lunch from 11:30 to 14:30 and dinner between 18:00 and 21:00. Each region has its own gastronomic twist, so order local house specials whenever possible. Pork, fresh water fish, and venison are good, and don't miss the bratwurst and sauerkraut. Potatoes are the standard vegetable. Great beers and white wines abound. Try the small local brands. Go with whatever beer is on tap. "Gummi Bears" are a local gumdrop candy with a cult following (beware of imitations—you must see the word "Gummi"), and Nutella is a chocolate nut spread specialty that may change your life. Service and tips are included in your restaurant bills, though it is polite to "round up," e.g., leave 20 DM for a 19.70 DM bill..

Banks are generally open from 8:00 to 12:00 and 14:00 to 16:00, other offices from 8:00 to 16:00. Beware: some banks charge a separate fee for each traveler's check you cash.

August is a holiday month for workers, but that doesn't really affect us tourists (unless you're on the road on the 15th, when half of Germany is going over the Alps one way and half returning the other).

Germany nitty-gritty
Country code: 49
International access: 00
AT&T: 0130-0010
MCI: 0130-0012
SPRINT: 0130-0013
Emergency: 110
Public phones are yellow. Many pay phones in cities take German phone cards, which cost 12 DM or 50 DM (Dutch phone cards also work in German phones). Coin-operated phones take three x 10 pf coins (a nice way to get rid of these), 1 DM or 5 DM coins, and give no change.
Senior/youth discount age: 65+
Bank hours: 8:00 - 16:00 M-F; closed for lunch from 12:00 to 14:00 in smaller cities.

Day 4: The Rhineland

Tour the Rhine's mightiest castle, take a scenic river cruise, and spend time browsing through two of the cutest towns you've ever laid eyes on.

Likely activities today...
Hike up to and tour Rheinfels Castle
Free time in Bacharach and St. Goar*
Rhine river cruise*
Dinner at the hotel*

You'll walk about 3 or 4 miles today, and sleep in Bacharach.

---

* Included as an activity on BB&B tours.

The Rhine
This is storybook Germany, a fairy-tale world of Rhine legends and castles. For hands-on castle thrills, climb through the Rhineland's greatest castle, Rheinfels, above the town of St. Goar. Then cruise the most castle-studded stretch of the romantic Rhine as you listen for the song of the treacherous Loreley.

Ever since Roman times, when this was the Empire's northern boundary, the Rhine has been one of the world's busiest shipping rivers. You'll see a steady flow of barges with 1,000- to 2,000-ton loads. Buses packed with tourists, hot train tracks, and highways line both banks.

Many of the castles were "robber baron" castles, put there by petty rulers (there were 300 independent little countries in medieval Germany) to levy tolls on all the passing river traffic. A robber baron would put his castle on, or even in, the river. Then, often with the help of chains and a tower on the opposite side of the river, he'd stop each ship and get his toll. There were ten customs stops between Mainz and Koblenz alone (no wonder merchants were early proponents of the creation of larger nation-states).

Some castles were built to control and protect settlements, and others were the residences of kings. As times changed, so did the life-styles of the rich and feudal. Many castles were abandoned for more comfortable mansions in the towns.

Most of the Rhine castles were originally built in the eleventh, twelfth, and thirteenth centuries. When the pope successfully asserted his power over the German emperor in 1076, local princes ran wild over the rule of their emperor. The castles saw military action in the

Best of the Rhine

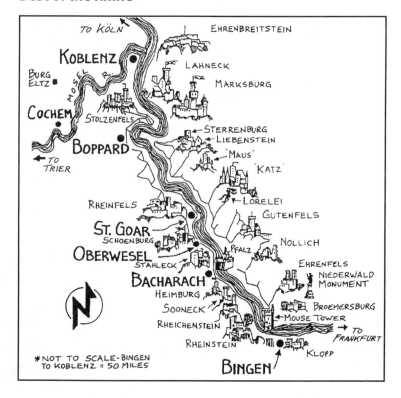

1300s and 1400s as emperors began reasserting their control over Germany's many silly kingdoms.

The castles were also involved in the Reformation wars that saw Europe's Catholic and "protesting" dynasties fight it out using a fragmented Germany as their battleground. The Thirty Years War (1618–1648) devastated Germany. The outcome: each ruler got the freedom to decide if his people would be Catholic or Protestant, and one-third of Germany was dead.

The French destroyed most of the castles prophylactically (Louis XIV in the 1680s, the Revolutionary army in the 1790s, and Napoleon in 1806). They were often rebuilt in neo-Gothic style in the romantic age—the late 1800s—and today are enjoyed as restaurants, hotels, youth hostels, and museums.

Getting Around the Rhine

While the Rhine flows from Switzerland to Holland, the stretch from Mainz to Koblenz is by far the most interesting. Studded with the crenelated cream of Germany's castles, it bustles with boats, trains, and highway traffic. Have fun exploring with a mix of big steamers, tiny ferries, bikes, and trains.

By boat, the most scenic hour is from St. Goar to Bacharach. Sit on the top deck and enjoy the parade of castles, towns, boats, and vineyards.

A Rhine cruise is included with your tour, but if you prefer to strike out on your own, here are the facts. There are several boat companies, but most travelers sail on the bigger, more expensive and romantic Köln–Düsseldorf line (free with Eurail, otherwise about 15 DM per hour, tel. 0221/2088). Boats run daily in both directions (no express boat on Monday) from May through September with fewer boats off-season. Complete, up-to-date, and more complicated schedules are posted in any station, Rhineland hotel, TI, or current Thomas Cook Timetable. Purchase tickets at the dock 5 minutes before departure. The boat is never full. (Confirm times at your hotel the night before.)

The smaller Bingen–Rüdesheimer line (tel. 06721/14140, Eurail not valid, buy tickets on the boat) is 25 percent cheaper than K-D with three 2-hour St. Goar–Bacharach trips daily in summer (departing St. Goar at 11:00, 14:10, and 16:10; departing Bacharach at 10:10, 12:30, 15:00; 11 DM one way, 14 DM round-trip).

You can rent **bikes** at the St. Goar TI or at Bacharach's Hotel Gelber Hof (ten speeds, 20 DM per day, 5 DM for child's seat). The best riverside bike path is from Bacharach to Bingen. The path is also good but closer to the highway from St. Goar to Bacharach. If you're on a BB&B tour, consider sailing to Bingen and biking back, visiting Rheinstein Castle (you're on your own to wander the well-furnished castle) and Reichenstein Castle (admittance with groups) and maybe even taking a ferry across the river to Kaub (where a tiny boat shuttles sightseers to the better-from-a-distance castle on the island). While there are no bridges between Koblenz and Mainz, several small ferries do their job constantly and cheaply.

Bacharach

Bacharach, which once prospered from its wood and wine trade, is just a pleasant medieval town that misses most of the tourist glitz (TI, Monday-Friday 10:00-12:00 and 15:00-17:00, tel. 06743/1297; look for "i" on the main street, then go through nearby door and follow signs to "Verkehrsamt" up the stairs, and down the squeaky hall). Some of the Rhine's best wine is from this town, whose name means "altar to

Bacharach

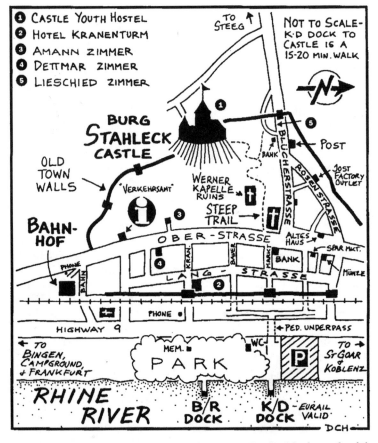

Bacchus." The huge Jost beer stein "factory outlet," a block north of the church carries everything a shopper could want (8:30-18:00, till 16:00 on Saturday, 11:00-15:00 on Sunday, 10% discount with this book). For one of the Rhine's best views, climb up the steep hill to the imposing 12th century Stahleck Castle, now a popular youth hostel.

St. Goar
St. Goar was named for a sixth-century hometown monk. It originated in Celtic times (really old) as a place where sailors would stop, catch their breath, send home a postcard, and give thanks after surviving the seductive and treacherous Loreley crossing.

St. Goar

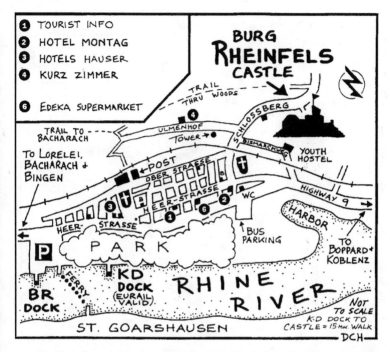

St. Goar is worth a stop to explore its **Rheinfels Castle**. Sitting like a dead pit-bull above St. Goar, this mightiest of Rhine castles rumbles with ghosts from its hard-fought past. Burg Rheinfels (b. 1245) withstood a siege of 28,000 French troops in 1692, but was creamed by the same team in 1797. It was huge, biggest on the Rhine, then used as a quarry. Today it's a hollow but interesting shell and offers your best single hands-on castle experience on the river. Follow the castle map with English instructions (.50 DM from the ticket window). If you follow the castle's perimeter, circling counterclockwise, and downward, you'll find an easy-to-explore chunk of the several miles of spooky tunnels. Bring your flashlight (and bayonet). These tunnels were used to lure in and entomb enemy troops. You'll be walking over the remains (from 1626) of 300 unfortunate Spanish soldiers. The reconstruction of the castle in the museum shows how much bigger it was before Louis XIV destroyed it. Climb to the top for the Rhine view (5 DM, daily 9:00-18:00, form a group of ten English-speaking tourists to get a cheaper ticket and a free English tour, tel. 383; 15 minutes' steep hike up from St. Goar, you can call a taxi at tel. 93100 for a 7-DM lift from the boat

Lower Rhine

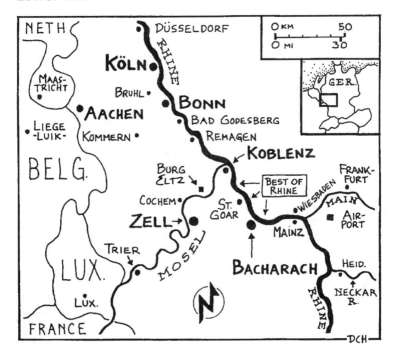

dock to the castle, 10 DM for a mini-bus).

The St. Goar TI (Monday - Friday 8:00-12:30, 14:00-17:00, Saturday 9:30-12:00, closed Sunday and earlier in winter, tel. 06741/383) now functions as the town's train station with free left-luggage service and budget bike rentals. They have information on which local wineries do English-language tours and tastings for individuals.

St. Goar has good shops (steins and cuckoo clocks, of course) and a waterfront park hungry for a picnic. The small supermarket (EDEKA) on Main Street is fine for picnic fixings. The friendly and helpful Montag family in the shop under the Hotel Montag has Koblenz-to-Mainz Rhine guidebooks, and fine steins. And across the street, you'll see what must be the biggest cuckoo clock in the world.

For a good two-hour hike from St. Goar: catch the ferry across to St. Goarshausen, hike to the Katz castle, and traverse along the hillside from there to the top of the Loreley. From there the trail winds down to the river and then takes you back to the St. Goarshausen-St. Goar ferry (4/hr., 2.50 DM round-trip).

Sights—The Romantic Rhine

Here's a quick and easy Rhine tour that skips the syrupy myths and the life story of Dieter V von Katzenelnbogen (und his lovely bride Brunhilda) that fill normal Rhine guides.

For more information than necessary, buy the handy *Rhine Guide from Mainz to Cologne* (6 DM book with foldout map, at most shops).

You'll notice large black-and-white kilometer markers along the riverbank, put up by Rick Steves years ago to make this tour easier to follow. They tell the distance from here to the Swiss Rhinefalls (where the Rhine first becomes navigable). Now the river-barge pilots have accepted these as navigational aids as well. We're tackling just 36 miles of the 820-mile-long Rhine. Just follow the kilometer markings.

Km 590: Koblenz—Not a nice city, Koblenz was really hit hard in World War II, but its place as the historic *Deutsches-Eck* (German corner)—the tip of land where the Mosel joins the Rhine—gives it a certain magnetism. "Koblenz," Latin for "confluence," has Roman origins. Walk through the park, noticing the blackened base of what was once a huge memorial to the Kaiser. Across the river, the yellow Ehrenbreitstein Castle is now a youth hostel.

Km 585: Burg Lahneck—This castle (above the modern autobahn bridge over the Lahn river) was built in 1240 to defend local silver mines, ruined by the French in 1688, and rebuilt in the 1850s in neo-Gothic style. Burg Lahneck faces the yellow Schloss Stolzenfels (open for touring, a 10-minute climb from the tiny car park, closed Monday).

Km 580: Marksburg (with the three modern chimneys behind it) is the best-looking of all the Rhine castles and the only surviving medieval castle on the Rhine. Because of its commanding position, it was never attacked. It's now open as a museum with a medieval interior second only to the Mosel's Burg Eltz (daily 10:00-17:00, by 7-DM tour only, tours generally in German, worth a visit only if you can tag along with a rare English tour, call ahead, tel. 02627/206).

Km 570: Boppard—Once a Roman town, Boppard has some impressive remains of fourth-century walls. Notice the Roman tower just after the Boppard's train station and the substantial chunk of Roman wall just before.

Boppard is worth a stop. Just above the market square are the remains of the Roman wall. Below the square is a fascinating church. Notice the carved Romanesque crazies at the doorway. Inside, to the right of the entrance, you'll see Christian symbols from Roman times. Also notice the painted arches and vaults. Originally, most Romanesque churches were painted this way. Down by the river, notice the high water (*Hochwasser*) marks on the arches from various flood years. (Throughout the Rhine valley you'll see these flood marks.)

Km 567: The "Hostile Brothers" castles (with the white square tower)—Take the wall between Burg Sterrenberg and Burg Liebenstein (actually designed to improve the defenses of both castles), add two greedy and jealous brothers and a fair maiden, and create your own legend. They are restaurants today.

Km 559: Burg Maus got its name because the next castle was owned by the Katzenelnbogen family. In the 1300s, it was considered a state-of-the-art fortification . . . until Napoleon had it blown up in 1806 with state-of-the-art explosives. It was rebuilt true to its original plans around 1900.

Km 557: St. Goar and Rheinfels Castle. See St. Goar above.

Km 556: Burg Katz—From the town of St. Goar, you'll see Burg Katz (Katzenelnbogen) across the river. Together, Burg Katz (b. 1371) and Rheinfels had a clear view up and down the river and effectively controlled traffic. There was absolutely no duty-free shopping on the medieval Rhine. Katz got Napoleoned in 1806 and rebuilt around 1900; today it's a convalescent home.

Km 554: The Loreley—Steep a big slate rock in centuries of legend and it becomes a tourist attraction, the ultimate Rhinestone. The Loreley (two flags on top, name painted near shoreline) rises 450 feet over the narrowest and deepest point of the Rhine. (The fine echoes here were thought to be ghostly voices in the old days, fertilizing the legendary soil.)

Because of the killer reefs just upstream (Km 552, called the "Seven Maidens"), many ships never made it to St. Goar. Sailors (after days on the river) blamed their misfortune on a wunderbar Fräulein whose long blond hair almost covered her body. (You can see her statue at about km 555.) Heinrich Heine's *Song of Loreley* (the *Cliffs Notes* version is on local postcards) tells the story of a count who sent his men to kill or capture this siren after his son was killed because of her. When the soldiers cornered the nymph in her cave, she called her father (Father Rhine) for help. Huge waves, the likes of which you'll never see today, rose out of the river and carried her to safety. And she has never been seen since.

But alas, when the moon shines brightly and the tour buses are parked, a soft, playful Rhine whine can still be heard from the Loreley. As you pass, listen carefully ("Sailors . . . sailors . . . over my bounding mane").

Km 550: Oberwesel—A Celtic town in 400 B.C., then a Roman military station, it has some of the best Roman wall-and-tower remains on the Rhine. Notice how many of the train tunnels have entrances designed like medieval turrets, built in the Romantic nineteenth century.

Km 546: Burg Gutenfels (white painted "Hotel" sign) and the ship-shape **Pfalz Castle** (built in the river in the 1300s, notice the overhanging his and hers "outhouses") worked very effectively to tax medieval river traffic. The town of Kaub grew rich as Pfalz raised its chains when boats came and lowered them only when the merchants had paid their duty. Those who didn't pay spent time touring its fascinating prison, on a raft at the bottom of its well. In 1504, a pope called for the destruction of Pfalz, but a six-week siege failed. Pfalz is tourable but pretty empty, accessible by 3-DM ferry from Kaub on the other side (4 DM, 9:00-13:00, 14:00-18:00, tel. 06774/570).

Km 543: Bacharach and Stahleck Castle. See Bacharach above.

Km 540: Lorch—This pathetic stub of a castle is barely visible from the road. Notice the small car ferry, one of several between Mainz and Koblenz, where there are no bridges.

Km 538: Castle Sooneck, built in the eleventh century, was twice destroyed by people sick and tired of robber barons.

Km 533: Burg Rheinstein and Burg Reichenstein (at km 534) are some of the first to be rebuilt in the Romantic era (both are privately owned, tourable and connected by a pleasant trail).

Km 530: Ehrenfels Castle—Opposite the Bingerbrück station, you'll see the ghostly Ehrenfels Castle (clobbered by the Swedes in 1636 and by the French in 1689). Since it had no view of the river traffic to the north, it built the cute little *Mäuseturm* (Mouse Tower) on an island (the yellow tower you'll see near the train station today). Rebuilt in the 1800s in neo-Gothic style, today it's used as a Rhine navigation signal station.

Km 528: Niederwald monument—Across from the Bingen station on a hilltop is the 120-foot-high Niederwald monument, a memorial built with 32 tons of bronze in 1877 to commemorate "the reestablishment of the German Empire." A lift takes tourists to this statue from the famous and extremely touristic wine town of Rüdesheim.

Day 5: To Rothenburg and Munich

After an early start and a four-hour drive you'll have the afternoon free
in Rothenburg, Germany's cutest medieval walled town. You may want
to see Reimenschneider's altarpiece (the best wood-carving in Germany),
walk the medieval wall, tour the medieval crime and punishment museum, or shop till you drop. We'll arrive in Munich in time for a late,
lively beerhall dinner.

Likely activities today...
4 hour drive to Rothenburg*
Free time to explore medieval Rothenburg*
3 hour drive to Munich*
Dinner at a Bavarian beerhall in Munich

You'll walk about 4 miles today, and sleep in Munich.

---

* Included as an activity on BB&B tours.

Rothenburg and the Romantic Road

From Frankfurt to Fussen, the Romantic Road takes you through
Bavaria's medieval heartland, a route strewn with picturesque villages,
farmhouses, onion-domed churches, Baroque palaces, and walled cities.

Dive into the Middle Ages via Rothenburg, Germany's best preserved walled town. Countless renowned travelers have searched for
the elusive "untouristy Rothenburg." There are many contenders (such
as Michelstadt, Miltenberg, Bamberg, Bad Windsheim, and Dinkelsbühl),
but none holds a candle to the king of medieval German cuteness. Even
with crowds, over-priced souvenirs, Japanese-speaking night watch-
men, and yes, even with schneeballs, Rothenburg is best.

Planning Your Time

Taking in Rothenburg's essential experiences is easy: the Criminal museum, the wood carving in the church, and a walk along the wall. With
more time there are several mediocre but entertaining museums, walking and biking possibilities in the nearby countryside, and a lifetime of
cafes and shops.

Rothenburg orientation (tel. code: 09861)

To orient yourself in Rothenburg (ROE-ten-burg), think of the town map
as a human head. Its nose—the castle garden—sticks out to the left, and
the neck is the skinny lower part.

Rothenburg on the Tauber

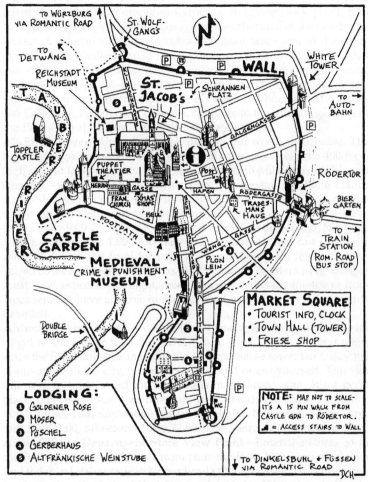

During Rothenburg's heyday, from 1150 to 1400, it was the crossing point of two major trade routes: Tashkent-Paris and Hamburg-Venice. Most of the buildings you'll see were built by 1400. The city was born around its long-gone castle (today's castle garden); built in 1142, destroyed in 1356. You can see the shadow of the first town wall, which defines the oldest part of Rothenburg, in its contemporary street plan. A few gates from this wall survive. The richest and therefore biggest houses were in this central part. The commoners built higgledy-piggledy (read: picturesquely) farther from the center near the present walls. Today, the great trade is tourism; two-thirds of the townspeople are employed serving you. Too often, Rothenburg brings out the shopper in visitors before they've had a chance to appreciate the historic city. True, this is a great place to do your German shopping, but first see the town.

Tourist Information: The TI is on the market square (Monday-Friday 9:00-12:30, 14:00-18:00, Saturday 9:00-12:00, 14:00-16:00, closed Sunday, tel. 40492). Pick up a map and the "sights worth seeing and knowing" brochure (a virtual walking guide to the town; read it all). The TI's free "Hotels and Pensions of Rothenburg" map has the most detail and names all streets. Confirm your sightseeing plans. The travel agency in the TI is a handy place to arrange train and couchette reservations. The best town map is available free at the Friese shop, two doors toward the nose. Rothenburg is a joy on foot. No sights are more than a 12 minute walk from each other.

Sights—Rothenburg

▲▲**Walk the Wall**—Just over a mile around, with great views, and providing a good orientation, this walk can be done (without ducking) by those under six feet tall in less than an hour and requires no special sense of balance. Photographers go through lots of film. The best fortifications are in the Spitaltor (south end). Walk from there counterclockwise to the forehead. Climb the Rödertor in route. The names you see along the way are people who donated money to repair the wall after WWII.

▲**Rödertor**—The wall tower nearest the train station is the only one you can climb. It's worth the hike up for the view and a fascinating rundown on the bombing of Rothenburg in the last weeks of World War II (the northeast corner of the city was destroyed; photos, English translation, 1 DM, daily 9:00-17:00, closed off-season).

Walking Tours—The TI on the market square offers 90-minute guided tours in English (daily, May-October at 14:00 from the market square, 6 DM). The equally informative but more dramatic Night Watchman's Tour leaves each evening at 20:00 (April-October, in English, 8 DM).

▲▲**Climb Town Hall Tower**—The best view of Rothenburg and the surrounding countryside and a closeup look at an old tiled roof from the inside (9:30-12:30, 13:00-17:00, off-season Saturday and Sunday 12:00-15:00 only) are yours for 1 DM and a rigorous (214 steps, 180 feet) but interesting climb. Ladies, beware, some men find the view best from the bottom of the ladder just before the top.

▲▲**Herrngasse and the Castle Garden**—Any town's Herrngasse, where the richest patricians and merchants (the *Herren*) lived, is your chance to see its finest old mansions. Wander from the market square down

Herrngasse (past the old Rothenburg official measurement rods on the City Hall wall) and drop into the lavish front rooms of a ritzy hotel or two. Pop into the Franciscan Church (from 1285, oldest in town, with a Riemenschneider altarpiece; daily 10:00-12:00, 14:00-16:00, free), continue on down past the old-fashioned puppet theater, through the old gate (notice the tiny after-curfew door in the big door and the frightening mask mouth from which hot tar was poured onto attackers) and into the garden that used to be the castle. (Great picnic spots and Tauber Riviera views at sunset.)

▲▲Medieval Crime and Punishment Museum—It's the best of its kind, full of fascinating old legal bits and Kriminal pieces, instruments of punishment and torture, even a special cage—complete with a metal gag—for nags. Exhibits are in English. (Fun cards and posters, daily 9:30-18:00, in winter 14:00-16:00, 6 DM.)

▲Toy Museum—Two floors of historic kinder cuteness is a hit with many (just off the market square, downhill from the fountain, Hofbronneng 13; 9:30-18:00 daily, 5 DM, 12 DM per family).

▲▲St. Jacob's Church—Here you'll find a glorious 500-year-old wooden altarpiece by Tilman Riemenschneider, located up the stairs and behind the organ. Riemenschneider was the Michelangelo of German woodcarvers. This is the one required art treasure in town (daily 9:00-17:30, off-season 10:00-12:00, 14:00-16:00, 2.50 DM, free helpful English info sheet).

Meistertrunk Show—Be on the main square at 11:00, 12:00, 13:00, 14:00, 15:00, 20:00, 21:00, or 22:00 for the ritual gathering of the tourists to see the less-than-breathtaking reenactment of the Meistertrunk story. In 1631, the Catholic army took the Protestant town and was about to do its rape, pillage, and plunder thing when, as the story goes, the mayor said, "Hey, if I can drink this entire 3-liter tankard of wine in one gulp, will you leave us alone?" The invading commander, sensing he was dealing with unbalanced people, said, "Sure." Mayor Nusch drank the whole thing, the town was saved, and the mayor slept for three days.

Hint: for the best show, don't watch the clock; watch the open-mouthed tourists gasp as the old windows flip open. At the late shows, the square flickers with flash attachments.

▲Historical Vaults—Under the town hall tower is a city history museum that gives a waxy but good look at medieval Rothenburg and a good-enough replica of the famous Meistertrunk tankard (well described in English, daily 9:00-18:00, closed off-season, 2.50 DM).

Museum of the Imperial City (Reichsstadt Museum)—This stuffier museum, housed in the former Dominican Convent, gives a more scholarly look at old Rothenburg with some fine art and the supposed Meistertrunk tankard, labeled "Kürfurstenhumpen" (daily 10:00-17:00, in winter 13:00-16:00, 4 DM).

St. Wolfgang's Church—This fortified Gothic church is built into the medieval wall at Klingentor (near the "forehead"). Explore its dungeon-like passages below and check out the shepherd's dance exhibit to see where they hot-oiled the enemy back in the good old days (daily 10:00-13:00, 14:00-17:00, closed off-season, 2 DM).

Alt Rothenburger Handwerkerhaus—This 700-year-old tradesman's house shows the typical living situation of Rothenburg in its heyday (Alter Stadtgraben 26, near the Markus Tower; daily 9:00-18:00, closed off-season, 3 DM).

▲**Walk in the Countryside**—Just below the Burggarten (castle garden) in the Tauber Valley is the cute, skinny, 600-year-old castle/summer home of Mayor Toppler (13:00-16:00 on Friday, Saturday, and Sunday in summer only, 2 DM). Intimately furnished, it's well worth a look. On the top floor, notice the photo of bombed-out 1945 Rothenburg. Then walk on past the covered bridge and huge trout to the peaceful village of Detwang. **Detwang** is actually older than Rothenburg, with another Riemenschneider altarpiece in its church (from 968, the second oldest in Franconia). For a scenic return, loop back to Rothenburg through the valley along the river past a café with outdoor tables, great desserts, and a town view to match.

A Franconian Bike Ride—For a fun, breezy look at the countryside around Rothenburg, rent a bike from the train station (12 DM per day, 8 DM with a train pass or ticket, extra gears available for 1 DM each, 5:00-18:30). For a pleasant half-day pedal, bike south down to Detwang via Topplerschloss. Go north along the level bike path to Tauberscheckenbach, then huff and puff uphill about twenty minutes to Adelshofen and south back to Rothenburg.

Swimming—Rothenburg has a fine modern recreation center, with an indoor/outdoor pool and a sauna, a few minutes walk down the Dinkelsbühl Road (8:00 or 9:00-20:00, tel. 4565).

Shopping

Rothenburg is one of Germany's best shopping towns. Do it here, mail it home, and be done with it. Lovely prints, carvings, wineglasses, Christmas tree ornaments, and beer steins are popular.

The Kathe Wohlfahrt Christmas trinkets phenomenon is spreading across the half-timbered reaches of Europe. In Rothenburg, tourists flock to the Kathe Wohlfahrt Kris Kringle Market and the Christmas Village (on either side of Herrngasse, just off the main square). This Christmas wonderland is filled with enough twinkling lights to require a special electric hookup, instant Christmas spirit mood music (best appreciated on a hot day in July), and American and Japanese tourists hungrily filling little woven shopping baskets with 5-to-10-DM goodies to hang on their trees. (Okay, I admit it, my Christmas tree dangles with a few

KW ornaments.) Note: prices have hefty tour-guide kickbacks built into them.

The Friese shop (just off the market square, west of the tourist office on the corner across from the public W.C.) offers a charming contrast. Cuckoo with friendliness, it gives shoppers with this book tremendous service: a 10 percent discount, 14 percent tax deducted if you have it mailed, and a free Rothenburg map. Anneliese, who runs the place with her sons, Frankie and Berni, charges only her cost to ship things, changes money at the best rates in town with no extra charge, and lets tired travelers leave their bags in her back room for free. Her pricing is generally but not always good. To comparison shop, go here last.

For characteristic wine glasses and oinkology gear, drop by the Weinluden am Plönlein at Plönlein on Spitalgasse.

For good prints, etchings, and paintings, 10% off of marked prices with this book, and a free shot of German brandy, visit the Ernst Geissendörfer print shop where the main square hits Schmiedgasse.

Those who prefer to eat their souvenirs shop the *Bäckerei* (bakeries). Their succulent pastries, pies, and cakes are pleasantly distracting. Skip the good-looking but bad-tasting "Rothenburger Schneeballs."

Eating in Rothenburg
Most restaurants serve meals only from 11:30 to 13:30 and 18:00 to 20:00. The **Hotel Goldener Rose** has good, reasonable meals, served by the stately Henni (who causes many monoglots to dream in fluent Deutsche). Galgengasse (Gallows Lane) has two cheap and popular standbys: **Pizzeria Roma** (19 Galgengasse, 11:30-24:00, 10-DM pizzas and normal schnitzel fare) and **Gasthof zum Ochsen** (26 Galgengasse, 11:30-13:30, 18:00-20:00, closed Thursday, decent 10-DM meals). **Zum Schmolzer** (corner of Stollengasse and Rosengasse) is a local favorite for its cheap beer and good food. Any place advertising "schnell imbiss" (fast food) serves cheap German fare in a jiffy. If you need a break from schnitzel, the **Hong Kong China Restaurant**, outside the town near the train tracks (1 Bensenstrasse, tel. 7377), serves good Chinese food. There are two supermarkets near the wall at Rödertor (the one outside the wall to the left is cheaper).

Evening Fun and Beer Drinking
If your group stays late in Rothenburg, the best beer garden for balmy summer evenings is just outside the wall at the Rödertor (red gate).

For a rare chance to mix it up with locals who aren't selling anything, bring your favorite slang and tongue-twisters to the English conversation club (Wednesdays, 20:00-24:00) at Mario's Altefränkische Weinstube. This dark and smoky pub is an atmospheric hangout any night but Tuesday, when it's closed (Klosterhof 7, off Klingengasse, behind St. Jacob's church, tel. 6404).

For mellow ambience, try the beautifully restored Alte Keller's Weinstube on Alterkellerstrasse under walls festooned with old toys. Wine lovers enjoy the Glocke Hotel's stube.

See tomorrow for information on Munich.

Day 6: Munich or Salzburg

After some sage orientation you'll be on your own in this most enter-taining of German cities. Munich offers wonderful museums, streetlife, beer gardens, parks and markets. If it's Monday (when most sights and shops are closed), you may want to hop a train for 90 minutes and spend the afternoon and evening in nearby Salzburg, Austria.

Likely activities today...
Walking tour of Munich*
Afternoon and evening free*

You'll walk from 3 to 10 miles today, and sleep in Munich.

Included as an activity on BB&B tours.

Munich (München)
Munich, Germany's most livable city, is also one of its most historic, artistic, and entertaining. It's big and growing, with a population of over 1,500,000. Just a little more than a century ago, it was the capital of an independent Bavaria. Its imperial palaces, jewels, and grand boule-vards constantly remind visitors that this was once a political as well as a cultural powerhouse. Its freshly-rebuilt look reminds us that it was heavily damaged by Allied bombers 50 years ago.

Orient yourself in Munich's old center with its colorful pedestrian mall. Immerse yourself in Munich's art and history—crown jewels, Baroque theater, Wittelsbach palaces, great art, and beautiful parks. Munich evenings are best spent in frothy beer halls—oompah bunny-hopping and belching Bavarian atmosphere. Pry big pretzels from no-nonsense buxom beer maids.

Munich Orientation (tel. code: 089)
The tourist's Munich is circled by a ring road (which was the town wall) marked by four old gates: Karlstor (near the train station), Sendlinger Tor, Isartor (near the river), and Odeonsplatz (near the pal-ace). Marienplatz is the city center. A great pedestrian-only street cuts this circle in half, running nearly from Karlstor and the train station through Marienplatz to Isartor. Orient yourself along this east-west axis. Most sights are within a few blocks of this people-filled walk. Our hotel and nearly all the sights we recommend are within about a 20-minute walk of Marienplatz and each other. Most Munich sights are closed on Monday.

Munich Center

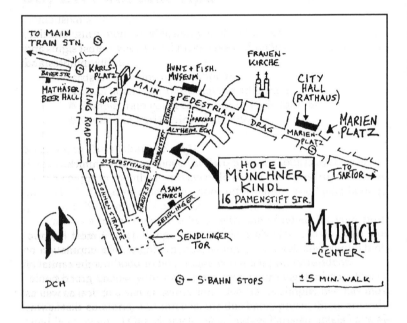

Tourist Info: The TI in the train station has lots of practical information (Monday-Saturday 8:00-22:00, Sundays 11:00-19:00, tel. 089/233-30-256, near street exit at track 11). Have a list of questions ready, confirm your sightseeing plans, and pick up brochures, the free and excellent city map, and subway map. Consider buying the 2.50 DM *Monatsprogram* for a German-language list of sights and calendar of events. The free monthly *In Munich* (available at the TI or any big cinema — one is next to Mathäser's Beerhall) lists all the movies and entertainment in town. If the TI line is worse than your questions are important, skip your questions, and go directly to the cash window to pick up the map and other brochures.

Munich's train station is a sight in itself, one of those places that stoke anyone's wanderlust. For a quick orientation in the station, use the big wall maps of the train station, Munich, and Bavaria (through the center doorway as you leave the tracks on the left). For a quick rest stop, the Burger King upstairs has toilets as pleasant and accessible as its hamburgers. Sussmann's Internationale Presse (across from track 24) is great for English language books, papers, and magazines including *Munich Found* (the informative English-speaking residents' monthly).

Getting Around Munich

By Subway: Most Munich sights are walkable, but if you're planning to visit the BMW museum, Olympic Grounds, or Nymphenburg Palace, take advantage of Munich's great subway system. Subways are called U- or S-bahns. Subway lines are numbered (e.g., S3 or U5). Regular tickets cost 3.50 DM and are good for 2 hours of changes in one direction. For the shortest rides (1 or 2 stops), get the smallest 2 DM ticket (Kurzstrecke). The 12-DM all-day pass is a great deal. One pass is good for up to 2 adults and 3 kids. If more than one adult is using it on a weekday, it's good only after 9:00. The cheaper 8-DM all-day pass is good for one adult only. Get a pass, validate it in a machine, and you have Munich by the rail for a day (purchase at tourist offices, subway booths, and in machines at most stops). The entire system (bus/tram/subway) works on the same tickets. You must punch your own ticket before boarding. (Plainclothes ticket checkers enforce this "honor system" rewarding free loaders with stiff fines.)

By bike: See the town by bike, rentable quick and easy at the train station. Munich—level, compact, with plenty of bike paths—feels good on two wheels. Near track 30 at the train station, **Radius Touristik** (daily, 10:00-18:00, May through mid-October, tel. 596114, run by Englishman Patrick Holder) rents three-speed bikes (5 DM/hour, 20 DM/day, 25 DM/24 hours) and organizes city bike tours. Patrick dispenses all the necessary tourist information (city map, bike routes).

By taxi: Taxis are expensive and needless.

Sights—Munich

▲▲**Marienplatz and the Pedestrian Zone**—The glory of Munich will slap your face into a smile as you ride the escalator out of the subway and into the sunlit Marienplatz (Mary's Place): great buildings bombed flat and rebuilt, the ornate facades of the new and old City Halls (the Neues Rathaus, built in neo-Gothic style from 1867 to 1910, and the Altes Rathaus), outdoor cafés, and people bustling and lingering like the birds and breeze they share this square with. From here the pedestrian mall (Kaufingerstrasse and Neuhauserstrasse) leads you through a great shopping area past carnivals of street entertainers, the twin-towering Frauenkirche (built in 1470, rebuilt after World War II), and several fountains, to Karlstor and the train station. The not-very-old Glockenspiel "jousts" on Marienplatz daily through the tourist season at 11:00, 12:00, 17:00, and a shorty at 21:00.

▲▲**City Views:** The highest viewpoint is from a 350-foot-high perch on top of the **Frauenkirche** (elevator, 4 DM, 10:00-17:00, closed Sunday). There's also a fine view from the **Neues Rathaus** (2 DM, elevator from under the Marienplatz Glockenspiel, 9:00-19:00, closed Sunday).

Munich

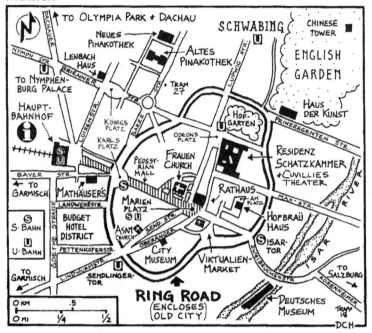

For a totally unobstructed view, but with no elevator, climb the **St. Peter's church** tower just a block away. It's a long climb, much of it with two-way traffic on a one-way staircase, but the view is dynamite (2.50 DM, 9:00-18:00, Sunday 10:00-18:00). Try to be two flights from the top when the bells ring at the top of the hour (and when your friends ask you about your trip, you'll say, "What?"). The church, built upon the hill where the first monks founded the city in the 12th century, has a fine interior with photos of the WWII bomb damage on a column near the entrance.

▲▲**Residenz**—For a long hike through rebuilt corridors of gilded imperial Bavarian grandeur, tour the family palace of the Wittelsbachs who ruled Bavaria for more than 700 years (10:00-16:30, closed Monday, 5 DM, enter on Max-Joseph Platz, 3 blocks from Marienplatz). The **Schatzkammer** (treasury) shows off a thousand years of Wittelsbach crowns and knickknacks (same hours, another 5 DM from the same window). Vienna's palace and jewels are better, but this is Bavaria's best.

▲**The Cuvillies Theater**—Attached to the Residenz, this National Theater, designed by Cuvillies, is dazzling enough to send you back to the days of divine monarchs (Monday-Saturday 14:00-17:00, Sunday 10:00-17:00, 3 DM).

▲▲Münchner Stadtmuseum—The underrated Munich city museum is a pleasant surprise. Exhibits include: life in Munich through the centuries (including WWII and Hitler's planned urban fantasy) illustrated in paintings, photos and models, beer history, antique puppets and carnival gadgets, a huge collection of musical instruments from around the world, old photography, and a first class medieval armory. No crowds, bored and playful guards (Tuesday-Sunday 10:00-17:00, Wednesday until 20:30, closed Monday, 5 DM, 7.50 DM for families; three blocks off Marienplatz at St. Jakob's Platz 1, a fine children's playground faces the entry).

▲▲Alte Pinakothek—Bavaria's best collection of art is closed for renovation at least through 1997. Thankfully most of its top masterpieces will be displayed in the normally much less interesting neighboring Neue Pinakothek (6 DM, Tuesday-Sunday 10:00-17:00, Tuesday and Thursday 10:00-20:00, closed Monday, tel. 238-05195). The collection's forte is Italian and North European artists, such as Rubens, Rembrandt, Fra Angelico, Botticelli, de Vinci, Raphael, and Dürer. (U-2 to Königsplatz or tram #27.)

▲Haus der Kunst—Built by Hitler as a temple of Nazi art, this bold and fascist building now houses modern art, much of which the Führer censored. It's a fun collection—Kandinsky, Picasso, Dali, and much more from this century (9:00-16:30, Thursday evenings 19:00-21:00, closed Monday, 3.50 DM).

Bayerisches Nationalmuseum—An interesting collection of Riemenschneider carvings, manger scenes, traditional living rooms, and old Bavarian houses (9:30-17:00, closed Monday, 5 DM, free on Sunday; tram #20 or bus 53 or 55 to Prinzregentenstrasse 3).

▲▲Deutsches Museum—Germany's answer to our Smithsonian Institution has everything of scientific and technical interest from astronomy to zymurgy. With 10 miles of exhibits, even those on roller skates will need to be selective. Technical types enjoy lots of hands-on gadgetry, a state-of-the-art planetarium and an IMAX theater (self-serve cafeteria, museum open daily 9:00-17:00, 9 DM; S-Bahn to Isartorplatz).

Schwabing—Munich's artsy, bohemian university district or "Greenwich Village" has been called "not a place but a state of mind." All I experienced was a mental lapse. The bohemians run the boutiques. I think the most colorful thing about Schwabing is the road leading back downtown. U3 or U6 will take you to the Münchener-Freiheit Center if you want to wander. Most of the jazz and disco joints are near Occamstrasse. The Haidhausen neighborhood (U-bahn: Max Weber Platz) is becoming the "new Schwabing."

▲**Englischer Garten**—One of Europe's great parks, Munich's "Central Park" is the Continent's largest, laid out in 1789 by an American. There's a huge beer garden near the Chinese Pagoda. Caution: while a local law requires sun-worshippers to wear clothes on the tram, this park is sprinkled with nude sunbathers. A rewarding respite from the city, it's especially fun on a bike under the summer sun (rental shop sometimes open where Veterinar Strasse hits the park).

Asam Church—Near the Stadtmuseum, this private church of the Asam brothers is a gooey drippy masterpiece by Bavaria's top two rococonuts, showing off their very popular Baroque-concentrate style.

The Centre of Unusual Museums is a collection of mediocre but occasionally interesting one-room museums featuring goofy topics such as padlocks, Easter bunnies, chamber pots, and so on (daily 10:00-18:00; near Marienplatz and Isartor at Westenriederstr. 26; not worth 8 DM).

▲**Olympic Grounds**—Munich's great 1972 Olympic stadium and sports complex is now a lush park offering a tower (commanding but so high it's boring view from 820 feet, 8:00-24:00, 5 DM), an excellent swimming pool (7:00-22:30, Monday from 10:00, Thursday closed at 18:00, 5 DM), a good look at its striking "cobweb" style of architecture, and plenty of sun, grass, and picnic potential. Take U3 to Olympiazentrum direct from Marienplatz.

BMW Museum—The BMW headquarters, located in a striking building across the street from the Olympic Grounds, offers a good 6 DM museum (daily 9:00-17:00, last ticket sold at 16:00, ask about their rare factory tours, tel. 382-25-652, closed much of August). The museum is popular with car buffs.

Bus Tours of Munich—Panorama Tours (at the train station, tel. 591504) offers 1-hour city orientation bus tours (at 10:00, 11:30, and 14:30, 15 DM).

▲▲**Nymphenburg Palace**—This royal summer palace is impressive, but if you've already seen the Residenz, it's only mediocre. If you do tour it, don't miss King Ludwig's "Gallery of Beauties"—a room stacked with portraits of Bavaria's loveliest women—according to Ludwig (who had a thing about big noses). The palace park, good for a royal stroll, contains the tiny, more-impressive-than-the-palace Amalienburg hunting lodge, a rococo jewel by Cuvillies. The sleigh and coach collection (Marstallmuseum) is especially interesting for "Mad" Ludwig fans (9:00-12:30 and 13:30-17:00, closed Monday, shorter hours October-March, admission to all 7 DM, less for individual parts, use the little English guidebook, tel. 179080, reasonable cafeteria; U1 to Rotkreuzplatz, then tram or bus 12).

Oktoberfest

When King Ludwig the First had a marriage party in 1810 it was such a success that they made it an annual bash. These days the Oktoberfest lasts 16 days ending with the first full weekend in October. It starts (usually on the third Saturday in September) with an opening parade of more than 6,000 participants and fills eight huge beer tents with about 6,000 people each. A million gallons of beer later, they roast the last ox.

The fairground, known as the Wies'n (a few blocks south of the train station), erupts in a frenzy of rides, dancing, strangers strolling arm-in-arm down rows of picnic tables, while the beer god stirs tons of beer, pretzels, and wurst in a bubbling cauldron of fun. The "three loops" roller coaster must be the wildest on earth (best before the beer drinking). During the fair, the city functions even better than normal, and it's a good time to sightsee even if beer hall rowdiness isn't your cup of tea. The Fasching carnival time (early January to mid-February) is nearly as crazy. And the Oktoberfest grounds are set up for a mini-Oktoberfest to celebrate spring for the two weeks around May Day.

Eating in Munich

Munich's most memorable budget meals are found in the beer halls. You have two basic choices: famous touristy places with music or mellower beer gardens with Germans.

The touristy ones have great beer, reasonable food, live music and are right downtown. These days Germans go there for the entertainment—to sing "Country Roads," see how Texas girls party, and watch salarymen from Tokyo chug beer. The music-every-night atmosphere is thick; the fat and shiny-leather band has even church mice standing up and conducting three-quarter time with a breadstick. Meals are inexpensive (for a light 10 DM meal, we like the local favorite, "*Schweinswurst mit Kraut*"); huge, liter beers called *ein Mass* (or "ein pitcher" in English) are 10 DM; white radishes are salted and cut in delicate spirals; and surly beermaids pull mustard packets from their cleavages. You can order your beer "*Helles*" (light, what you'll get if you say "ein beer"), "*Dunkel*" (dark) or "*Radler*" (half lemonade, half light beer). Notice the vomitoriums in the WC.

The most famous beer hall, the **Hofbräuhaus** (Platzl 9, near Marienplatz, tel. 221676, music for lunch and dinner), is most touristy. But check it out; it's fun to see 200 Japanese people drinking beer in a German beer hall. (They have a gimmicky folk evening upstairs in the "Festsaal" nightly at 19:00, 8 DM, tel. 290136-10, food and drinks are sold from the same menu.) My long-time favorite, **Mathäser Bierstadt** (dinner #94 is light, good, typical and cheap, tel. 592896, Bayerstrasse 5, halfway between the train station and Karlstor, music after 17:00) has joined the Hofbräuhaus as the tour-group beer hall. For typical Bavarian fast food, try the self-serve at Mathäser's entry.

The **Weisses Bräuhaus** (Tal 10, between Marienplatz and Isartor) is more local and features the local fizzy *"Weizenbier"* (wheat beer). Hitler met with fellow fascists here in 1920 when his Nazi party had yet to ferment. The **Augustiner Beer Garden** (across from the train tracks, three blocks from the station away from the center on Arnulfstrasse) is a sprawling haven for local beer-lovers on a balmy evening. Upstairs in the tiny **Jodlerwirt** (4 Altenhofstrasse, between the Hofbräuhaus and Marienplatz, after 19:00, closed Sunday) is a woodsy, smart-aleck, yodeling kind of pub. For a classier evening stewed in antlers and fiercely Bavarian, eat under a tree or inside at the sometimes-smoke-filled **Nürnberger Bratwurst Glöckl am Dom** (Frauenplatz 9, under the twin-domed cathedral, 20 DM dinners, tel. 220385, closed Sunday).

For outdoor atmosphere and a cheap meal, spend an evening at the **Englischer Garten's Chinese Pagoda** (Chinesischer Turm) **Biergarten**. You're welcome to BYO food and grab a table or buy from the picnic stall (*Brotzeit*) right there. Don't bother to phone ahead: there are six thousand seats! For similar BYOF atmosphere right behind Marienplatz, eat at the **Viktualien Markt** beer garden. Lunch or dinner here taps you into about the best budget eating in town. Countless stalls surround the beer garden selling wurst, sandwiches, produce, and so on. This BYOF tradition goes back to the days when monks were allowed to sell beer but not food. Now those were the days. Bare wooden tables are for picnics. A tablecloth means you need to order from the menu. This is a good place to grab the most typical meal in town: Weisswurst (white sausage) with süss (sweet) mustard, a salty pretzel, and Weissbier. The **Suppenkücke** (soup kitchen, 5 DM-8 DM soup meals, in the Viktualien Market near Rosental Street, everyone knows where it is) is fine for a small, cozy, sit-down lunch.

The crown in its emblem indicates that the royal family assembled its picnics in the historic, elegant, and expensive **Alois Dallmayr** delicatessen at 14 Dienerstrasse just behind the Rathaus (9:00-18:30, Saturday 9:00-14:00, closed Sunday). Wander through this dieter's purgatory, put together a royal picnic, and eat it in the nearby, adequately royal Hofgarten. To save money, browse at Dallmayr's, but buy in the basement supermarket of the Kaufhof department store across the Marienplatz.

Optional day trip to Salzburg
Munich is a world-class city. But if your free day falls on a Saturday or Sunday (when most shops are closed) or Monday (when most sights are closed), consider hopping a train to Mozart's Austrian home town for the afternoon. If you get a bunch of friends together and travel as a

group both ways, the round trip will cost you only about 32 DM ($20) each. Remember to bring your passport. You can spend German marks in Austria. You'll get your change back in Austrian shillings.

Salzburg

With a well-preserved old town, gardens, churches, and lush surroundings, set under Europe's biggest intact medieval castle, and forever smiling to the tunes of Mozart and *The Sound of Music*, Salzburg knows how to be popular. Eight million tourists crawl its cobbles each year. That's a lot of Mozart balls.

Orientation (tel. code: 0662)

Salzburg, a city of 150,000 (Austria's fourth largest) is divided into old and new. The old town, sitting between the Salzach River and the 1,600-foot-high hill called Mönchsberg, is a bundle of Baroque holding all the charm and most of the tourists.

Tourist Info: The helpful tourist office (at the train station, and on Mozartplatz in the old center, tel. 88987) is your essential first stop. Ask for a city map, a list of sights with current hours, and a schedule of events.

Arriving by Train: The tourist information office is at track 2A. Downstairs is the place to rent bikes and get train information. This lower street level faces the bus station (where buses numbered 1, 5, 6, and 51 go to the old center). To walk downtown (15 minutes), leave the station ticket hall near window #8 through the door marked "Zentrum" and walk absolutely straight down Rainerstrasse, which leads you under the tracks past Mirabellplatz, changes its name to Dreitaltigkeitsgasse, and takes you to the *Staatsbrucke* (bridge) which deposits you in the old town. For a more dramatic approach, leave the same way but follow the tracks to the river, turn left, and walk the riverside path toward the castle.

Getting Around: Salzburg is served by a fine bus system (info tel. 87 21 45). Single-ride tickets are sold on the bus for 21 AS. Twenty-four-hour passes cost 30 AS. Salzburg is bike-friendly and the train station rents good bikes all day until midnight for 50 AS (90 AS if you have no train ticket or pass, no deposit required, go to counter #3 to pay, then pick it up at "left luggage").

Helpful Hints: The American Express office is on Mozartplatz 5 (open Monday-Friday 9:00-17:30, Saturday 9:00-12:00, tel. 842501).

Sights—Salzburg

▲Salzburg Cathedral (daily 8:00-17:00, free) claims to be the first Baroque building north of the Alps. It's modeled after St. Peter's and is three-quarters the size of Europe's biggest church. Back then, the bishop

Salzburg

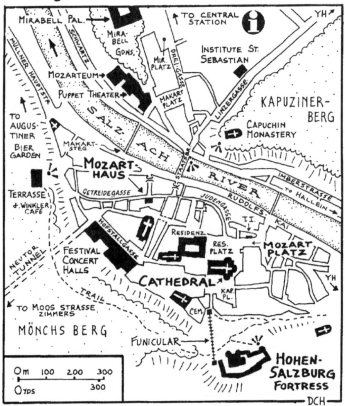

of Salzburg was number-two man in the church hierarchy and Salzburg fancied itself as the "Northern Rome." Check out its 6,000-pipe organ. Sunday Mass (10:00) is famous for its music. For a fee you can tour the excavation site under the church and the Dom Museum in the church. **Residenz**—It was Archbishop Wolf Dietrich (not Mozart or Julie Andrews) who had the greatest impact on Salzburg. His grandiose vision of Salzburg shaped the city into the Baroque beauty you'll see today. His palace, the Residenz, next to the cathedral is impressive—unless you've seen any others. Admission is by German-language tour only (hourly 10:00-15:00, 45 AS).

▲**Carillon**—The bell tower on Mozartplatz chimes throughout the day. Its carillon of 35 17th-century bells (cast in Antwerp) plays a tune daily at 7:00, 11:00, and 18:00.

▲**Getreidegasse**—Old Salzburg's lively and colorful main drag, famous for its many old wrought-iron signs, still looks much as it did in Mozart's day.

▲**Mozart's Birthplace (Geburtshaus, 1756)**—The birthplaces of famous people are usually as dead as they are. But this best Mozart sight in town is almost a pilgrimage, and if you're a fan, you'll have to check it out. It's right in the old town on colorful Getreidegasse, #9 (daily 9:00-19:00, shorter hours off-season, 62 AS). In 1996, Mozart's Residence (just over the river at Markplatz 8) will open with a new expanded exhibit on Mozart's life.

▲**Hohensalzburg Fortress**—This castle, one of Europe's mightiest, dominates Salzburg's skyline. The interior is so-so unless you catch a tour (30 AS, confirm that it will be in English as well as German). The basic entry fee (30 AS) gives you only the view and the courtyard. The museum has the noisiest floorboards in Europe. Even so the prince had a chastity belt. You can see it next to other gruesome torture devices that need no explanation. Upstairs is a mediocre military museum offering a chance to see photos of nice-looking young Nazi officers whose government convinced them that their operation was a just cause.

The funicular zips you effortlessly to the castle (32 AS round-trip, every 10 minutes) or you can hike up (20 minutes). The castle is open daily, 9:00 to 19:00, less in off-season.

▲**Mirabell Gardens and Palace (*Schloss*)**—The bubbly gardens are always open and free, but to properly enjoy the lavish Mirabell Palace, get a ticket to a *Schlosskonzerte*. Baroque music flying around a Baroque hall is a happy bird in the right cage. Tickets are around 330 AS (cheaper at the palace and for students) and rarely sold out (tel. 848-586).

▲**City Walking Tour**—A mediocre two-language 1-hour guided walking tour of the old town leaves from the tourist information office at Mozartplatz (80 AS, 12:15, Monday-Saturday, May-October, tel. 847568).

While walking on your own, be sure to browse through St. Peter's Cemetery (at the base of the castle lift, tours of early Christian catacombs, this was where the Trapp family hid out in the *S.O.M.*) and through the morning open-air market (daily except Sunday) on Universitätsplatz.

And for a most enjoyable approach to the castle, consider riding the elevator to the Café Winkler and walking 20 minutes through the woods high above the city to Festung Hohensalzburg (stay on the high trails or you'll have a needless climb back up to the castle).

Eating in Salzburg
Augustiner Bräustübl (Augustinergasse 4, walk through the Mirabellgarten, over the Müllnersteg bridge and ask for "Müllnerbräu," its local nickname, 1,000 seats, open daily 15:00-23:00). This monk-run

brewery is very rustic and crude, but we recommend it. It's like a Munich beer hall with no music but the volume turned up, a historic setting with beer-sloshed smoke-stained halls, and a pleasant outdoor beer garden serving a fine monastic brew. Here you can eat hearty slabs of schnitzel with your fingers or cold meals from the self-serve picnic counter.

Stiftskeller St. Peter (next to St. Peter's church at the foot of Mönchsberg, outdoor and indoor seating, tel. 8412680) has been in business for over a thousand years. It's classier, more central, not too expensive, and your best splurge for traditional Austrian cuisine in medieval sauce. The "Monastery Pot" (hearty soup in a bowl made of dark bread) is cheap and filling.

Gasthaus "Zum Wilder Mann" (enter from Getreidegasse 20 or Griesgasse 17, tel. 841-787, food served 11:00-21:00) is the place if the weather's bad and you're in the mood for Hofbräu atmosphere in one small well-antlered room and a hearty cheap meal at a shared table, 2 minutes from Mozart's place. For a quick 100-AS lunch, get the Bauernschmaus, a mountain of dumpling, kraut, and peasant's meats.

Stieglkeller (50 yards uphill from the lift to the castle, tel. 842-681), a huge, atmospheric institution with several rustic rooms and outdoor garden seating offering a great rooftop view of the old town, is an inexpensive way to get really schnitzeled.

You'll see a mountainous sweet souffle served all over town. The memorable "Salzberger Nockerl" is worth a try (if you have someone to split it with). It's really big enough for four. (The Goldenen Ente Restaurant does a fine one.)

Day 7: To Austria

We'll take a short drive out of Munich to the Dachau concentration camp. After this powerful pilgrimage we'll drive south along the Romantic Road, making an old-fashioned pilgrimage to the Wies Church, before popping just over the Austrian border to Reutte, our small-town Tirolean home base.

> **Likely activities today...**
> 30 minute drive to Dachau*
> Visit to the Dachau Concentration Camp*
> 3 hour drive to Wies Church*
> 1 hour drive to Reutte, Austria*
> Dinner at hotel*
>
> You'll walk about 2 miles today, and sleep in Reutte.

* Included as an activity on BB&B tours.

▲▲**Dachau**—Dachau was the first Nazi concentration camp (1933). Today it's the most accessible camp to travelers and a very effective voice from our recent but grisly past, warning and pleading "Never Again," the memorial's theme. This is a valuable experience and when approached thoughtfully, well worth the trouble. In fact, it may change your life. See it. Feel it. Read and think about it. After this most powerful sightseeing experience, many people gain more respect for history

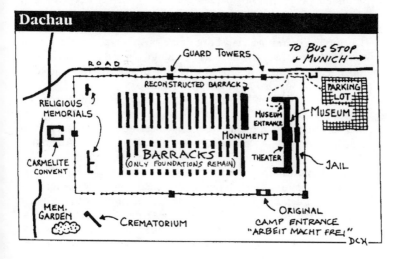

and the dangers of not keeping tabs on their government.

Upon arrival, pick up the mini-guide and note when the next documentary film in English will be shown (25 minutes, normally at 11:30 and 15:30). The museum and the movie are exceptional. Notice the Expressionist fascist-inspired art near the theater, where you'll also find English books, slides, and a WC. Outside, be sure to see the reconstructed barracks and the memorial shrines at the far end (9:00-17:00, closed Monday).

▲▲Wies Church—Germany's greatest Rococo-style church, Wieskirche (the church in the meadow), is newly restored and looking as brilliant as the day it floated down from heaven. With flames of decoration, over-ripe but bright and bursting with beauty, this church is a divine droplet, a curly curlicue, the final flowering of the Baroque movement. The ceiling depicts the Last Judgment.

This is a pilgrimage church. In the early 1700s, a carving of Christ, too graphic to be accepted by that generation's church, was the focus of worship in a peasant's private chapel. Miraculously, it wept. And pilgrims came from all around. Bavaria's top Rococo architects, the Zimmerman brothers, were then commissioned to build this church which features the amazing carving above its altar and still attracts countless pilgrims. Take a commune-with-nature-and-smell-the-farm detour back through the meadow to the car park (daily, 8:00-20:00).

Austria (Österreich, the Kingdom of the East)
■ 32,000 square miles (the size of South Carolina, or two Switzerlands).
■ 7.6 million people (235 per square mile and holding, 85 percent Catholic).
■ About 10 AS = US$1. Figure a dime each.

During the grand old Habsburg days, Austria was Europe's most powerful empire. Its royalty built a giant kingdom of more than 50 million people by making love, not war (having lots of children and marrying them into the other royal houses of Europe).

Today this small, landlocked country does more to cling to its elegant past than any other in Europe. The waltz is still the rage. Austrians are very sociable; more so than anywhere else, it's important to greet people you pass on the streets or meet in shops. The Austrian's version of "Hi" is a cheerful *Grüss Gott* (may God greet you). You'll get the correct pronunciation after the first volley—listen and copy.

While they speak German, accept German currency (at least in Salzburg, Innsbruck, and Reutte), and talked about unity with Germany long before Hitler ever said "*Anschluss*," the Austrians cherish their distinct cultural and historical traditions. They are not Germans. Austria is mellow and relaxed compared to Deutschland. *Gemütlichkeit* is the lo-

Austria

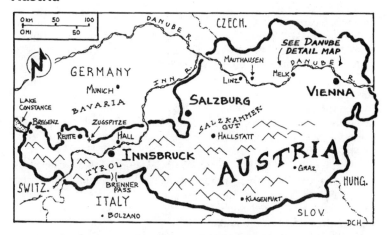

cal word for this special Austrian cozy-and-easy approach to life. It's good living—whether engulfed in mountain beauty or bathed in lavish high culture. The people stroll as if every day were Sunday, topping things off with a visit to a coffee or pastry shop.

It must be nice to be past your prime—no longer troubled by being powerful, able to kick back and be as happy as an Edelweiss in the clean, untroubled mountain air. While the Austrians make less money than their neighbors, they enjoy a short work week and a long life span. Austria was a neutral country throughout the cold war. It's now free to get closer to Europe's economic community.

The Austrian schilling (S or AS) is divided into 100 groschen (g). Divide prices by ten to get approximate costs in dollars (e.g., 420 AS is $42). About 7 AS = 1 DM. Most Austrian waiters and merchants (except post offices) are happy to accept German DMs, but you cannot use German postage stamps in Austria.

Austrians eat on about the same schedule we do. Treats include *Wiener Schnitzel* (breaded veal cutlet), *Knödel* (dumplings), *Apfelstrudel*, and fancy desserts like the *Sachertorte*, Vienna's famous chocolate cake. Service is included in restaurant bills.

Shops are open from 8:00 to 17:00 or 18:00. Banks keep roughly the same hours but usually close for lunch.

Austria nitty-gritty
Country code: 43
International access: 00
AT&T: 022-903-011

MCI: 022-903-012
SPRINT: 022-903-014
Telephone cards cost 50, 100 or 200 AS.
When you make a phone call in Austria, you'll pay for the amount of time you were on the line, even if you get a busy signal or no answer (this includes calls from your hotel room).

Reutte, Austria

Reutte (pronounced "ROY-teh," rolled "r"), population 5,000, is a relaxed town, far from the international tourist crowd but popular with Germans and Austrians for its climate. Doctors recommend its "grade 1" air.

You won't find Reutte in any American guidebook. Its charms are subtle. It never was rich or important. Its castle is ruined, its buildings have paint-on "carvings," its churches are full, its men yodel for each other on birthdays, and lately its energy is spent soaking its Austrian and German guests in gemütlichkeit.

Because most guests stay for a week, the town's attractions are more time-consuming than thrilling. If the weather's good, hike to the mysterious Ehrenberg ruins or ride the luge.

Orientation

Tourist Info (TI): The Reutte TI, a block in front of the train station, is very helpful (open weekdays 8:30-12:00 and 13:00-17:00 or 18:00, Saturday 8:00-12:00, and from mid-July to mid-August on Saturday and Sunday afternoons from 16:00-18:00; tel. 05672/2336, or direct and cheap from Germany, 0043-5672/2336). Go over your sightseeing plans, ask about a folk evening, and pick up a city map. Don't ask about a laundromat. Unless you can infiltrate the local campground, the town has none.

Getting Around: While Reutte is a short bus ride from Fussen (departures at 8:35, 12:10, 13:50, 16:45; returning from Fussen to Reutte at 9:30, 12:50, 15:20 and 17:10), its train line goes to Garmisch (2/hr., 60-minute ride). The station rents bikes cheaply. From Reutte in the summer, you can bus directly to the castle at Neuschwanstein (11:25-12:00) and return (15:45-16:10).

Sights—Reutte

Folk Museum—The town's *Heimatmuseum* (10:00-12:00, 14:00-17:00, closed Monday; in the Green House on Untermarkt, around the corner from Hotel Goldener Hirsch) offers a quick look at the local folk culture and the story of the castle, but so do the walls and mantels of most of the hotels.

Reutte in Tirol

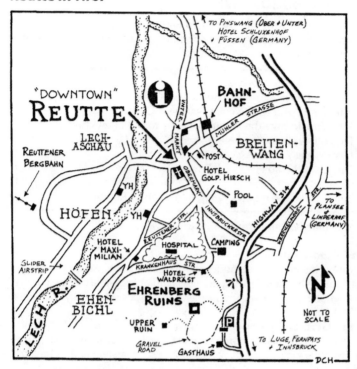

Swimming—Plunge into Reutte's Olympic-sized swimming pool to cool off after your castle hikes (10:00 to 21:00, off-season 14:00-21:00, closed Monday, 58 AS).

The Reuttener Bergbahn (mountain lift) swoops you high above the tree line to a starting point for several hikes and an Alpine flower park with special paths leading you past countless local varieties.

Flying and Gliding—For a major thrill on a sunny day, drop by the tiny airport in Hofen across the river and fly. A small single-prop plane (three people for 30 minutes, 1,200 AS; 60 minutes for 2,100 AS) can buzz the Zugspitze and Ludwig's castles and give you a bird's-eye peek at Reutte's Ehrenberg ruins (that's about the cost of three lift tickets up the Zugspitze, and a lot easier). Or for something more angelic, how about Segelfliegen? For 260 AS, you get 30 minutes in a glider for two (you and the pilot). Just watching the tow rope launch the graceful glider like a giant slow motion rubber-band gun is thrilling (late May through October, 11:00-19:00, in good weather, tel. 05672/3207).

Day 8: Castle Day

We'll tour "Mad King" Ludwig's Neuschwanstein Castle, take a wild ride on the luge, and hike to the Ehrenburg ruins above our home base town of Reutte.

Likely activities today...
30 minute drive to Neuschwanstein Castle*
Hike up to and tour Neuschwanstein Castle*
Free time to hike the Pöllat Gorge or tour Hohenschwangau*
Drive to and ride the luge (if open)*
Hike to the Ehrenberg ruins*
Dinner at the hotel*

You'll walk 3 to 6 miles today, and sleep in Reutte.

---

* Included as an activity on BB&B tours.

Bavaria and Tirol
Straddling the border, two hours south of Munich, between Germany's Bavaria and Austria's Tirol is a timeless land of fairy-tale castles, painted buildings shared by cows and farmers, and locals who still yodel when they're happy.

In Germany's Bavaria, tour "Mad" Ludwig's ornate Neuschwanstein Castle, Europe's most spectacular. In Austria's Tirol, hike up to the very different castles of Neuschwanstein and Ehrenberg, then scream down a nearby ski slope on an oversized skateboard.

Sights in Bavaria
▲▲▲Neuschwanstein and Hohenschwangau Castles (Königsschlösser)—
The fairy-tale castle, Neuschwanstein, looks medieval, but it was built after the American Civil War. Created to suit the whims of Bavaria's King Ludwig II, it's a textbook example of the romanticism that was popular in nineteenth-century Europe.

Beat the crowds. See Neuschwanstein, Germany's most popular castle, early in the morning. The castle is open every morning at 8:30; by 11:00, it's packed. Rushed 25-minute English-language tours are less rushed early. They leave regularly, telling the sad story of Bavaria's "mad" king.

It's a steep 20-minute uphill hike to the castle. Or, you can take advantage of the buses (3.50 DM up, 5 DM round-trip, dropping you near Mary's Bridge, a steep 10 minutes above the castle) or horse car-

Neuschwanstein

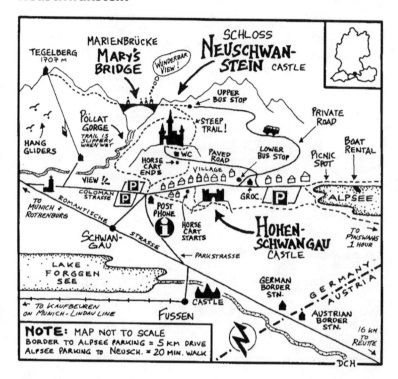

riages (slower than walking, stops 5 minutes short of the castle, 7 DM up, 3.50 DM down) that go constantly (watch your step). Your work continues inside the castle as your tour takes you up and down more than 300 stairs. Signposts and books often refer to these castles in the German, "Königsschlösser."

After the tour, climb up to Mary's Bridge to marvel at Ludwig's castle, just as Ludwig did. This bridge was quite an engineering accomplishment a hundred years ago. From the bridge, the frisky can hike even higher to the "Beware—Danger of Death" signs and an even more glorious castle view. For the most scenic descent, follow signs to the Pöllat Gorge. (The turn-off is midway between the castle and Mary's Bridge -- look for steps leading down. This route takes about 20 minutes longer and is extremely slippery when wet.)

The big, yellow Hohenschwangau Castle nearby was Ludwig's boyhood home. It's more lived-in and historic and actually gives a better glimpse of Ludwig's life. (Each castle costs 10 DM and is open daily

Bavaria and Tirol Castle Loop

8:30-17:30, October-March 10:00-16:00, tel. 08362/81035. If not enough
English-speakers gather, you may have to do Hohenschwangau with a
German group. TI tel. 08362/8198-40.)

The "village" at the foot of the castles was created for and lives off
the hungry, shopping tourists who come in droves to Europe's "Disney"
castle. The big yellow Bräustüberl restaurant by the lakeside parking
lot is cheapest. Next door is a little family-run, open-daily souvenir/
grocery store with the makings for a skimpy picnic and a microwave
fast-food machine. Picnic in the lakeside park or in one of the old-fashioned rent-by-the-hour rowboats. The bus stop, the post/telephone office, and a helpful TI cluster around the main intersection.

▲▲**Ehrenberg Ruins**—The brooding ruins of Ehrenberg (two castle
ruins atop two neighboring hills) are a mile outside of Reutte on the
road to Lermoos and Innsbruck. These thirteenth-century rock piles, a
great contrast to King Ludwig's "modern" castles, are a great opportu-

nity to let your imagination off its leash. Hike up from the parking lot at the base of the hill; it's a 15-minute walk to the small (*kleine*) castle for a great view from your own private ruins. (Facing the hill from the parking lot the steeper but more scenic trail is to the right, the easy gravelly road is to the left.) Imagine how proud Count Meinrad II of Tirol (who built the castle in 1290) would be to know that his castle repelled 16,000 Swedish soldiers in the defense of Catholicism in 1632.

You'll find more medieval mystique atop the taller neighboring hill in the big (*gross*) ruins. You can't see anything from below and almost nothing when you get there, but these bigger, more desolate and overgrown ruins are a little more romantic (and a lot harder to get to).

The easiest way down is via the small road from the gully between the two castles. The car park, with a café/guest house (with a German language flyer about the castle), is just off the Lermoos/Reutte road. Reutte is a pleasant 60-minute walk away. The town museum and many Reutte hotels have sketches of the intact castle.

▲▲**Sommerrodelbahn, the Luge**—Near Lermoos, on the Innsbruck-Lermoos-Reutte road, you'll find two rare and exciting luge courses. In the summer, these ski slopes are used as luge courses, or Sommerrodelbahn. To try one of Europe's great $5 thrills, take the lift up, grab a sled-like go-cart, and luge down. The concrete bobsled course banks on the corners, and even a novice can go very, very fast. Most are cautious on their first run and speed demons on their second. (Keep both hands on the stick at all times, especially if you plan to go fast. Ignoring this rule is the surest way to flip off the course and lose some skin.) No one emerges from the course without a windblown hairdo and a smile-creased face. Both places charge a steep 70 AS per run, with five-trip or ten-trip discount cards; both are open weekends from late May, and daily (from 9:00 or 10:00 until about 17:00) from about mid-June through September, and into October if weather permits. They shut down at the slightest hint of moisture on the track.

The small and steep luge: The first course (100-meter drop over 800-meter course) is 6 kilometers beyond Reutte's castle ruins. Call ahead, tel. 05674/5350, the local TI at 05674/5354 speaks more English).

The longest luge: The Biberwier Sommerrodelbahn, 15 minutes closer to Innsbruck, just past Lermoos in Biberwier, is the longest luge in Austria—1,300 meters—but has a shorter season. (9:00-16:30, tel. 05673/2111, local TI tel. 05673/2922.) A block or two downhill from this luge, behind the Sport und Trachtenstüberl shop, is a wooden church-dome with a striking Zugspitze backdrop. If you have sunshine and a camera, don't miss it.

Day 9: To Venice

We'll drive to Innsbruck or Hall-in-Tirol for a short stop, then an all-afternoon drive into Italy—a whole new world of sunshine, cappuccino, gelato, and *la dolce vita*! We'll leave the bus on the outskirts of Venice and ride a boat to our ancient and very Venetian pension near the historic Rialto bridge. After dinner we'll have an evening orientation walk.

Likely activities today...
2-hour drive to the Inn Valley*
Short stop in Innsbruck or Hall*
5-hour drive to Venice*
Dinner and evening walk in Venice

You'll walk from 2 to 5 miles today, and sleep in Venice.

---

* Included as an activity on BB&B tours.

Sightseeing Highlights
▲**Innsbruck**—A very popular mountain sports center and home of the 1964 and 1976 Winter Olympics, Innsbruck is surrounded by 150 mountain lifts, 1,250 miles of trails, and 250 hikers' huts. But the tastiest part of Innsbruck is its chewy center. The building with the Golden Roof (Goldenes Dachl), built with 2,657 gilded copper tiles in 1496 by Emperor Maximilian as an impressive viewing spot for his medieval spectacles, is in the historic center of town. On this square you'll see the Baroque-style Helblinghaus, the city tower (climb it for a great view, 20 AS), and the Olympics museum (behind the Golden Roof, 22 AS, 9:30-17:30 daily) with exciting action videos for winter sports lovers. The tourist information is three blocks in front of the Golden Roof at Berggraben #3 (8:00-19:00 daily, tel. 0512/5356, the train station branch is open until 22:00).

Nearby are the pastel yellow palace (Hofburg) and church (Hofkirche) and the unique Tiroler Volkskunst Museum. This museum (40 AS, open 9:00-17:00 daily, closed Sunday afternoons) is the best look anywhere at traditional Tirolean life-styles. Fascinating exhibits range from wedding dresses and babies' cribs to nativity scenes. Use the helpful English guidebook.

Our home in Venice, **Albergo Guerrato**, is warmly run by English-speaking Piero and Roberto. Their ancient building is old world simple, airy, wonderfully characteristic, and just an earplug's-throw from a colorful morning produce market. To get there, walk over the Rialto bridge away from San Marco, go straight past the pink arcaded building, turn right on Calle drio La Scimia ("the Alley of the Monkey's Behind"), and you'll see the red sign at Calle drio la Scimia 240a, Rialto.

ITALY
- 116,000 square miles (the size of Arizona).
- 60 million people (477 people per square mile).
- 800 miles tall, 100 miles wide.
- 1,600 lire = U.S.$1; 1,000 lire = about 65 cents.
- Country telephone code: 39; international access code: 00.

Ah, Italy! It has Europe's richest, craziest culture. If we have to choose just one, Italy is our favorite. If you take it on its own terms and accept the package deal, Italy is wonderful. Some people, often with considerable effort, manage to hate it. Italy bubbles with emotion, corruption, stray hairs, inflation, traffic jams, indiscretions, body odor, strikes, rallies, holidays, crowded squalor, and irate ranters shaking their fists at each other one minute and walking arm in arm the next. Have a talk with yourself before you cross the border. Promise yourself to relax and be militantly positive. Become a temporary Italian.

With so much history and art in Venice, Florence, and Rome, you'll need to do some reading ahead to maximize your experience. There are two Italys: the north is relatively industrial, aggressive, and "time-is-money" in its outlook. The Po River basin and the area between Milan, Genoa, and Turin have the richest farmland and comprise the industrial heartland. The south is more crowded, poor, relaxed, farm oriented, and traditional. Families here are very close and usually live in the same house for many generations. Loyalties are to the family, city, region, soccer team, and country—in that order. The Appenine mountains give Italy a rugged north-south spine.

Economically, Italy has its problems, but things somehow work out. It is the Western world's seventh biggest industrial power. Italians now make more per capita than the British. Italy is a leading wine producer and is sixth in the world in cheese and wool output. And tourism (your dollars) is big business in Italy. Cronyism is an integral part of the economy.

Italy, home of the Vatican, is Catholic, but the dominant religion is life—motor scooters, soccer (*calcio*), fashion, girl-watching, boy-watching, good coffee, good wine, and *la dolce far niente* (the sweetness of doing nothing).

The language is fun. Be melodramatic and move your hand with your tongue. Hear the melody, get into the flow. Fake it, let the farce be with you. Italians are outgoing characters; they want to communicate and try harder than any other Europeans. Play with them.

Italy

Italy, a land of extremes, is also the most thief-ridden country you'll visit. Tourists suffer virtually no violent crime—but plenty of petty purse-snatchings, pickpocketings, and short-changings. Only the sloppy get stung. Wear your money belt! Unfortunately, you'll need to assume any Gypsy woman or child on the street is after your wallet or purse.

Traditionally, Italy uses the siesta plan: people work from 8:00 or 9:00 to 13:00 and from 15:30 to 19:00, six days a week. Many businesses have adopted the government's new recommended 8:00 to 14:00 work-day. In tourist areas, shops are open longer.

Sightseeing hours are always changing in Italy, and many of the hours given in this book will be wrong by the time you travel. Double check your sightseeing plans at the local tourist office. For extra sightseeing information, take advantage of the cheap, colorful, hard-to-read but informative city guidebooks sold on the streets all over. Many dark interiors can be brilliantly lit for a coin. Whenever possible, let there be light.

Some important Italian churches require modest dress—no shorts or bare shoulders on men or women. With a little imagination (except at the Vatican), those caught by surprise can improvise something—a tablecloth for your knees and maps for your shoulders. I wear a super lightweight pair of long pants for my hot and muggy big city Italian sightseeing.

The Italian autostrada is lined with some of Europe's best rest stops, with gas, coffee bars, W.C.'s, long-distance telephones, grocery stores, restaurants, and often change facilities and tourist information.

While no longer a cheap country, Italy is still a hit with shoppers. Glassware (Venice), gold, silver, leather, and prints (Florence), and high fashion clothes (Rome) are good souvenirs.

Many tourists are mind-boggled by the huge prices: 20,000 lire for dinner! 70,000 for the room! 126,000 for the taxi ride! That's still real money—it's just spoken of in much smaller units than a dollar. Since there are roughly 1600 lire in a dollar (at this writing), figure Italian prices by covering the last three zeros with your finger and taking about two-thirds of the remaining figure. That L20,000 dinner costs $14 in U.S. money; the L70,000 room, $50; and the taxi ride... oh-oh!

Beware of the "slow count." After you buy something, you may get your change back in groups. The salesperson (or bank teller) hopes you are confused by all the zeros and will gather up your first group of money and say *"Grazie"* before he or she finishes the count. Always do your own rough figuring beforehand and understand the transaction. This trick is routine at subway and bus ticket windows.

Italians eat a skimpy breakfast, a huge lunch between 12:30 and 15:30, and a light dinner around 20:00. Food in Italy is given great importance and should be thought of as sightseeing for your tongue. Focus on regional specialties, wines, and pastas. In restaurants, you'll be billed a small cover charge (*coperto*) and a 10 to 15 percent service charge (*servizio*). A salad and minestrone or pasta, while not considered a proper meal by Italian standards, is cheap and filling. Many big city eateries have a three-tiered price system based on where you eat: at a stand-up bar (cheapest), an indoor table, or on the terrace (most expensive). Coffee and *gelato* (ice cream) are art forms in Italy. When ordering gelato, ask for an "Assortito, per favore" (assortment) to get two flavors per scoop.

The bar/cafeteria procedure can be frustrating. Decide what you want, check the price list on the wall, pay the cashier, give the receipt to the bartender (whose clean fingers handle no dirty lire), and tell him what you want. *Panini* is sandwich. *Da portar via* is "for the road."

La dolce far niente is a big part of Italy. Zero in on the fine points. Don't dwell on the problems; accept Italy as Italy. Savor your cappuccino, dangle your feet over a canal (if it smells, breathe with your mouth), and imagine what it was like centuries ago. Ramble through the rubble of Rome and mentally resurrect those ancient stones. Look into the famous sculpted eyes of Michelangelo's David, and understand Renaissance man's assertion of himself. Sit silently on a hilltop rooftop. Get chummy with the winds of the past. Write a poem over a glass of local wine in a sun-splashed, wave-dashed Riviera village. If you fall off your moral horse, call it a cultural experience. Italy is for romantics.

Italy nitty-gritty
Country code: 39
International access: 00
AT&T: 172-1011
MCI: 172-1022
SPRINT: 172-1877
Emergency: 113
Police: 113
Many Italian pay phones take both coins and phone cards. Telephone cards cost 5,000 or 10,000L.
Senior/youth discount age: none.
Banking hours: 8:30-13:35 & 14:45-15:45, but this varies greatly.

See tomorrow for Venice information.

Day 10: Venice

After an optional morning glass-blowing demonstration, your day is free for wandering, shopping, churches and museums. If your group is interested, your guide may organize an evening pub crawl or gondola ride.

Likely activities today (all optional)...
Glass blowing demonstration
Free time to wander on your own
Neighborhood pub crawl
Gondola ride

You'll walk from 3 to 8 miles today, and sleep in Venice.

Note: No activities are planned for BB&B tours today.

Venice (Venezia)
Soak all day in this puddle of elegant decay. Venice is Europe's best-preserved big city, a car-free urban wonderland of 100 islands, laced together by 400 bridges and 2000 alleys.

Born in a lagoon 1500 years ago as a refuge from barbarians, Venice is overloaded with tourists and slowly sinking (unrelated facts). In the Middle Ages, after the Venetians created a great trading empire, they smuggled in the bones of St. Mark (San Marco), and Venice gained religious importance as well.

Today, Venice is home to about 75,000 people in its old city, down from a peak population of around 200,000. While there are about 500,000 in greater Venice (counting the mainland, not counting tourists), the old town has a small-town feel. To see small-town Venice through the touristic flak, explore the back streets and try a Stand-Up-Progressive-Venetian-Pub-Crawl-Dinner.

Planning Your Time
For a one day visit: cruise the Grand Canal, do the major San Marco sights (square, palace, church), see the Church of the Frari for art, and wander the back streets on a pub crawl. Venice's greatest sight is the city itself. Make time to simply wander. The most magical times are early in the morning and after dark. Stay up late. Venice is a medieval cookie jar, and nobody's looking.

Orientation (tel. code: 041)
The island city of Venice is shaped like a fish. Its major thoroughfares are canals. The Grand Canal snakes through the middle of the fish, start-

Venice

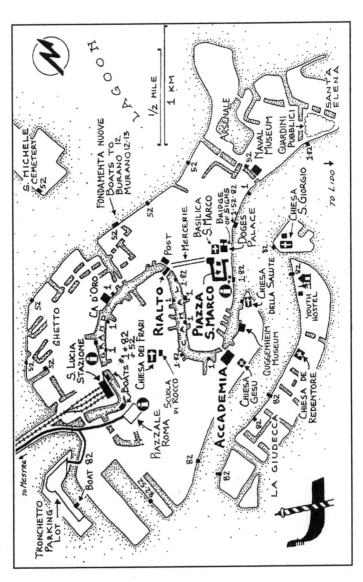

ing at the mouth where all the people and food enter, passing under the Rialto Bridge, and ending at St. Mark's Square (San Marco). Park your twentieth-century perspective at the mouth, and let Venice swallow you whole.

Venice is a car-less kaleidoscope of people, bridges, and odorless canals. The city has no real streets, and addresses are hopelessly confusing. There are six districts, each with about 6,000 address numbers. Luckily, it's easy to find your way, since many street corners have a sign pointing you to the nearest major landmark (such as San Marco, Accademia, and Rialto). To find your way, navigate by landmarks, not streets. Obedient visitors stick to the main thoroughfares as directed by these signs and miss the charm of back street Venice.

Tourist Information

The best tourist information office is tucked between St. Mark's Square and the San Marco vaporetto stop (tel. 522 6356, open maybe 9:00-13:00 and 14:00-16:00, closed Sunday). Pick up a city map, public transit map, the latest museum hours, and confirm your sightseeing plans. Drop into any fancy hotel (as if you're sleeping there) and pick up the free periodical entertainment guide, *Un Ospite de Venezia* (a handy listing of events and the latest museum hours). The cheap Venice map on sale at postcard racks has much more detail than the TI map. Also consider the little sold-with-the-postcards guidebook with a city map and explanations of the major sights.

Getting Around Venice

The public transit system is a fleet of bus-boats called *vaporetti*. They work like city buses except that they never get a flat, the stops are docks, and if you get off between stops you may drown. While route numbers seem to change every year, for now only three lines matter: #1 is the slow boat, taking 45 minutes to make every stop along the entire length of the Grand Canal; #82 is the fast boat down the Grand Canal, stopping only at the car park, train station (ferrovia), Rialto, and San Marco and making the trip in 20 minutes; and #52 gives you an interesting circular tour of the island city. Buy tickets (L4000) before boarding or for an extra fee from a conductor on board.

Only three bridges cross the Grand Canal, but seven *traghetti* (little L600 ferry gondolas, marked on better maps) shuttle locals and in-the-know tourists across the canal, where necessary. Take advantage of these "time savors."

Good city maps show boat stops, routes, and traghetti crossings. The TI, boat information office at Piazzale Roma, and some hotels can give you the free ACTV Venice public transportation map (which has a good city map on the back).

Helpful Hints

The Venice fly-trap lures us in and takes our money, any way it can. Expect to be shortchanged by any ticket-taker. Wait through the delay payment of change trick. Count your change carefully. Accept the fact that Venice was a tourist town 400 years ago. It was, is, and always will be crowded. Eighty percent of Venice is actually an untouristy place. Eighty percent of the tourists never notice. Hit the back streets.

Get Lost: Venice is the ideal town to explore on foot. Walk and walk to the far reaches of the town. Don't worry about getting lost. Get as lost as possible. Keep reminding yourself, "I'm on an island and I can't get off." When it comes time to find your way, just follow the directional arrows on building corners, or simply ask a local, *"Dové* (DOH-vay) *San Marco*?" ("Where is St. Mark's?"). People in the tourist business (that's most Venetians) speak some English.

Money: Bank rates vary. I like the Banco di Sicilia a block towards San Marco from Campo San Bartolomeo. American Express, between San Marco and the Accademia, is convenient but has bad rates. Thomas Cook on San Marco is open on Sundays, and charges no fee for Thomas Cook traveler's checks. Non-bank exchange bureaus can cost you $10 more than a bank for a $200 exchange. There's a 24 hour cash machine near the Rialto vaporetto stop that exchanges U.S. dollars and other currencies into lire at a fair rate.

Water: Venetians pride themselves in having pure, safe, and tasty tap water, which is piped in from the foothills of the Alps (which you can actually see from Venice on a crisp winter day).

Pigeon Poop: If bombed by a pigeon, resist the initial response to wipe it off immediately—it'll just smear into your hair. Wait until it dries and flake it off cleanly.

Modest Dress: If you'll be visiting St. Mark's or the other major churches, cover your knees and shoulders.

Sights—Venice

▲▲▲**Grand Canal Tour**—Grab a front seat on boat #82 (fast, 20 minutes) or #1 (slow, 45 minutes) to cruise the entire Canale Grande from the car park (Tronchetto) or train station (Ferrovia) to San Marco. While Venice is a barrage on the senses that hardly needs a narration, these notes give the cruise a little meaning and help orient you to this great city. Some city maps (on sale at postcard racks) have a handy Grand Canal map on the back side.

Venice, built in a lagoon, sits on pilings—pine trees driven 15 feet into the mud. Over 100 canals, about 25 miles in length, drain the city, dumping like streams into the Grand Canal.

Venice is a city of palaces. The most lavish were built fronting this canal. This cruise is the only way to really appreciate the front doors of

Downtown Venice

LODGING:

❶ GUERRATO	❻ DONI	⓫ GAMBERO
❷ STURION	❼ CORONA	⓬ PAGANELLI
❸ CANADA	❽ PIAVE	⓭ MARIN
❹ RIVA	❾ MASETTO	⓮ ALBORETTI
❺ SAN GALLO	❿ CASA PETRARCA	

this unique and historic chorus line of mansions from the days when Venice was the world's richest city. Strict laws prohibit any changes in these buildings, so while landowners gnash their teeth, we can enjoy Europe's best-preserved medieval city—slowly rotting. Many of the grand buildings are now vacant. Others harbor chandelliered elegance above mossy basements.

Start at Tronchetto (the bus and car park) or the train station. FS stands for "Ferrovie dello Stato," the Italian state railway system. The bridge at the station is one of only three that cross the Canale Grande.

Vaporetto stop #4 (San Marcuola-Ghetto) is near the world's original ghetto. When this area was set aside as the local Jewish quarter in 1516 it was a kind of urban island which developed into one of the most closely knit business and cultural quarters of any Jewish community in Italy.

As you cruise, notice the traffic signs. Venice's main thoroughfare is busy with traffic. You'll see all kinds of boats: taxis, police boats, garbage, even brown-and-white UPS boats.

Venice's 500 sleek, black, graceful gondolas are a symbol of the city. They cost about $35,000 apiece and are built with a slight curve so that one oar propels them in a straight line.

At the Ca d'Oro stop, notice the palace of the same name. For years it's been under a wooden case of scaffolding for reconstruction. Named the "House of Gold," and considered the most elegant Venetian Gothic palace on the canal, today it's an art gallery with a few important paintings. Unfortunately its interior shows nothing of its palatial origins.

Just before the Rialto Bridge, on the right, the outdoor produce market bustles with people in the morning but is quiet with only a few grazing pigeons the rest of the day. Can you see the traghetto gondola ferrying shoppers back and forth? The huge post office, usually with a postal boat moored at its blue posts, is on the left.

A symbol of Venice, the Rialto Bridge, is lined with shops and tourists. Built in 1592, with a span of 42 meters, it was an impressive engineering feat in its day. Locals call the summit of this bridge the "icebox of Venice" for its cool breeze.

The Rialto, a separate town in the early days of Venice, has always been the commercial district, while San Marco was the religious and governmental center. Today a street called the Merceria connects the two, providing travelers with a gauntlet of shopping temptations.

Take a deep whiff of Venice. What's all this nonsense about stinky canals? By the way, how's your captain? Smooth dockings? To get to know him, stand up in the bow and block his view.

Notice how the rich marble facades are just a veneer covering no-nonsense brick buildings. And notice the characteristic chimneys.

After passing the British consulate, you'll see the wooden Accademia Bridge, leading to the Accademia Gallery, filled with the best Venetian paintings. The bridge was put up in 1932 as a temporary fix for the original iron one. Locals liked it and it became permanent.

Cruising under the bridge, you'll get a classic view of the Salute Church, built as a thanks to God when the devastating plague of 1630 passed. It's claimed over a million trees were used for the foundation alone. Much of the surrounding countryside was deforested by Venice. Trees were needed both to fuel the furnaces of its booming glass industry and to prop up this city in the mud.

The low white building on the right (before the church) is the Peggy Guggenheim Gallery. She willed the city a fine collection of modern art.

The building on the right with the golden dome is the Dogana da Mar, a sixteenth-century customs house. Its two bronze Atlases hold a statue of Fortune riding the dome.

As you prepare to de-boat at stop #15—San Marco—look from left to right out over the lagoon. A wide harborfront walk leads past the town's most elegant hotels to the green area in the distance. This is the public gardens, the only sizable park in town. Farther out is the Lido, tempting with its beaches and casinos. The dreamy church that seems to float is the architect Palladio's San Giorgio (interesting visit, fine Tintoretto paintings, great view from its bell tower, L2000, 9:30-12:30, 14:00-18:00 daily). And farther to the right is a residential chunk of Venice called the Guidecca.

For more Vaporetto fun, ride boat 52 around the city. Plenty of boats leave from San Marco for the beach (Lido), as well as speedboat tours of Burano (a quiet, picturesque fishing and lace town), Murano (the glassblowing island), and Torcello (has the oldest churches and mosaics but is an otherwise dull and desolate island). Boat 12 takes you to these remote points slower and cheaper.

▲▲▲**St. Mark's Square (Piazza San Marco)**—Surrounded by splashy and historic buildings, Piazza San Marco is filled with music, lovers, pigeons, and tourists from around the world by day and serves as your private rendezvous with the Middle Ages late at night. Europe's greatest dance floor is the romantic place to be. This is the first place to flood, is near Venice's best tourist information office (near vaporetto stop), and has fine public rest rooms (behind Napoleon's wing).

With your back to the church, survey one of Europe's great urban spaces and the only square in Venice to merit the title piazza. Nearly two football fields long, it's surrounded by the offices of the republic. On the right are the "old offices," (16th century, Renaissance). On the left, the "new offices" (17th century, Baroque style). Napoleon enclosed the square with the more simple and austere Neoclassical wing across the far end and called this "the most beautiful drawing room in Europe."

For a slow and pricey thrill, invest L15,000 in a beer or coffee in one of the elegant cafés with the dueling orchestras. If you're going to sit awhile, and savor the scene, it's worth the splurge. Caution: ask if there's an extra music fee. For the most thrills L1500 can get you in Venice, buy a bag of pigeon seed and become popular in a flurry.

▲▲**Doge's Palace (Palazzo Ducale)**—The seat of the Venetian government and home of its ruling duke or "Doge," this was the most powerful half acre in Europe for 400 years. It was built to show off the power

St. Mark's Square

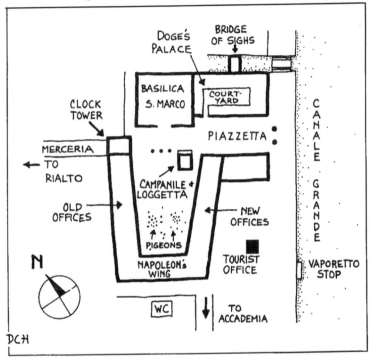

and wealth of republic and remind all visitors that Venice was number one. Built in Venetian Gothic style the bottom has pointy arches and the top has an eastern or Islamic flavor. Its columns sat on pedestals but in the thousand years since they were erected, the palace has settled into the mud and they have vanished.

Entering the palace (before the ticket booth) notice grand staircase (with nearly naked Moses and Paul Newman at the top). Even the most powerful visitors climbed this to meet the Doge. This was the beginning of an architectural power trip. The Doge, the elected king of this "dictatorial republic," lived on the first floor (now used for special exhibits). You'll tour the public rooms of the top floor. The place is wallpapered by masterpieces by Veronese and Tintoretto. Don't worry much about the great art. Enjoy the building.

In room 12, the Senate Room, the 200 senators met, debated and passed laws. From the center of the ceiling, Tintoretto's "Triumph of Venice" shows the city in all her glory. Lady Venice, in heaven with the Greek Gods, stands high above the lesser nations who swirl respectfully at her feet with gifts.

The Armory shows the military might of the empire which was employed to keep the east-west trade lines open (and the local economy booming). Squint out the window at the far end for a fine view of Palladio's San Georgio church and the Lido in the distance.

After the huge old globes, you'll enter the giant Hall of the Grand Council (180 feet long, capacity 2000) where the entire nobility met to elect the senate and doge. Ringing the room are portraits of 76 doges (in chronological order). One, who opposed the will of the Grand Council, is blacked out. Behind the doge's throne, you can't miss Tintoretto's monsterpiece, Paradise. At 1700 square feet, this is the world's largest oil painting. Christ and Mary are surrounded by 500 saints.

Walking over the Bridge of Sighs, you'll enter the prisons. The doges could sentence, torture, and jail their opponents secretly and in the privacy of their own home. As you walk back over the bridge, wave to the gang of tourists gawking at you. (L10,000, daily 9:00-19:00, last entry at 18:00, WC near exit).

▲▲**St. Mark's Basilica**—For well over a thousand years, it has housed the saint's bones. The mosaic above the door at the far left of the church shows two guys carrying Mark's coffin into the church. Mark looks pretty grumpy after the long voyage from Egypt. The church has 4000 square meters of Byzantine mosaics. The best and oldest are in the atrium (turn right as you enter and stop under the last dome). Face the piazza, gape up (it's okay, no pigeons) and study the story of Noah, the arc and flood (two by two, the wicked drowning, Noah sending out the dove, happy rainbow, sacrifice of thanks). Now face the church and read clockwise the story of Adam and Eve that rings the bottom of the dome. Step inside the church (stairs on right lead to horses) and notice the rolling mosaic marble floor. Stop under the central dome and look up for the ascension. (Modest dress, no shorts or bare shoulders, 9:00-17:00, Sunday 14:00-17:00, free, tel. 522 5205, see the schedule board in the atrium listing free English guided tours of the church, beautifully lit at the 18:45 mass on Saturday, 14:00-17:00 Sunday, and some mid-days).

Upstairs you can see an up-close mosaic exhibition, a fine view of the church interior, a view of the square from the horse balcony, and the newly restored original bronze horses (L3000, daily 9:45-17:00). These horses, made during the days of Alexander the Great (4th century B.C.), were taken to Rome by Nero, to Constantinople by Constantine, to Venice by crusaders, to Paris by Napoleon, back "home" to Venice when Napoleon fell, and finally inside out of the acidic air.

The treasures of the church (requiring two more L3000 admissions) give you the best chance outside of Istanbul or Ravenna to see the glories of Byzantium. Venetian crusaders looted the Christian city of Constantinople and brought home piles of lavish loot (until the advent of TV evangelism, perhaps the lowest point in Christian history). Much of this plunder is stored in the *tesaro* (treasury) of San Marco. As you view these treasures, remember most were made in A.D. 500, while western Europe was still rooting in the mud. Behind the high altar lies the body of St. Mark ("Marxus") and the Pala d'Oro, a golden altarpiece made (A.D. 1000-1300) with 80 Byzantine enamels. Each shows a religious scene set in gold and precious stones. Both of these sights are interesting and historic, but neither are as much fun as two bags of pigeon seed.

▲**Campanile di San Marco**—Ride the elevator 300 feet to the top of the bell tower for the best view in Venice. Photos on the wall inside show how this bell tower crumbled into a pile of bricks in 1902, one thousand years after it was built. For an ear-shattering experience, be on top when the bells ring (daily 9:30-19:00, L5000). The golden angel at its top always faces into the wind.

Clock Tower—From Piazza San Marco you can see the bronze men (Moors) swing their huge clappers at the top of each hour. Notice the world's first "digital" clock on the tower facing the square (flips dramatically every 5 minutes).

▲▲**Galleria dell' Accademia**—Venice's top art museum is packed with the painted highlights of the Venetian Renaissance (Bellini, Giorgione, Veronese, Tiepolo, and Canaletto). It's just over the wooden Accademia Bridge (L12,000, 9:00-14:00, Sunday 9:00-13:00, expect delays as they allow only 180 visitors at a time, tel. 522 2247).

▲**Museo Civico Correr**—The interesting city history museum offers dusty bits of Venice's glory days and fine views of Piazza San Marco. Entry is on the square opposite the church (L8000, 10:00-17:00, closed Tuesday).

▲▲▲**Chiesa dei Frari**—This great Gothic Franciscan church, an artistic highlight of Venice featuring three great masters, offers more art per lira than any other Venetian sight. Freeload on English-language tours to get the most out of the Titian Assumption above the high altar. Then move one chapel to the right to see Donatello's wood carving of St. John the Baptist almost live. And for the climax, continue right into the sacristy to sit before Bellini's Madonna and the Saints. Perhaps the greatest Venetian painter, Bellini's genius is obvious in the pristine clarity, believable depth, and reassuring calm of this three-paneled altarpiece. Notice the rich colors of Mary's clothing and how good it is to see a painting in its intended setting. For many, these three pieces of art make a visit to the Accademia Gallery unnecessary. Before leaving, check out the Neoclassical pyramid-shaped tomb of Canova and (opposite) the grandiose tomb of Titian, the Venetian. Compare the carved marble Assumption behind his tombstone portrait with the painted original above the high altar (L1,000, 9:00-12:00, 14:30-18:00, Sunday 15:00-18:00).

▲**Scuola di San Rocco**—Next to the Frari church, another lavish build-ing bursts with art, including some 50 Tintorettos. The best paintings are upstairs, especially the *Crucifixion* in the smaller room. View the neck-breakingly splendid ceiling paintings with one of the mirrors (*specchio*) available at the entrance. (L8000, daily 9:00-17:30, last entrance 17:00.) For lots of Tiepolo (14 stations of the cross), drop by the nearby Church of San Polo.

▲**Peggy Guggenheim Collection**—This popular collection of far-out art, including works by Picasso, Chagall, and Dali, offers one of Europe's best reviews of the art styles of the 20th century. (L10,000, 11:00-18:00, closed Tuesdays.)

Ca' Rezzonico—This eighteenth century Grand Canal palazzo is now open as the Museo del '700 Veneziano, offering a good look at the life of Venice's rich and famous 200 years ago. (L5000, 10:00-16:00, closed Fri-day, tel. 522 4543, at a vaporetto stop by the same name).

▲**Gondola Rides**—A traditional must for many but a rip-off for some, gondoliers charge about L100,000 for a 40-minute ride. You can divide the cost—and the romance—by up to six people (some take seven if you beg and they're hungry). For cheap gondola thrills, stick to the L600 1-minute ferry ride on a Grand Canal *traghetti*, or hang out on a bridge along the gondola route and wave at the romantics.

▲**Glassblowing**—It's unnecessary to go all the way to Murano Island to see glassblowing demonstrations. For the best show, wait near one of several glassworks near St. Mark's Square and follow any tour group into the furnace room for a fun and free 10-minute show. You'll usually see a vase and a "leetle orse" made from molten glass. The commercial that always follows in the showroom is actually entertaining. Prices around St. Mark's have a sizable tour-guide commission built in. Seri-ous glass-shoppers buy at small shops on Murano Island.

Santa Elena—For a pleasant peek into a completely untouristy residen-tial side of Venice, catch the boat from San Marco to the neighborhood of Santa Elena (at the fish's tail). This 100-year-old suburb lives as if there was no tourism. You'll find a kid-friendly park, a few lazy restau-rants, and great sunsets over San Marco.

▲▲**Evening: The Stand-up Progressive Venetian Pub Crawl Dinner**—Venice's residential back streets hide plenty of characteristic bars with countless trays of interesting toothpick munchie food (*cicheti*). Partaking in the "*giro di ombre*" (pub crawl) tradition is a great way to mingle and have fun with the Venetians. Real *cicheti* pubs are getting rare in these fast-food days, but locals can point you in the right direction or you can follow the plan below. As always, the best way to find a landmark is to ask locals "Dové...?" and go where they point.

Italian *cicheti* (hors d'oeuvre) wait under glass in bars. Try fried mozzarella cheese, blue cheese, calamari, artichoke hearts, and anything ugly on a toothpick. Ask for a *piatto misto* (mixed plate). Drink the house wines. A small glass of house red or white wine (*ombre rosso* or *ombre bianco*) or a small beer (*birrino*) costs about L1,000, meat and fish munchies are expensive, veggies are around L4,000 for a meal-sized plate. A good last drink is the local sweet red wine called Fragolino. To be safe, you might give each pub L20,000 (or whatever) for your group and explain you want to eat and drink until it's *finito*. A liter of wine costs around L7000. Bars don't stay open very late, and the *cicheti* selection is best early, so start your evening by 18:30. (I'd appreciate any feedback on this plan.)

First course: Start on Campo San Bartolomeo near the Rialto Bridge. If the statue walked backwards 20 yards, turned left, went under a passageway he'd hit Rosticceria San Bartolomeo. This isn't really a pub but they have a likeably surly staff, great fried *mozzarella e prosciutto* (L1800) and L800 glasses of wine. Continue over a bridge to Campo San Lio (landmark), take a left past Hotel Canada and walk straight over another bridge and into Alberto's Osteria, called simply Osteria on Calle Malvasia. This fine local-style bar has plenty of snacks and *cicheti*. Say "hi" to Alberto, order with your best Italian (and by pointing), then sit or stand for the same price (9:00-15:00, 17:30-21:00, closed Sunday, tel. 522-9038). Alberto will make a fine L10,000 piatto misto with wine.

Second course: Leaving Alberto's, turn left on Calle Malvasia and go basically straight with a jog to the left through a couple of squares to Campo Santa Maria di Formosa. (Ask *"Dové Santa Maria di Formosa?"*) You could split a pizza with wine on the square (Piero's Bar all' Orologio, opposite the canal, has best setting.) *Capricciosa* means the house specialty. You can get "pizza to go" on the square from Cip Ciap Pizza Rustica (over the bridge behind the SMF gelateria on Calle del Mondo Novo, open until 21:00, closed Tuesday).

Third course: Fresh fruit and vegetables from the stand on the square next to the water fountain (open until about 20:00).

Fourth course: More *cicheti* and wine. From Bar all' Orologio (on Campo S.M. di Formosa), with your back to the church (follow yellow sign to SS Giov e Paolo), head down the street to Osteria Mascaron (Gigi's bar, best selection by 19:30, closes at 23:00 and on Sunday).

Fifth course: Gigi also runs **Enoteca Mascareta**, another good bar 30 yards further down the street (#5183, tel. 523-0744). The piano sounds like they dropped it in the canal. The wine was saved. If you're feeling like the painting of Bacchus on the wall looks, it's time for...

Sixth course: Gelato. The unfriendly but delicious gelateria on Campo di Formosa closes at about 20:00 and on Thursday. (The owner, Mario, promised me that even if you buy a cone for the L1,000 take-away price, you can sit on his chairs for 5 minutes.) Or head toward San Marco where the gelaterias stay open later (the best is opposite the Doge's Palace, by the two columns, on the bay). There's also a good late-hours gelateria (L1,000 small cones) midway between Campo San Bartolomeo and the Rialto Bridge.

You're not a tourist, you're a living part of a soft Venetian night . . . an alley cat with money. Streetlamp halos, live music, floodlit history, and a ceiling of stars make St. Mark's magic at midnight. Shine with the old lanterns on the gondola piers where the sloppy Grand Canal splashes at the Doge's Palace...reminiscing. Comfort the four frightened tetrarchs (ancient Byzantine emperors) under the moon near the Doge's Palace entrance. Cuddle history.

Rialto pub crawl: There are also a lot of *cicheti* bars around the Rialto market (between the bridge, Campo San Polo, Chiesa di San Cassiano and recommended Hotel Guerrato). You could track down: Do Mori, Cantina Do Spade, Vini da Pinto, All' Arco, Ostaria Antico Dolo, and Osteria Enoteca Vivaldi (all within a block or two of each other, most closed on Sunday). You'll notice the same local crowd popping up at each of these characteristic places.

Sights—Venice's Lagoon

Several interesting islands hide out in the Venice Lagoon. **Burano**, famous for its lace making, is a sleepy island with a sleepy community—village Venice without the glitz. Lace fans enjoy Burano's Scuola di Merletti (L3000, 10:30-12:30, 14:00-17:00, closed Monday, tel. 730034). **Torcello**, another lagoon island, is dead except for its church, which claims to be the oldest in Venice (L2000, 10:00-12:30, 14:00-17:00, closed Monday, tel. 730084). It's impressive for its mosaics but not worth a look on a short visit unless you really have your heart set on Ravenna but aren't able to make it there. The island of **Murano**, famous for its glass factories, has the Museo Vetrario, which displays the very best of 700 years of Venetian glassmaking (L5000, 10:00-16:00, closed Wednesday, tel. 739586). The islands are reached easily but slowly by vaporetto (catch at Fondamente Nove). Four-hour speedboat tours of these three lagoon destinations leave twice a day from the dock near the Doges Palace.

Eating in Venice

For low-stress, but not necessarily low-price, meals, you'll find plenty of self-service restaurants (*self-service* in Italian). One is right at the Rialto Bridge. Pizzerias are cheap and easy. Those that sell take-out food by the slice or gram are cheapest. Menus should clearly explain the *coperto* (cover charge) and *servizio* (service charge).

You'll pay a premium to eat in the tourist center. For reasonable Grand Canal-side meals, try the places along the canal opposite the Rialto vaporetto stop.

A key to cheap eating in Venice is bar snacks, especially stand-up mini-meals in out-of-the-way bars. Order by pointing. *Panini* (sandwiches) are sold fast and cheap at bars everywhere. My favorite Venetian dinner is the pub crawl described above under Sights. Any of the listed bars would make a fine one-stop, sit-down dinner.

The produce market that sprawls for a few blocks just past the Rialto Bridge (best 8:00-13:00, closed Sunday, closed Sunday) is a great place to assemble a picnic. The nearby street, Ruga Vecchia, has good bakeries and cheese shops. Side lanes in this area are speckled with fine little hole-in-the-wall munchie bars.

The Mensa DLF (to the right of the train station as you face the tracks, 12:30-13:30, 18:00-21:00, closed Saturday, Sunday, and during lunch on Tuesdays and Thursdays, tel. 716242), the public transportation workers' cafeteria, is cheap and open to the public.

Near Campo San Bartolomeo: While these places aren't worth hiking to, they're handy, near the central Campo San Bartolomeo (a block toward San Marco from the Rialto Bridge). Directions are based on the statue in this square's center.

The very local, hustling **Rosticceria San Bartolomeo/Gislon** (Calle della Bissa 5424, 20 yards behind the statue to its left, under a passageway, tel. 5223569, 9:30-14:30, 17:00-21:00, closed Monday) is a cheap--if confusing--self-service restaurant on the ground floor (L6000 pasta, L800 wine, prices listed at door, no cover or service charge if you sit at stools along the window). Good but pricier meals are served at the full-service restaurant upstairs. Get a take-out meal to eat on a nearby bridge or campo.

If the statue on the square were to jump off his pedestal, walk ahead 50 yards, and go down a narrow alley to the left, he'd find the **Devil's Forest Pub**, with English decor and self-service Italian food (L7000 pasta, no cover, open late).

Ristorante Pizzeria da Nane Mora (behind the statue, past post office, over the bridge, and right at the red Santuario Madonna della Grazie church, on a tiny triangular square, open at 19:00) has good pizza and indoor/outdoor seating.

Day 11: All-day drive to Rome

We'll spend all day driving south to Rome. Depending on your guide's grand scheme for the next two days, you may spend this evening getting oriented to Rome with a hike across the heart of the Eternal City, and a late-night metro ride home.

Likely activities today...
8-hour drive to Rome*
Free time for dinner on your own*
Nighttime walk across the heart of Rome

You'll walk from 1 to 3 miles today, and sleep in Rome.

---

* Included as an activity on BB&B tours.

Here are some Rome sights you may see this evening. **See tomorrow's section for more Rome orientation and information.**

▲▲▲**Floodlit Rome Hike: Trastevere to the Spanish Steps**—Rome can be grueling. But a fine way to enjoy this historian's fertility rite is an evening walk lacing together Rome's flood-lit night spots. Fine urban spaces, real-life theater vignettes, sitting close enough to the Bernini fountain to hear no traffic, water flickering its mirror on the marble, jostling with local teenagers to see all the gelati flavors, enjoying lovers straddling more than the bench, jay-walking past flak-vested *polizia,* marveling at the ramshackle elegance that softens this brutal city for those who were born here and can imagine living nowhere else—these are the flavors of Rome best tasted after dark.

Taxi or ride the bus (#23 from the Vatican area) to Trastevere, the colorful neighborhood across (*tras*) the Tiber (*tevere*). Start your hike at Santa Maria in Trastevere. Trastevere offers the best look at medieval-village Rome. The action all marches to the chime of the church bells. Go there and wander. Wonder. Be a poet. This is Rome's Left Bank.

Santa Maria in Trastevere from the third century (8:00-12:00, 16:00-19:00, free) is one of Rome's oldest churches. Notice the ancient basilica floor plan and early Christian symbols in the walls near the entry.

From the square, Via del Moro leads to the river and Ponte Sisto, a pedestrian bridge with a good view of St. Peter's dome. Cross the bridge and continue straight ahead for one block. Take the first left, which leads through the scary and narrow darkness to Piazza Farnese with the imposing Palazzo Farnese. The palace's beautiful interior, designed in part by Michelangelo, is closed to the public. One block from there is **Campo di Fiori** (Field of Flowers), an affordable outdoor dining room after dark (Trattoria Virgilio is one of several decent restaurants).

If the statue on the square did a hop, step, and a jump forward and turned right, he'd cross the busy Corso Vittorio Emanuele and find **Piazza Navona.** Rome's most interesting night scene features street music, artists, fire eaters, local Casanovas, ice cream, outdoor cafés (splurge-worthy if you've got time to sit and enjoy the human river of Italy), and three fountains by Bernini, the father of Baroque art. Its Tartufo "death by chocolate" ice cream (L5000 to go) made the Tre Scalini café world-famous among connoisseurs of ice cream and chocolate alike. This oblong square is molded around the long-gone stadium of Domitian, an ancient chariot race track that was often flooded so the masses could enjoy major water games.

Leave Piazza Navona directly across from the Tre Scalini café, go past rose peddlers and palm readers, jog left around the guarded building, and follow the yellow sign to the **Pantheon** straight down Via del Salvatore (cheap pizza place on left just before the Pantheon). From the obelisk (facing the Pantheon), head left to Casa del Caffe, then left down Via degli Orfani. At the square, pass the church on the left down Via Aquiro. At the obelisk (if it's gelati time, take a detour left behind Albergo Nazionale), turn right, walk between the Italian parliament and the huge Il Tempo newspaper building to the busy Via del Corso. You'll pass the huge second-century column honoring Marcus Aurelius, cross the street, and go into the lofty gallery. Take the right branch of this Y-shaped gallery and exit continuing straight down Via de Crociferi to the roar of the water, light, and people of the Trevi fountain.

The **Trevi fountain** is an example of how Rome took full advantage of the abundance of water brought into the city by its great aqueducts. This watery Baroque avalanche was built in 1762. Romantics toss two coins over their shoulder thinking it will give them a wish and assure their return to Rome. Try it. It's worked well for our tour guides.

Take some time to people-watch (whisper a few breathy *bellos* or *bellas*) before leaving. Facing the fountain, go past it on the right down Via delle Stamperia to Via del Triton. Cross the busy street and continue to the Spanish Steps (ask: *Dové Piazza di Spagna*?) a few short blocks and thousands of dollars of shopping opportunities away.

The **Piazza di Spagna** (rhymes with lasagna), with the very popular Spanish Steps, got its name 300 years ago when this was the site of the Spanish Embassy. It's been the hangout of many romantics over the years (Keats, Wagner, Openshaw, Goethe, and others). The Boat Fountain at the foot of the steps was done by Bernini's father, Bernini.

Facing the steps, walk to your right about a block to tour one of the world's biggest and most lavish McDonalds (a handy bathroom stop). About a block on the other side of the steps is the subway, or *Metropolitana*, which (until 23:30) will zip you home.

Day 12: Rome

Today you'll do the "Caesar Shuffle," visiting the essential ancient sights—Colosseum, Forum, and Pantheon. After a siesta we'll visit St. Peter's, the greatest church in Christendom and you'll have a chance to climb to the top of Michelangelo's dome for a memorable view of the Vatican grounds, with all of Rome at your feet.

Likely activities today...
Metro ride to the Colosseum
Tour of the Colosseum and Forum
Walk to and tour the Pantheon
Free time for lunch and siesta
Orientation tour of St. Peter's
Free time for afternoon Mass or dome-climbing

You'll walk 5 or 6 miles today, and sleep in Rome.

Note: No activities are planned for BB&B tours today.

Rome (Roma)

Rome is magnificent and brutal at the same time. Your ears will ring, your nose will turn your hankie black, the careless will be run down or pickpocketed, you'll be frustrated by chaos that only an Italian can understand. You may even come to believe Mussolini was necessary. But Rome is required. If your hotel provides a comfortable refuge; if you pace yourself, accept and even partake in the siesta plan; if you're well-organized for sightseeing; and if you protect yourself and your valuables with extra caution and discretion, you'll do fine. You'll see the sights and leave satisfied.

Rome at its peak meant civilization itself. Everything was either civilized (part of the Roman Empire, Latin- or Greek-speaking) or barbarian. Today, Rome is Italy's political capital, the capital of Catholicism, and a splendid . . . "junkpile" is not quite the right word . . . of Western Civilization. As you wander, you'll find its buildings, people, cats, laundry, and traffic endlessly entertaining. And then, of course, there are its magnificent sights.

Tour St. Peter's, the greatest church on earth, and scale Michelangelo's 100-yard-tall dome, the world's largest. Learn something about eternity by touring the huge Vatican Museum. You'll find paradise--bright as the day it was painted--in the Sistine Chapel. Do the "Caesar shuffle" walk from the historic Colosseum through the ancient Forum, and over the Capitoline Hill. Take an early evening *dolce vita* (sweet life) stroll down the Via del Corso with Rome's beautiful people.

Planning Your Time

Rome is best done fast. It's great, but exhausting. If you only have a day, be brutally selective: Vatican (two hours in museum and Sistine and an hour in St. Peter's), march over river to Pantheon, then over the Capitoline Hill, through the Forum and to the Colosseum. Dinner on Campo di Fiori and evening stroll (Piazza Navona to Spanish Steps). If you've been here before, skip some of the biggies and take in the Borghese Gallery (Caravaggio paintings and Bernini sculptures), St. Peter in Chains (Michelangelo's Moses), and a trip to Ostia Antica, Rome's ancient seaport.

Orientation (tel. code: 06)

The modern sprawl of Rome is of no interest to us. Our Rome is the old core—within the triangle formed by the train station, Colosseum, and Vatican. Get a handle on Rome by considering it in these chunks: **The ancient city** had a million people. Tear it down to size by walking through just the core. The best of the classical sights stand in a line from the Colosseum to the Pantheon. In the time of **Medieval Rome,** the population dipped as low as 50,000, and a good part of them were thieves. The medieval city, a colorful tangle of lanes, lies between the Pantheon and the river. **Window shoppers' Rome** twinkles with nightlife and ritzy shopping near medieval Rome, on or near Rome's main drag, the Via del Corso. **The Vatican City** is a compact world of its own with two great sights: a huge basilica and the museum. And **Trastevere**, the seedy/colorful wrong-side-of-the-river neighborhood-village is Rome at its crustiest. **Baroque Rome** is an overleaf that embellishes great squares throughout the town with fountains and church facades.

Tourist Information (TI)

Rome offers less tourist information per capita than any city in the first world. Most available publications are two years old, and nobody seems to know or care what is actually going on. If all you need is a map, forget the TI. Most hotels offer a free city map. Fancy hotels carry a free and helpful English monthly, *Un Ospite a Roma* (A Guest in Rome).

   Tourist Info. offices: The Ente Provinciale Per il Turismo (EPT) has three offices (8:15-19:15): at the airport, in the train station (near track #1, very crowded, the only one open Sunday), and the central office (5 Via Parigi, just a 5-minute walk out the front of the station, near Piazza della Republica's huge fountain, less crowded and more helpful, air-conditioned with comfortable sofas and a desk to plan on--or sit and overcome your frustration, tel. 06/48899255 or 48899253). Get the free EPT city map and a monthly periodical guide if there is one.

   Enjoy Rome (8:30-13:00, 15:30-18:00, closed Saturday afternoon and Sunday, 3 blocks northeast of the station at Via Varese 39, tel. 4451843,

English-speaking) is a free and friendly new information service providing maps and museum hours.

Walking tours: American students in Rome lead "Secret Walks" (May-October). Three or four different walks are given daily (L20,000 per tour or L15,000 for students, children under 15 go free, tel. 39728728).

Trains and Buses

The Termini train station is a minefield of tourist services: a late-hours bank, 24-hour thievery, the city bus station, and a subway stop. Handy multilingual charts make locations very clear. La Piazza, inside the station, is a bright and cheery self-service restaurant (open 11:00-22:30).

Getting Around Rome

Sightsee on foot, by city bus, or taxi. We've grouped your sightseeing options into walkable neighborhoods. Public transportation is efficient, cheap, and part of your Roman experience.

Subway: The Roman subway system (Metropolitan) is simple, with two clean, cheap, fast lines. While much of Rome is not served by its skimpy subway, these stops may be helpful to you: Termini (central train station, National Museum), Republica (main tourist office), Barberini (Cappuccin Crypt, Trevi Fountain), Spagna (Spanish Steps, Villa Borghese, classiest shopping area), Flaminio (Piazza del Popolo, start of the Via del Corso Dolce Vita stroll), Ottaviano (the Vatican, recommended hotels), Colosseo (the Colosseum, Roman Forum), and EUR (Mussolini's futuristic suburb). Buy your L1500 subway tickets at subway ticket counters or neighborhood *tabacchi* (tobacco shops). Beware of getting short-changed.

Buses: Bus routes are clearly listed at the stops. Bus #64 is particularly useful, connecting the station, Victor Emmanuel Monument (near the Forum), and the Vatican. Ride it for a city overview and to watch pickpockets in action. Buy tickets at newsstands, tobacco shops or at major bus stops but not on board (L1500, good for 75 minutes — one Metro ride and unlimited buses, punch them yourself as you board). Buy a bunch so you can hop a bus without searching for an open tobacco shop. (Riding without a ticket, while relatively safe, is still stressful. Inspectors fine even innocent-looking tourists L50,000 if found on a bus or subway without a ticket.) If you hop a bus without a ticket, locals who use tickets rather than a monthly pass can sell you a ticket from their wallet bundle. All-day bus/Metro passes cost L6000. Learn which buses serve your neighborhood.

Buses, especially the touristic #64, and the subway, are havens for thieves and pickpockets. Assume any commotion is a thief-created distraction. Hug your pack, wear no wallet or fanny/waist pack, and keep your moneybelt tucked out of sight in your pants/skirt. When it's

Rome

crowded, a giggle or a jostle can be expensive. On every trip we've witnessed at least one pickpocketing attempt.

Taxis: Taxis' big drop-charge (L6400) covers you for 3 kilometers. (L5000 surcharge after 22:00.) From the Alimandi Hotel to the Piazza Navona costs L11,000 to L15,000. Three or four traveling together with more money than time should taxi almost everywhere. Rather than wave and wave, ask in local shops for the nearest taxi stand (*Dov'e una fermata dei tassi?*). The meter is fair.

Helpful Hints

General Museum Hours: 9:00-14:00, closed on Mondays (except the Vatican) and at 13:00 on Sundays. Outdoor sights like the Colosseum, Forum, and Ostia Antica are open 9:00 to 19:00 (or one hour before sunset), and are often closed one day a week. The Capitoline Hill museums, Rome's only nocturnal museums, are open on Tuesday and Saturday nights. There are absolutely no absolutes in Italy. These hours will vary. Confirm sightseeing plans each morning with a quick L200 telephone call asking, "Are you open today?" (*Aperto oggi?*) and "What time do you close?" (*A che ora chiuso?*). I've included telephone numbers for this purpose. The last pages of the daily "Messaggero" newspaper lists current events, exhibits and hours.

Churches: Churches open early, close for lunch, and reopen from about 16:00 to 19:00. Modest dress means no bare shoulders, mini-skirts, or shorts (men or women). Kamikaze tourists maximize their sightseeing hours by visiting churches before 9:00, seeing the major sights that don't close for siesta (St. Peter's and the Forum) when all good Romans are taking it cool and easy, and doing the nocturnal museums after dark.

Shop Hours: Usually 9:00-13:00 and 16:00-20:00. In the holiday month of August, many shops and restaurants close up for vacation—*Chiuso per ferie* (and closed for restoration) signs decorate locked doors all over town.

Theft Alert: With sweet-talking con artists, thieves on buses, and thief gangs at the ancient sights, Rome is a gauntlet of rip-offs. Other than getting run down, there's no great physical risk. But green tourists will be ripped off. Thieves strike when you're distracted. Don't trust kind strangers and keep nothing important in your pockets. Assume you're being stalked. (Then relax and have fun.)

Buyer Beware: Carefully understand the final price before you order *anything* and deliberately count your change. Expect the "slow count." Wait for the last bits of your change straggle over to you. There are legitimate extras (café prices skyrocket when you sit down, taxis get L5000 extra after 22:00, and so on) to which paranoid tourists wrongly take offense. But the waiter who charges you L70,000 for the pizza and beer assumes you're too polite to involve the police. If you have any

Metropolitana: Rome's Subway

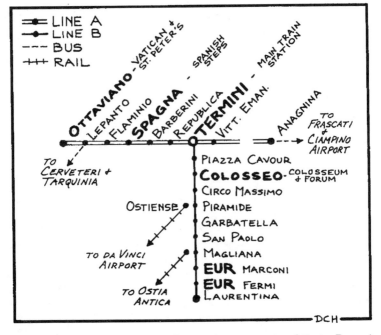

problem with a restaurant, hotel, or taxi, get a cop to arbitrate. Rome is trying to civilize itself.

Siesta: The siesta is a key to survival in summertime Rome. Lie down and contemplate the extraordinary power of gravity in the eternal city. I drink lots of cold, refreshing water from Rome's many drinking fountains (the Forum has three). If you get sick, call the International Medical Center (tel. 488 2371).

Sights—Rome

▲ **Thief Gangs**—If you wear a moneybelt and you know what to look out for, the omnipresent groups of children picking the pockets and handbags of naive tourists are no threat but an interesting, albeit sad, spectacle. Gangs of city-stained children, too young to prosecute but old enough to rip you off, troll through the tourist crowds around the Forum, Colosseum, train and metro stations. Watch them target tourists distracted with a video camera, overloaded with bags, or lulled into thinking a "fanny pack" is secure. They look like beggars and use newspapers or cardboard signs to distract their victims. Every year they get bolder, but they'll still scram like stray cats if you're on to them (wave your arm and menacingly yell, "Basta!" if they try to get close to you). A fast-fingered mother with a baby is often nearby.

▲▲▲**Colosseum**—This is the great example of Roman engineering, 2,000 years old. The Romans, using concrete, brick, and their trademark round arches, were able to construct much larger buildings than the Greeks. But in deference to the higher Greek culture, notice how they finished their no-nonsense mega-structure by pasting all three orders (Doric, Ionic, and Corinthian) of Greek columns as decorations on the outside. The Flavian Amphitheater's popular name "Colosseum" comes from the colossal statue of Nero that used to stand in front of it.

Romans were into "big." By putting two theaters together, they created a circular amphitheater. They could fill and empty its 50,000 numbered seats as quickly and efficiently as we do our super-stadiums. They had teams of sailors who could hoist canvas awnings over the stadium to give the fans shade. This was where the ancient Romans, whose taste was nearly as violent as modern America's, enjoyed their Dirty Harry and Terminator. Gladiators, criminals, and wild animals fought to the death in every conceivable scenario. They could even flood the place to wage mock naval battles (daily 9:00-19:00, Sunday and Wednesday 9:00-13:00, less off-season, free, L8000 to go upstairs, tel. 7004261).

▲**St. Peter-in-Chains Church (San Pietro in Vincoli)**—The original chains and Michelangelo's able-to-stand-and-toss-those-tablets *Moses* are on exhibit in an otherwise unexceptional church. Just a short walk uphill from the Colosseum (free, 6:30-12:30, 15:30-19:00, modest dress required).

▲▲▲**Roman Forum (Foro Romano)**—Ancient Rome's birthplace and civic center, the Forum was the common ground between Rome's famous seven hills. To help resurrect this confusing pile of rubble, study the before-and-after pictures in the cheap city guidebooks sold on the streets. (Check out the small red *Rome, Past and Present* books with plastic overleafs to un-ruin the ruins. They're priced at L25,000, but groups wanting five or more can bargain the price to half that).

Start at the Basilica Aemilia, on your right as you walk down the entry ramp. This ancient palace's floorplan shows how medieval churches adopted the "basilica" design. Then walk the Via Sacra, the main street of ancient Rome, running from the Arch of Septimus Severus on the right, past Basilica Aemilia, up to the Arch of Titus and the Colosseum on the left. The plain, intact brick building near the Arch of Septimus Severus was the Curia where the Roman senate sat. (Peek inside.) Only the giant barrel vault remains of the huge Basilica Maxentius, looming crumbly and weed-eaten to the left of Via Sacra as you walk to the Arch of Titus (direction: Colosseum).

As you stand in the shadow of the Bas Max, reconstruct the place in your mind. The huge barrel vaults were just side niches. Extend the broken nub of an arch out over the vacant lot and finish your imaginary Roman basilica with rich marble and fountains. People it with toga-clad Romans. Yeow.

The Arch of Titus is carved with propaganda celebrating the defeat, in A.D. 70, of the Jews (find the menora). This began the Diaspora that ended only with the creation of Israel in 1947.

From the Titus drinking fountain, walk up the Palatine Hill to the remains of the Imperial palaces. We get our word "palace" from this hill where the emperors chose to live. The pleasant garden overlooks the Forum, and, on the far side, look down on the dusty old Circus Maximus. (Forum open 9:00-19:00, Sunday 9:00-13:00, 9:00-15:00 in off-season, last tickets sold an hour before closing, L12,000, tel. 6990110. Just past the entry, there's a W.C. and a handy headless statue for you to pose behind.)

▲**Mammertine Prison**—The 2,500-year-old converted cistern that once imprisoned Saints Peter and Paul is worth a quick look if it's open. On the walls are lists of prisoners (Christian and non-Christian) and how they were executed: Strangolati, Decapitato, Morto di Fame . . . (donation requested, 9:00-12:00, 14:30-17:00). At the top of the stairs leading to the Campidoglio you'll find a refreshing water fountain. Block the spout with your fingers; it spurts up for drinking (or surprising a friend).

▲▲**Capitoline Hill (Campidoglio)**—This hill was the religious and political center of ancient Rome. It's still the home of the city's government. Michelangelo's lovely Renaissance square is bounded by two fine museums and the mayoral palace.

The Capitoline Museum (Musei Capitolini) in the Palazzo Nuovo (the building closest to the river) is the world's oldest museum (500 years old) and more important than its sister (opposite). Outside the entrance, notice the marriage announcements (and, very likely, wedding party photo ops). Inside the courtyard, have some photo fun with chunks of a giant statue of Emperor Constantine. (A rare public toilet hides near the museum ticket taker.) The museum is worthwhile, with lavish rooms housing several great statues including the original (500 B.C.) Etruscan Capitoline wolf and the enchanting Commodus as Hercules. Across the square is a museum full of ancient statues—great if you like portrait busts of forgotten emperors or want to see the restored equestrian statue of Marcus Aurelius which used to sit on the pedestal in the square. (Both open Tuesday-Saturday 9:00-13:30, summer Tuesdays and Saturdays 20:00-23:00, winter Tuesdays and Saturdays 17:00-20:00, Sunday 9:00-13:00, closed Monday, L10,000, tel. 67102475.) There's a fine view of the Forum from the terrace just past the mayor's palace on the right.

To approach the great square the way Michelangelo wanted you to, walk halfway down the grand stairway toward Piazza Venezia, spin

Downtown Ancient Rome

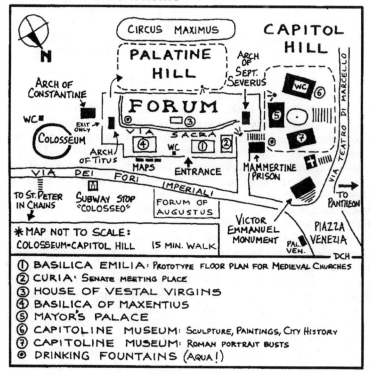

① **BASILICA EMILIA:** Prototype floor plan for Medieval Churches
② **CURIA:** Senate meeting place
③ **HOUSE OF VESTAL VIRGINS**
④ **BASILICA OF MAXENTIUS**
⑤ **MAYOR'S PALACE**
⑥ **CAPITOLINE MUSEUM:** Sculpture, Paintings, City History
⑦ **CAPITOLINE MUSEUM:** Roman portrait busts
◉ **DRINKING FOUNTAINS** (Aqua!)

around and walk back up. At the bottom of the stairs, look up the long stairway to your right for a good example of the earliest style of Christian church and be thankful it's not worth climbing up to see.

Way down the street on your left, you'll see a modern building actually built around surviving ancient pillars and arches. Farther ahead (toward Piazza Venezia), look into the ditch (on the right) and see how everywhere modern Rome is built on the countless bricks and forgotten mosaics of ancient Rome.

Piazza Venezia—This square is the focal point of modern Rome. The Via del Corso, starting here, is the city's axis, surrounded by the classiest shopping district. From the Palazzo di Venezia's balcony above the square (to your left with back to Victor Emmanuel Monument), Mussolini whipped up the nationalistic fervor of Italy. Fascist masses filled the square screaming, "Four more years!" or something like that. (Fifteen years later, they hung him outside a gas station in Milan.)

Victor Emmanuel Monument—This oversize monument to an Italian king loved only by his relatives and the ignorant is known to most Romans as "the wedding cake," "the typewriter," or "the dentures." It wouldn't be so bad if it weren't sitting on a priceless acre of Ancient Rome. Soldiers guard Italy's Tomb of the Unknown Soldier as the eternal flame flickers.

▲▲▲**Pantheon**—For the greatest look at the splendor of Rome, antiquity's best-preserved interior is a must (normally open 9:00-18:00, Sunday 9:00-13:00, less in winter, tel. 683-00230, free). Walk past its one-piece granite columns and through the original bronze door. Sit inside under the glorious skylight and study it. The dome, 140 feet high and wide, was Europe's biggest until Brunelleschi's dome was built in Florence 1,200 years later. You'll understand why this wonderfully harmonious architecture was so inspirational to the artists of the Renaissance, particularly Raphael; along with Italy's first two kings, he chose to be buried here. As you walk around the outside of the Pantheon, notice the "rise of Rome"—about 15 feet since it was built.

▲**Curiosities near the Pantheon**—The only Gothic church you'll see in Rome is **Santa Maria sopra Minerva**. On a little square behind the Pantheon to the left, past the Bernini elephant and the Egyptian obelisk statue, it was built *sopra*, or over, a pre-Christian Temple of Minerva. Rome was at its low ebb, almost a ghost town through much of the Gothic period, and the little building done from this time was later redone Baroque. This church is a refreshing exception. St. Catherine's body lies under the altar (her head is in Siena) and a little-known Michelangelo statue, *Christ Bearing the Cross*, stands to the left. Fra Angelico's tomb is in the left, or north, transept. Nearby (head out the church's rear door behind the Michelangelo statue and turn left) you'll find the **Chiesa di St. Ignazio** church, a riot of Baroque illusions. Study the ceiling in the back of the nave. Then stand on the yellow disk on the floor between the two stars. Look at the central (black) dome. Keeping your eyes on the dome, walk under and past it. Did the congregation run out of building funds? Turn around and look at the fresco over the entry. Walk left, then right . . . then look at the altar. What is painted and what is real? (These churches are open until 19:00, take a 12:30-16:00 siesta, are free, and welcome modestly dressed visitors.)

A few blocks away, back across Corso Victor Emmanuel, is the very rich and Baroque **Gesu Church**, headquarters of the Jesuits in Rome. The Jesuits powered the Church's Counter-Reformation. With Protestants teaching that all roads to heaven didn't pass through Rome, the Baroque churches of the late 1500s were painted with spiritual road maps that said they did.

Vatican City, St. Peter's, and the Museum

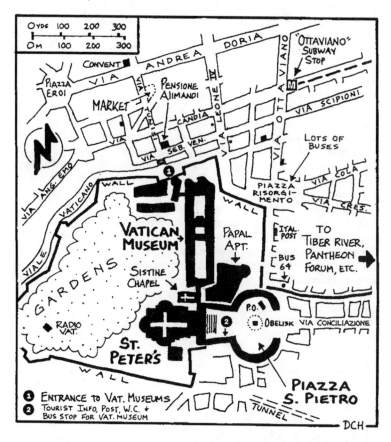

▲▲Vatican City—This tiny independent country of just over 100 acres is contained entirely within Rome. Politically powerful, the Vatican is the religious capital of 800 million Roman Catholics. If you're not one already, become a Catholic for your visit. Start by dropping by the helpful tourist office just to the left of St. Peter's Basilica (Monday-Saturday, 8:30-19:00, tel. 6988 4466.) Check out the glossy L5000 guidebooklet (crowded piazza on cover) which doubles as a classy souvenir. Telephone them if you're interested in the pope's schedule (Sunday at noon for a quick blessing for the crowds in Piazza San Pietro from the window of his study above the square, or Wednesday mornings when a reservation is necessary), or in their sporadic but very good tours of the

Vatican grounds or the church interior. If you don't care to see the pope, remember that the times he appears are most crowded. Handy buses shuttle visitors between the church and the museum (twice an hour, 8:45 until museum closes, L2000). This is far better than the exhausting walk around the Vatican wall, and it gives you a rare, pleasant peek at the garden-filled Vatican grounds.

▲▲▲St. Peter's Basilica—There is no doubt: this is the richest and most impressive church on earth. To call it vast is like calling God smart. Marks on the floor show where the next largest churches would fit if they were put inside. The ornamental cherubs would dwarf a large man. Birds roost inside, and thousands of people wander about, heads craned heavenward, hardly noticing each other. Don't miss Michelangelo's *Pietà* (behind bullet-proof glass) to the right of the entrance. Bernini's altar work and huge bronze canopy (*baldacchino*) are brilliant.

For most visitors the treasury (in the sacristy) is not worth the admission, but the crypt is free and worth a wander. Directly under the dome, stairs will lead you down to the level of the earlier church and the tombs of many of the popes, including the very first one . . . Peter.

The dome, Michelangelo's last work, is (you guessed it) the biggest anywhere. Taller than a football field is long, it's well worth the sweaty climb (330 steps after the elevator, allow an hour to go up and down) for a great view of Rome, the Vatican grounds, and the inside of the Basilica--particularly heavenly while there is singing. The elevator (just

St. Peter's Basilica

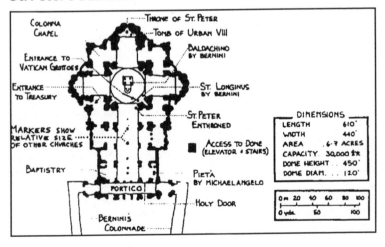

outside the church to the right as you face it) takes you to the rooftop of the nave. From there a few steps bring you to a balcony at the base of the dome looking down into the church interior. After that, the one-way (for some people claustrophobic) 300-step climb to the cupola begins. The rooftop level (below the dome) has a gift shop, WC, drinking fountain, and a commanding view (L6,000 elevator, allow an hour to go up and down.) The church strictly enforces its dress code. Dress modestly—a dress or long pants, shoulders covered. You are usually required to check any bags at a cloak room near the entry. St. Peter's is open daily from 7:00 to 19:00, 18:00 in winter; ticket booths to the treasury and dome close an hour early. All are welcome to join in the mass (most days at the front altar, 17:00).

Volunteers who want you to understand and appreciate St. Peter's give free 90-minute "Pilgrim Service" tours in English often at 10:00 and 15:00 (as you enter the church, check for the day's schedule at the desk just after the dress code guards). Seeing the *Pietà* is neat, understanding it is divine.

See tomorrow for information on the Vatican Museum.

Other sights in and near Rome
▲▲**The Dolce Vita Stroll down Via del Corso**—The city's chic and hip "cruise" from the Piazza del Popolo (Metro: Flaminio) down a wonderfully traffic-free section of the Via del Corso and up Via Condotti to the Spanish Steps each evening around 18:00. Shoppers, take a left on Via Condotti for the Spanish Steps and Gucci (after siesta, shops open from 16:30 to 19:30). Historians, start with a visit to the Baroque Church of Santa Maria del Popolo (with Raphael's Chigi Chapel and two Caravaggio paintings) continue down the Via del Corso to the Victor Emmanuel Monument, climb Michelangelo's stairway to his glorious Campidoglio Square, and visit Rome's Capitoline Museum, open Tuesday and Saturday evenings. Catch the lovely view of the Forum (from past the mayor's palace on right) as the horizon reddens and cats prowl the unclaimed rubble of ancient Rome.
▲**Villa Borghese**—Rome's unkept "Central Park" is great for people-watching (plenty of modern-day Romeos and Juliets). Take a row on the lake, or visit its fine museums. The **Borghese Gallery** has some world-class Baroque art, including the exciting Bernini statue of Apollo chasing Daphne, and paintings by Caravaggio and Rubens (L4000, 9:00-14:00, Sunday 9:00-13:00, closed Monday, tel. 8548577, for a few years the paintings will be in Trastevere at via de San Michele 22, 9:00-19:00, closed Monday and Sunday afternoon). Also in the Villa Borghese, the

Museo di Villa Giulia is a fine Etruscan museum (9:00-19:00, Sunday 9:00-13:00, closed Monday, L8000, call 3201951).

▲**National Museum of Rome (Museo Nazionale Romano delle Terme)**—Directly in front of the train station, it houses much of the greatest ancient Roman sculpture (9:00-14:00, Sunday until 13:00, closed Monday, L12,000, tel. 4880530). At the far side of the Palace, facing Piazza Republica, the Aula Ottagona (Rotunda of Diocletian, free, daily 10:00-13:00, 15:00-18:00) is an impressive space decorated with fine ancient statues and worth a quick peek.

▲**Cappuccin Crypt**—If you want bones, this is it: below the church of Santa Maria della Immaculata Concezione on Via Veneto, just off Piazza Barberini, are thousands of skeletons, all artistically arranged for the delight—or disgust—of the always wide-eyed visitor. The monastic message on the wall near the entry explains that this is more than just a macabre exercise. Pick up a few of Rome's most interesting postcards (L10,000 donation, 9:00-12:00, 15:00-18:30). A bank with long hours and good exchange rates is next door and the American Embassy is just up the street.

▲**E.U.R.**—Mussolini's planned suburb of the future (60 years ago) is a 10-minute subway ride from the Colosseum to Metro: Magliana. From the Magliana subway stop, walk through the park uphill to the Palace of the Civilization of Labor (Pal. d. Civilta d. Concordia), the essence of Fascist architecture with its giant, no-questions-asked, patriotic statues and its this-is-the-truth simplicity. On the far side is the Museo della Civilta Romana (history museum, Piazza G. Agnelli; Metro: EUR Fermi; 9:00-13:30, Tuesday and Thursday 15:00-18:00, closed Monday, L5000, tel. 592 6041), including a large-scale model of ancient Rome.

▲▲**Ostia Antica**—Rome's ancient seaport (80,000 people in the time of Christ, later a ghost town, now excavated), less than an hour from downtown, is the next best thing to Pompeii. Start at the 2,000-year-old theater, buy a map, explore the town, and finish with its fine little museum. To get there, take the subway's B Line to the Magliana stop, catch the Lido train to Ostia Antica (twice an hour), walk over the overpass, go straight to the end of that road, and follow the signs to (or ask for) "scavi" Ostia Antica. Open daily from 9:00 to one hour before sunset. The L8000 entry fee includes the museum (which closes at 14:00, tel. 565-0022). Just beyond is the filthy beach (Lido), an interesting anthill of Roman sun-worshipers.

Overrated Sights—The Spanish Steps are a disappointment for those who would rather not pass around bottles of cheap wine with with the young backpacking crowd (with one of the world's largest McDonald's–McGrandeur at its greatest—just down the street). The commercialized

Catacombs, which contain no bones, are way out of the city, and are not worth the time or trouble. The venerable old Villa d'Este garden of fountains near Hadrian's Villa outside of town at Tivoli are now run-down, overpriced, and a disappointment.

Eating in Rome
The cheapest meals in town are picnics (from *alimentari* shops or open-air markets), self-serve **Rostisseries**, and stand-up or take-out meals from a **Pizza Rustica** (pizza slices sold by the weight). One hundred grams, or an *etto*, is a hot cheap snack; 200 grams (2 *etti*) make a light meal. Most alimentari will slice and stuff a sandwich (*panini*) for you if you buy the stuff there.

In Trastevere or on the Campo di Fiori: For the best of Rome's Vespa street ambience, find your own place in Trastevere (bus #23 from the Vatican area) or on Campo di Fiori. Guidebooks list Trastevere's famous places, but more enjoyable is wandering the fascinating maze of streets around the Piazza Santa Maria in Trastevere and find a mom-and-pop place with barely a menu, like **Da Meo Petaca** (L15,000 menu, Piazza de Mercanti 30, tel. 581-6198). For the basic meal with lots of tourists, eat amazingly cheap at **Mario's** (three courses with wine and service for L17,000, near the Sisto bridge at via del Moro 53, tel. 5803809, closed Sunday). For the ultimate romantic square setting, eat at whichever place looks best on Campo di Fiori: **Virgilio's** (tel. 68802746, closed Wednesday), **Il Capitello** (tel. 656-573), and **Om Shanti** are all reasonable.

Near the Pantheon: Il Delfino is a handy self-service cafeteria on the Largo Argentina square (7:00-21:00, closed Monday, not cheap but fast). The alimentari on the Pantheon square will make you a sandwich for a temple porch picnic.

On Via Firenze, near Hotel Nardizzi: **Lon Fon**, at #44, serves reasonably priced Chinese food with elegant atmosphere (closed Wednesday). There's also **Snack Bar Gastronomia** (#34, really cheap hot meals dished up from under glass counter, open until 20:00, closed Sunday) and an alimentari (grocery store, at #54). McDonald's on Piazza della Republica has free piazza seating and a L6,000 great salad bar that no American fast-food joint would recognize.

Near the Vatican Museum and Pension Alimandi: Viale Giulio Cesare is lined with cheap fun eateries (such as **Cipriani Self-Service Rosticceria** near the Ottaviano subway stop at Via Vespasiano, with pleasant outdoor seating). Don't miss the wonderful **Via Andrea Doria** open-air market in front of the Vatican Museum, 2 blocks between Via Tunisi and Via Andrea Doria (closed by 13:30, Monday-Saturday). **Antonio's Hostaria dei Bastioni** is a tasty, friendly place for a good sit-down meal (L9,000 pastas, at the corner of the Vatican wall, Via Leone IV 29, tel. 397-23034, closed Sunday).

Day 13: Rome, Città, Florence

After an art-packed morning tour of the Vatican Museum and Sistine Chapel, we'll drive north to hike and unwind at Città di Bagnoregio, Italy's quintessential Back Door hilltown. We'll end the day checking into our hotel in the heart of Italy's treasure chest of art, Florence.

> **Likely activities today...**
> Tour of Rome's Vatican Museum
> 2-hour drive to Bagnoregio*
> 40-minute hike to Città*
> Free time in Città, hike back*
> 3-hour drive to Florence*
>
> You'll walk 5 to 10 miles today, and sleep in Siena.

Included as an activity on BB&B tours.

▲▲▲**The Vatican Museum**—Too often, the immense Vatican Museum is treated as an obstacle course, with four nagging miles of displays, separating the tourist from the Sistine Chapel. Even without the Sistine, this is one of Europe's top three or four houses of art. It can be exhausting, so plan your visit carefully, focusing on a few themes, and allow several hours. The museum uses a nearly-impossible-not-to-follow, one-way system.

Required minimum stops, in this order: Egyptian mummies and statues; *Apollo Belvedere* and *Laocoön* in Octagonal Courtyard, *Belvedere Torso* (all three showing the classical mastery of the body and very influential to Renaissance artists); past the rooms of animals, the giant porphyry hot tub, between the porphyry sarcophagi of Constantine's mother and daughter, then down the hall of broken penises and past the corridor of maps to huge rooms plastered with church propaganda (Constantine's divine vision and his victory at Milvian Bridge which led him to become Christian, and the 19-century Vatican declaration of the immaculate conception of the Virgin Mary), past a small chapel frescoed by Fra Angelico and into the Raphael rooms.

The masterpiece here is the newly restored School of Athens, remarkable for its blatant pre-Christian classical orientation wallpapering the apartments of Pope Julius II. Raphael honors the great pre-Christian thinkers—Aristotle, Plato, and company—who are portrayed as the leading artists of Raphael's day: the bearded figure of Plato is Leonardo da Vinci, and Michelangelo broods in the foreground—supposedly added late, after Raphael snuck a peek at the Sistine Chapel and decided that his arch-competitor was so good he had to put their personal differences aside and include him in this tribute to the artists of his generation. Today's St. Peter's was under construction as Raphael was working. In this fresco he gives us a sneak preview of the unfinished church.

Next (unless you detour through the refreshing modern Catholic art section) is the newly restored Sistine Chapel. Michelangelo's pictorial culmination of the Renaissance shows the story of creation with a powerful God weaving in and out of each scene through that busy week. This is an optimistic and positive expression of the high Renaissance. Later, after the Reformation wars had begun and after the Catholic army of Spain had sacked the Vatican, the reeling church began to fight back. As part of its Counter-Reformation, Michelangelo was commissioned to paint the Last Judgment (behind the altar). Newly restored, the message is as brilliant and clear as the day Michelangelo finished it: Christ is returning, some will go to hell and some to heaven, and some will be saved by the power of the rosary.

The Vatican's small but fine collection of paintings, the Pinacoteca (with Raphael's *Transfiguration* and Caravaggio's *Deposition*) is near the entry/exit. Early Christian art is the final possible side-trip before exiting via the souvenir shop.

The museum clearly marks out four color-coded visits of different lengths. Rentable headphones (L8000) give a recorded tour of the Raphael rooms and Michelangelo's Sistine masterpiece. (April, May, September, and October hours: 8:45-16:45, Saturday 8:45-14:00, closed Sunday, except last Sunday of month when museum is free; the rest of the year it's open 8:45-13:45. Last entry an hour before closing. Many minor rooms close from 13:45 to 14:45 or from 13:30 on. The Sistine Chapel is closed 30 minutes before the rest of the museum. A small door at the rear of the Sistine Chapel is used by speedy tour groups to escape via St. Peter's. If you squirt out here you're done with the museum. The Pinacoteca is the only important part left. Consider doing it at the start. Otherwise, it's a 10-minute heel-to-toe slalom through the tourists from the Sistine to the entry/exit, L15,000, tel. 69883333. The museum is closed on 5/1, 6/29, 8/15, 11/1, 12/8 and on church holidays.)

The museum's excellent book and card shop offers a priceless (L12,000) black-and-white photo book (by Hupka) of the *Pietà*—great for gifts. The Vatican post has an office in the museum and one on Piazza San Pietro (comfortable writing rooms, Monday-Friday 8:30-19:00, Saturday 8:30-18:00). The Vatican post is the only reliable mail service in Italy and the stamps are a collectible bonus (Vatican stamps are good if mailed in Rome, Italian stamps are not good at the Vatican). The Vatican bank has sinfully bad rates.

Cività di Bagnoregio
Perched on a pinnacle in a grand canyon, this is our favorite tiny hill town. Immerse yourself in the traffic-free village of Cività. Curl your toes around its Etruscan roots.

Cività is terminally ill. Only 15 residents remain, as bit by bit the town is being purchased by rich big-city Italians who will escape to their villas here. Apart from its permanent (and aging) residents and those who have weekend villas here, there is a group of Americans, mostly Seattle-ites, introduced to the town through a small University of Washington architecture program, who have bought into the rare magic of Cività. When the program is in session, 15 students live with residents and study Italian culture and architecture.

Hill Towns of Central Italy

Cività is connected to the world and the town of Bagnoregio by a long donkey path. While Bagnoregio lacks the pinnacle-town romance of Cività, it rings true as a pure bit of small-town Italy. It's actually a healthy, vibrant community (unlike Cività, the suburb it calls "the dead city"). Get a haircut, sip a coffee on the square, walk down to the old

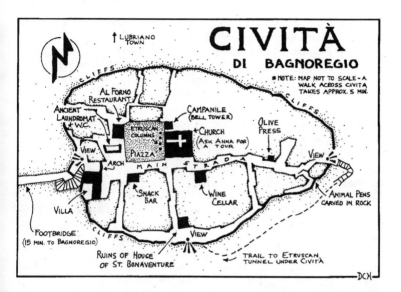

laundry (ask, *Dové la lavandaria vecchia?*). From Bagnoregio, yellow signs direct you along its long and skinny spine to its older neighbor, Cività. Enjoy the view as you head up the long donkey (and now, Vespa) path to Cività and its main (and only) square. A shuttle bus runs between Bagnoregio and the base of Cività's bridge about hourly in season (L1,000).

At the church on the main square, Anna will give you a tour (tip her and buy your postcards from her). Around the corner, on the main street, is a cool and friendly wine cellar with a dirt floor and stump chairs, where Domenica serves local wine—L1000 a glass and worth it, if only for the atmosphere. Step down into her cellar and note the traditional wine-making gear and the provisions for rolling huge kegs up the stairs. Tap on the kegs in the cool bottom level to see which are full. Most village houses are connected to cellars like this which often date from Etruscan times.

Down the street is Victoria's **Antico Mulino** (L1500), an atmospheric room of old olive presses. On weekends her grandson toasts delicious *bruschetta* (toast topped with olive oil, garlic, and tomatoes). Just down the way, Maria (for L1,000) will show you through her garden with a fine view (**Maria's Giardino**). Continuing through the town, the main drag peters out and a trail leads you down and around to the right to a tunnel that has cut through the hill under the town since Etruscan times. Slowly the town is being bought up by wealthy, big-city Italians. The

"Marchesa," who married into the Fiat family, owns the house at the town gate—complete with Cività's only (for now) hot tub.

Have cappuccino and rolls at the small café on the town square. **Al Forno** (green door on main square, June-October only, tel. 0761/793586, open daily), run by the Paolucci family, is the only real restaurant in town and serves up a good reasonable pasta and wine lunch or dinner.

Whenever you visit, stop halfway up the donkey path and listen to the sounds of rural Italy. Reach out and touch one of the monopoly houses. If you know how to turn up the volume up on the crickets, do so.

Eating in Florence
Near Santa Maria Novella: **Trattoria il Contadino** (Via Palazzuolo 69 red, a few blocks south of the train station, 12:00-14:30, 18:00-21:30, closed Sunday, tel. 238-2673) and **Trattoria da Giorgio** (Via Palazzuolo 100 red, 12:00-15:00, 18:30-22:00, closed Sunday) each offer a L14,000 hearty family-style, fixed-price menu with a bustling working-class/budget-Yankee-traveler atmosphere. Get there early or be ready to wait. **La Grotta di Leo** (Via della Scala 41 red, tel. 219-265, closed Wednesday) has a cheap, straightforward menu and decent food.

Il Latini is an internationally famous but popular-with-the-locals traditional Florentine eatery. You'll share a large table under hanging hams. There's no menu and the wine's already on the table. Just order as you go. This isn't cheap, but it can provide a memorable evening's experience, not to mention a wonderful dinner (Via del Palchetti 6, just off Moro between S.M. Novella and the river, tel. 210-916, open from 19:30, closed Monday).

South of the River: There are several good and colorful restaurants in Oltrarno near Piazza Santo Spirito. **Trattoria Casalinga** (just off Piazza Santo Spirito, near the church at 9 Via dei Michelozzi, tel. 218-624, closed Sunday) is an inexpensive and popular standby, famous for its home cooking. Good values but more expensive are **Trattoria Sabitino** on Borgo S. Frediano and **Osteria del Cinghiale Bianco** at Borgo S. Jacopo 43 (closed Tuesday and Wednesday). For a splurge, **Trattoria Oreste** (on Piazza S. Spirito at #16), with a renowned cook and on-the-piazza ambience, may have the best L50,000 dinner in the area. The **Ricchi** bar on the same square has fine homemade gelati and a particularly pleasant interior.

See tomorrow for more information on Florence.

Day 14: Florence and the Cinque Terre

Florence is Italy's blockbuster art center. You'll fall under the spell of Michelangelo's David at the Accademia and the sublime Renaissance art in the Uffizi Gallery. Take a Renaissance walk through the historic core of town. In the afternoon, head for the beaches.

To get to your remote village Riviera homebase, you'll leave the bus in Levanto and take a 15-minute train ride into the Cinque Terre, five perfectly preserved port towns hiding in the most rugged part of the Italian Riviera, surrounded by vineyards, and the Mediterannean.

Likely activities today...
Accademia (Michelangelo's David)
Renaissance Walk
Uffizi Gallery
4-hour drive to the Cinque Terre*

You'll walk about 3 miles today, and sleep in Vernazza.

---

* Included as an activity on BB&B tours.

Florence (Firenze)
Florence, the home of the Renaissance and birthplace of our modern world, is a "supermarket sweep" and the groceries are the best Renaissance art in Europe. Get your bearings with a Renaissance walk. Florentine art goes beyond paintings and statues—there's food, fashion, and handicrafts. You can lick Italy's best gelato while enjoying Europe's best people-watching.

Planning Your Time
For a day in Florence, see Michelangelo's David, tour the Uffizi gallery (best Italian paintings), tour the under-rated Bargello (best statues), and do the Renaissance ramble (explained below). Get an early start, and watch your sightseeing hours -- many sights close at 2:00 p.m. Weekend afternoons and Mondays can have especially slim pickins.

Orientation (tel. code: 055)
The Florence we're interested in lies mostly on the north bank of the Arno River. Everything is within a 20-minute walk from the train station, cathedral, or Ponte Vecchio (Old Bridge). Just over the bridge is the less awesome but more characteristic Oltrarno (south bank) area.

Orient yourself by the huge red-tiled dome of the cathedral (the Duomo) and its tall bell tower (Giotto's Tower). This is the center of historic Florence.

Tourist Info (TI): Normally overcrowded, under-informed, and under-staffed, the train station's tourist information office is not worth a stop if you're a good student of this book. If there's no line, pick up a map, a current museum-hours listing, and the periodical entertainment guide or tourist magazine (daily in summer 9:00-21:00, tel. 282893 or 219537). There's a smaller, less crowded tourist office in the alley to the right of the Loggia dei Lanzi on the Piazza della Signoria. The free monthly *Florence Concierge Information* magazine lists the latest museum hours and events. It's stocked by the expensive hotels (pick one up, as if you're staying there).

Getting Around: Taxis are expensive. Buses are cheap. A L1400 ticket lets you ride anywhere for 60 minutes and L1900 gives you two hours, (tickets not sold on bus, buy in tobacco shop, validate on bus). If you organize your sightseeing with some geographic logic you'll do it all on foot.

Helpful Hints

Museums and Churches: See everyone's essential sight, *David*, right off. In Italy, a masterpiece seen and enjoyed is worth two tomorrow; you never know when a place will unexpectedly close for a holiday, strike, or restoration. The Uffizi has 1- to 2-hour lines on busy days. Many museums close at 14:00 and stop selling tickets 30 minutes before that. Most close Mondays and at 13:00 or 14:00 on Sunday. Churches usually close from 12:30 to 15:00 or 16:00. Hours can change radically and no one knows exactly what's going on tomorrow. Local guidebooks are cheap and give you a decent commentary on the sights and a map.

Addresses: Street addresses list businesses in red and residences in black or blue (color coded on the actual street number, and indicated by a letter following the number in printed addresses: n=black, r=red).

Theft Alert: Florence has particularly hardworking thief gangs.

Sights—Florence

▲▲▲**The Accademia (Galleria dell' Accademia)**—This museum houses Michelangelo's *David* and his powerful (unfinished) *Prisoners*. Eavesdrop as tour guides explain these masterpieces. More than any other work of art, when you look into the eyes of David, you're looking into the eyes of Renaissance man. This was a radical break with the past. Man is now a confident individual, no longer a plaything of the supernatural. And life is now more than just a preparation for what happens after you die.

The Renaissance was the merging of art and science. In a humanist vein, David is looking at the crude giant of medieval darkness and thinking, "I can take this guy." Back on a religious track (and, speaking of veins), notice how big and overdeveloped David's right hand is. This is symbolic of the hand of God that powered David to slay the giant . . . and, of course, enabled Florence to rise above its crude neighboring city-states.

Beyond the magic marble, there are two floors of interesting pre-Renaissance and Renaissance paintings including a couple of lovely Botticellis (Via Ricasoli 60, 9:00-19:00, Sunday 9:00-14:00, closed Monday, L12,000, tel. 2388609.)

There's a good book-and-poster shop across the street. Behind the Accademia is the Piazza Santissima Annunziata, with its lovely Renaissance harmony, and the Hospital of the Innocents (Spedale degli Innocenti, not worth going inside) by Brunelleschi, with terra-cotta medallions by della Robbia. Built in the 1420s, it is considered the first Renaissance building.

▲▲▲▲ **A Florentine Renaissance Walk**—Even during the Dark Ages, people knew they were in a "middle time." It was especially obvious to the people around here—sitting on the rubble of Rome—that there was a brighter age before them. The long-awaited rebirth, or "Renaissance," happened in Florence for good reason. Wealthy for its cloth industry, trade and banking; powered by a fierce city-state pride (locals would pee into the Arno with gusto, knowing rival city-state Pisa was downstream); and fertile with more than its share of artistic genius (imagine guys like Michelangelo and Leonardo attending the same high school); Florence was a natural home for this cultural explosion.

Take a walk through the core of Renaissance Florence by starting at the Accademia (home of Michelangelo's *David)* and cutting through the heart of the city to the Ponte Vecchio on the Arno River. (A ten-page, self-guided tour of this walk is outlined in my museum guidebook, *Mona Winks.* Otherwise, you'll find brief descriptions below.)

At the Accademia you'll look into the eyes of Renaissance man—humanism at its confident peak. Then walk to the Cathedral (Duomo) to see the dome that kicked off the architectural Renaissance. Step inside the Baptistery to see a ceiling covered with preachy, flat, 2-D, medieval mosaic art. Then, to see what happened when art met math, see the realistic 3-D reliefs on the doors. The painter, Giotto, designed the bell tower—an early example of how a Renaissance genius was broad and well-rounded. Continue toward the river on Florence's great pedestrian mall, Via de' Calzaioli (or "Via Calz"), which was part of the original grid plan given the city by the ancient Romans. Down a few blocks, compare medieval and Renaissance statues on the exterior of

Florence

❶ CASA RABATTI	❼ PENSIONE CENTRALE	⓭ SORELLE BANDINI
❷ HOTEL ENZA	❽ PENS. BURCHIANTI	RESTAURANTS :
❸ HOTEL UNIVERSO	❾ PENSIONE MAXIM	⓮ TRAT. CASALINGA
❹ HOTEL VISCONTI	⓾ PENS. BRETAGNA	⓯ TRAT. CONTADINO
❺ HOTEL ELITE	⓫ PENS. ALESSANDRA	⓰ GROTTA DI LEO
❻ PENSIONE SOLE	⓬ HOTEL SCALETTA	⓱ IL LATINI

the Orsanmichele Church. Via Calz connects the cathedral with the central square (Piazza della Signoria), the city palace (Palazzo Vecchio), and the Uffizi Gallery, which contains the greatest collection of Italian Renaissance paintings in captivity. Finally, walk through the Uffizi courtyard, a statuary think-tank of Renaissance greats, to the Arno River and the Ponte Vecchio.

▲▲**The Duomo**–Florence's mediocre Gothic cathedral has the third longest nave in Christendom (10:00-18:00, with an occasional lunch break, daily, free). The church's noisy neo-Gothic facade, from the 1870s, is covered with pink, green, and white Tuscan marble. Since all of its great art is stored in the Museo dell' Opera del Duomo, behind the church, the best thing about the inside is the shade. But it's capped by Brunelleschi's magnificent dome—the first Renaissance dome and the model for domes to follow. When planning St. Peter's in Rome, Michelangelo said, "I can build a dome bigger, but not more beautiful, than the dome of Florence."

Giotto's Tower—Climbing Giotto's Tower (Campanile, daily 9:00-16:30, until 19:30 in summer, L5000) beats climbing the neighboring Duomo's dome because it's fifty fewer steps, faster, not so crowded, and offers the same view plus the dome.

▲**The Baptistery**—Michelangelo said its bronze doors were fit to be the gates of paradise. Check out the gleaming copies of Ghiberti's bronze doors facing the Duomo, and the famous competition doors around to the right. Making a breakthrough in perspective, Ghiberti used mathematical laws to create the illusion of 3-D on a 2-D surface. Go inside Florence's oldest building, and sit and savor the medieval mosaic ceiling. Compare that to the "new, improved" art of the Renaissance (13:00-16:30, Sunday 9:00-13:00, free, bronze doors are on the outside so always "open"; original panels are in the Museo dell' Opera del Duomo).

▲**Orsanmichele**—Mirroring Florentine values, this was a combination church-granary. The best L200 deal in Florence is the machine which lights its glorious tabernacle. Notice the grain spouts on the pillars inside. Also study the sculpture on its outside walls. You can see man stepping out of the literal and figurative shadow of the church in the great Renaissance sculptor Donatello's *St. George*. (On Via Calzaioli, 8:00-12:00, 15:00-18:00, free.)

▲**Palazzo Vecchio**—The interior of this fortified palace, which was once the home of the Medici family, is worthwhile only if you're a real Florentine art and history fan. (L12,000, 9:00-19:00, Sunday 8:00-13:00, closed Thursday, handy public W.C. inside on ground floor.) Until 1873, Michelangelo's *David* stood at the entrance, where the copy is today. The huge statues in the square are important only as the whipping boys of art critics and as pigeon roosts. The important art is in the nearby Loggia dei Lanzi. Notice Cellini's bronze statue of Perseus (with the head of Medusa). The round plaque on the pavement in front of the palace marks the spot where Savonarola was burned.

▲▲▲**Uffizi Gallery**—The greatest collection of Italian painting anywhere is a must, with plenty of works by Giotto, Leonardo, Raphael, Caravaggio, Rubens, Titian, Michelangelo, and a roomful of Botticellis, including his *Birth of Venus*. There are no official tours, so buy a book on the street before entering (or follow *Mona Winks*). The museum is nowhere near as big as it is great: few tourists spend more than 2 hours inside. The paintings are displayed (behind obnoxious reflective glass) on one comfortable floor in chronological order from the thirteenth through the seventeenth century.

Essential stops are (in this order): the Gothic altarpieces by Giotto and Cimabue (narrative, pre-realism, no real concern for believable depth); Uccello's *Battle of San Romano*, an early study in perspective; Fra Lippi's cuddly Madonnas; the Botticelli room filled with masterpieces including the small *La Calumnia*, showing the *glasnost* of Renaissance free-thinking being clubbed back into the darker age of Savonarola; two minor works by Leonardo; the octagonal classical sculpture room with a copy of Praxiteles' *Venus de Medici*, considered the epitome of beauty in Elizabethan Europe; view of the Arno through two dirty panes of glass; Michelangelo's only surviving easel painting, the round Holy Family; Raphael's *Madonna of the Goldfinch*; Titian's *Venus of Urbino*; and an interesting view of the palace and cathedral from the café terrace at the end (9:00-19:00, Sunday 9:00-14:00, closed Monday, last ticket sold 45 minutes before closing, L12,000).

Enjoy the Uffizi square, full of artists and souvenir stalls. The surrounding statues honor the earthshaking Florentines of 500 years ago. You'll see all the great artists, plus philosophers (Machiavelli), scientists (Galileo), writers (Dante), explorers (Amerigo Vespucci), and the great patron of so much Renaissance thinking, Lorenzo (the Magnificent) Medici. The Florentine Renaissance involved more than just the visual arts.

▲▲▲**Bargello (Museo Nazionale)**—The city's underrated museum of sculpture is behind the Palazzo Vecchio (4 blocks from the Uffizi) in a former prison that looks like a mini-Palazzo Vecchio. It has Donatello's *David* (the very-influential first male nude to be sculpted in a thousand years), works by Michelangelo, and much more (Via del Proconsolo 4; 9:00-14:00, closed Monday, L8000). Dante's house, across the street and around the corner, is interesting only to his Italian-speaking fans.

▲▲**Museo dell' Opera di Santa Maria del Fiore del Duomo**—The underrated cathedral museum, behind the church at #9, is great if you like sculpture. It has masterpieces by Donatello (a gruesome wood carving of Mary Magdalene clothed in her matted hair, and the *cantoria*, the delightful choir loft bursting with happy children), Luca della Robbia (another choir loft, lined with the dreamy faces of musicians praising the Lord), a late Michelangelo Pietà (Nicodemus, on top, is a self-portrait), Brunelleschi's models for his dome, and the original restored panels of Ghiberti's doors to the Baptistery. (9:00-19:30, closed Sunday, L8000, tel. 2302885.)

▲▲**Museum of San Marco**—One block north of the Accademia on Piazza San Marco, this museum houses the greatest collection anywhere of dreamy medieval frescoes and paintings by the early Renaissance master, Fra Angelico. You'll see why he thought of painting as a form of prayer and couldn't paint a crucifix without shedding tears. Each of the monks' cells has a Fra Angelico fresco. Don't miss the cell of Savonarola, the charismatic monk who threw out the Medici, turned Florence into a theocracy, sponsored "bonfires of the vanities" (burning books, paintings, and so on), and was finally burned when Florence decided to change channels (L8000, 9:00-14:00, closed Monday).

▲**Medici Chapel (Cappelle dei Medici)**—This chapel, containing two Medici tombs, is drenched in incredibly lavish High Renaissance architecture and sculpture by Michelangelo (L8000, 9:00-14:00, closed Monday). Behind San Lorenzo on Piazza Madonna, it's surrounded by a lively market scene that, for some reason, I find more interesting.

▲**Michelangelo's Home, Casa Buonarroti**—Fans enjoy Michelangelo's house at Via Ghibellina 70 (L8000, 9:30-13:30, closed Tuesday).

▲**The Pitti Palace**—Across the river, it has the giant Galleria Palatina collection with works of the masters (especially Raphael), plus the enjoyable Galleria d'Arte Moderna (upstairs) and the huge semi-landscaped Boboli Gardens—a cool refuge from the city heat (L12,000 for the five museums, 9:00-14:00, closed Monday; gardens cost L4000 and are open 9:00-17:30 except Monday).

▲**Brancacci Chapel**—For the best look at the early Renaissance master Masaccio, see his newly restored frescoes here (L5000, 10:00-17:00, holidays 13:00-17:00, closed Tuesday, across the Ponte Vecchio and turn left a few blocks to Piazza del Carmine).

▲**Piazzale Michelangelo**—Across the river overlooking the city (look for the huge statue of David), this square is worth the half-hour hike or the drive for the view. After dark it's packed with local school kids sharing slices of watermelon with their dates. Just beyond it is the strikingly beautiful, crowd-free, Romanesque San Miniato church. (Bus #13 from the train station.)

▲▲**Gelato**—Gelato is a great Florentine edible art form. Italy's best ice cream is in Florence. Every year we repeat our taste test, and every year Vivoli's (on Via Stinche, see map, closed Mondays and the last three weeks in August) wins. Festival del Gelato and Perche Non!, just off Via Calz, are also good. That's one souvenir that can't break and won't clutter your luggage. Get a free sample of Vivoli's *riso* (rice) before ordering.

Shopping—Florence is a great shopping town. Busy street scenes and markets abound, especially near San Lorenzo (closed Sunday and Monday), on the Ponte Vecchio, and near Santa Croce. Leather, gold, silver, art prints, and tacky plaster "mini-Davids" are most popular.

A Quick Lunch near Florence's Sights: We keep lunch fast and simple, eating in one of countless self-service places, Pizza Rusticas (holes in walls selling cheap, delicious pizza by weight), or just picnicking (juice, yogurt, cheese, roll: L8000). For mountains of picnic produce or just a cheap sandwich and piles of people watching, visit the huge multi-storied Mercato Centrale (farmers' market open 7:00-14:00, closed Sunday) in the middle of the San Lorenzo street market. Behind the Duomo, **Snack** (15 Pronconsolo) serves decent cheap lunches. For a reasonably priced pizza with a Medici-style view, try one of the pizzerias on Piazza della Signori.

Next to Santa Croce, **Osteria/Pizzeria Baldo Vino** (via San Giuseppe 22r, tel. 241-773, closed Tuesday) makes budget travelers feel welcome.

See tomorrow for information on Vernazza and the Cinque Terre.

Day 15: The Cinque Terre

Ahh, today is your vacation from your vacation. You couldn't see a museum here if you wanted to! This is simply hard-core traditional Italy with nothing to do but hike through the vineyards that connect the five villages, hang out on the beaches, swim, or lounge around your town as if you lived there.

Likely activities today...
Free day to explore the Cinque Terre*

You'll walk anywhere from zero to 6 miles today, and sleep in Vernazza.

---

* Included as an activity on BB&B tours.

Planning Your Time
Your guide/escort will update you on coastal trail conditions and closures. For a good Cinque Terre day consider this: Pack your beach and swim gear, wear your walking shoes, and catch the train to Riomaggiore (town #1). Walk the cliff-hanging Via dell' Amore to Manarola (#2) and buy food for a picnic, then hike to Corniglia (#3) for a rocky but pleasant beach. Swim here or in Monterosso (#5). From #5, hike or catch the boat home to Vernazza (#4).

If you're into *la dolce far niente* (the sweetness of doing nothing) and don't want to hike, you could enjoy the blast of cool train tunnel air that announces the arrival of every Cinque Terre train and go directly to Corniglia or Monterosso to maximize beach time.

Getting Around the Cinque Terre
While you can hike or catch the irregular boats, the easy way to zip from town to town is by train. These *locale* trains (that's Italian for "milk run") are so tiny they don't even register on the Thomas Cook train timetable. But they go nearly hourly and are cheap. To orient yourself, remember that directions are *"per* (to) *Genoa"* or *"per La Spezia,"* and virtually any train that stops at one of the five villages will stop at all five. The five towns are just minutes apart by train. Know your stop. After leaving the town before your destination, move down to the door. Since the stations are small and the trains are long, you may need to get off the train deep in a tunnel and you may need to open the door yourself. Since a one-town hop costs the same as a five-town hop (L2,000), and every ticket is good all day with stopovers, you can save money by exploring the region in one direction on one ticket.

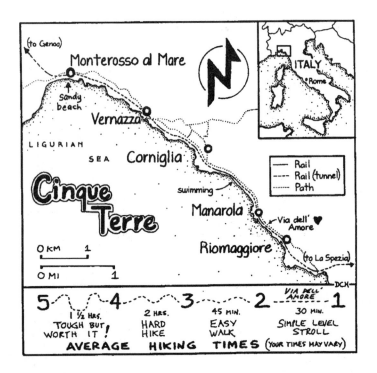

Vernazza

With the closest thing to a natural harbor, overseen by a ruined castle and an old church, and only the occasional noisy slurping up of the train by the mountain to remind you these are the 1990s, Vernazza is the best 5-Terre home base.

The action is at the harbor, where you'll find a kids' beach, plenty of sunning rocks, outdoor restaurants, a bar hanging on the edge of the castle (great for evening drinks), the tiny town soccer field, and a tail-gate party street market each Tuesday morning.

The town's thousand residents, proud of their Vernazzan heritage, brag that "Vernazza is locally owned. Portofino has sold out." Fearing the change it would bring, they stopped the construction of a major road into the region. Families are tight, go back centuries, and several generations stay together. Leisure time is spent wandering lazily together up and down the main street. Sit on a bench and study Vernazza's "passeggiata." Then explore the characteristic alleys called *carugi*. In October the cantinas are draped with drying grapes. In the winter the population shrinks as many people move to more comfortable big city apartments.

An hourly boat service connects Vernazza and Monterosso (L5,000 one way, L8,000 round-trip, calm summer days only). A 5-minute hike in either direction from Vernazza gives you a classic village photo stop. Franco's bar with a panoramic terrace is at the tower on the trail towards Corniglia.

Sights—Vernazza

The Burned-Out Sightseer's Visual Tour of Vernazza—Sit facing the town on the harbor breakwater and you'll see...

    The harbor: In a moderate storm you'd be soaked as waves routinely crash over the "molo" (breakwater, made in 1972). Below the waterfall are the town's most popular sunning rocks. The train line (above) was built in 1930s. Plastered on the breakwater concrete is the schedule for the tiny shuttle boat service from here to Monterosso. Vernazza's fishing fleet is down to three small fishing boats--the town's restaurants buy up everything they can catch. Vernazzans are more likely to own a boat than a car.

Vernazza

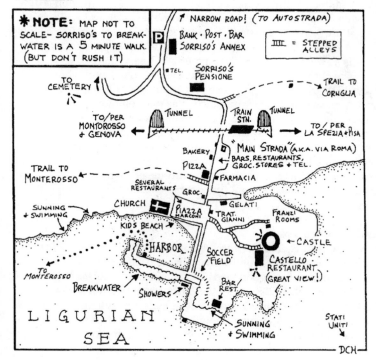

The castle: On the far right, the castle still guards the town. The Belforte Bar (originally named "bea forte" or the "fort of warning screams," for the tower's function in pirating days) is a great perch. The lowest deck (follow the rope) is great for a glass of wine. (Inside the submarine-strength door, a photo of a major storm shows the entire tower under a wave.) The highest umbrellas mark the recommended Castello restaurant.

The town: From the lower castle, the houses were interconnected with an interior arcade--ideal for fleeing in times of attack. The pastel colors are regulated by a commissioner of good taste in the community government. The square before you is famous locally for some of the region's finest restaurants. The big red central house, the 12th century site where Genoan ships were built, used to be a guard house of sorts.

Above the town: The ivy-covered tower, another part of the city fortifications, reminds us of Vernazza's importance in the Middle Ages when it was an important ally of Genoa (whose arch enemies were the other maritime republics of Pisa, Amalfi and Venice). Franco's bar, just behind the tower, welcomes hikers finishing (starting, or simply con-templating) the Corniglia-Vernazza hike with great town views. Vine-yards fill the mountainside beyond the town. Wine production is down now days as the younger residents choose less physical work. But lo-cals still work their plots and proudly serve their family wine. A single steel train line (barely visible) winds up the gully behind the tower. This is a "trenino" line for the vintner's tiny service train.

The church and city hall: Vernazza's Ligurian Gothic church dates from 1318. The red house above and to the left of the spire is the city hall. Vernazza and Corniglia function as one community. In 1995 they elected their popular major, a Communist, to his second 5-year term. The party's banner (now the PDS or "people's democratic party of the left") decorates town walls. Also in the city hall is the elementary school. High school is in the "big city," La Spezia. Finally, on the top of the hill, with the best view of all, is the town cemetery where most locals al-ready have a niche reserved (tutto completo...but a new wing is under construction).

Eating in Vernazza

If you're into Italian cuisine, Vernazza's restaurants are worth the splurge. The **Castello**, run by charming and English-speaking Monica and her family, serves good food just under the castle (12:00-22:00, closed Wednesday, tel. 812296). On the harborfront, **Trattoria Franzi** and **Trattoria del Capitano** are more atmospheric and famous. **Trattoria da Sandro** (often with an entertaining musical flair) is also popular. The more off-beat **Trattoria Piva** is less expensive with good food and late night guitar strumming. The town's only gelateria is good, and most harborside bars will let you take your glass on a breakwater stroll. You can get good pizza by the L3,500 slice on the main street. Grocery store hours are 7:30-13:00, 17:00-19:30.

Pesto: This is the birthplace of pesto. Try it on spaghetti, trofie, or trenette. Basil, which loves the temperate Ligurian climate, is mixed with cheese (half parmigiano cow cheese and half pecorino sheep cheese), garlic, olive oil, and pine nuts, poured over pasta, and then into visitors. If you become addicted, small jars of it are sold in the local grocery stores.

Wine: The Vino delle Cinque Terre, famous throughout Italy, flows cheap and easy throughout the region. If you like sweet, sherry-like wine, the local *Sciachetra* (shock-ee-TRA) wine is worth the splurge (L5000 per glass, often served with a cookie). While ten kilos of grapes yield seven liters of local wine, Sciachetra is made from near-raisins and ten kilos of grapes make only 1.5 liters of Sciachetra. If your room is up a lot of steps, be warned: Sciachetra is 18% alcohol while regular wine is only 11%. In the cool, calm evening, sit on the Vernazza break-water with a glass of wine, and watch the phosphorous in the waves.

Cinque Terre Swimming

Wear your walking shoes and pack your swim gear. Each beach has showers that may work better than your hotel's. (Bring soap and sham-poo.) Monterosso's beaches, immediately in front of the train station, are by far the best (and most crowded). It's a sandy resort with every-thing rentable...lounge chairs, umbrellas, paddle boats and usually even beach access (L2,000). Vernazza has a sandy children's cove, sunning rocks by a little waterfall and showers by the breakwater. The tiny "Acque Pendente" (waterfall) cove that locals call their "laguna blu" between Vernazza and Monterosso is accessible only by small hired boat. Forget Manarola or Riomaggiore for beaches. I do my 5-Terre swim-ming on the pathetic but peaceful manmade beach below the Corniglia station. Unfortunately, much of it has washed away and it's almost non-existent when the surf's up. It has a couple of buoys to swim to, and is clean and less crowded than the Monterosso beach. The beach bar has showers, drinks, snacks, and goils. The nude Guvano (GOO-vah-noh) beach (between Corniglia and Vernazza, 30-45 minute hike or hire a boat) made headlines in Italy in the 1970's as clothed locals in a make-shift armada of dinghies and fishing boats retook their town beach. But big city nudists still work on all around tans in this remote setting.

Cinque Terre Hiking

All five towns are connected by good trails. Experience the area best by hiking from one end to the other. The entire hike can be done in about three hours but allow five for dawdling. While you can detour to hill-top sanctuaries, I'd keep it simple by following the easy, blue and white marked low trails between the villages. A good L5000 hiking map (sold in all the towns, not necessary for this described walk) covers the expanded version of this hike from Porto Venere through all the 5-Terre towns to Levanto.

Riomaggiore-Manarola (20 minutes): From the Riomaggiore station (town #1) the Via dell' Amore affords a film-gobbling promenade (wide enough for baby strollers) down the coast to Manarola. While there's no beach here, stairs lead down to sunbathing rocks.

Manarola-Corniglia (45 minutes): From the Manarola (#2) waterfront, it's easiest to take the high trail out of town. The broad and scenic low trail ends with steep stairs leading to the high road. The walk from #2 to #3 is a little longer, and a little more rugged, than from #1 to #2. If it's closed (as it has been for several years) you can scramble around the fence. Any cat burglar can handle it. If you're concerned, ask other travelers about its current status.

Corniglia-Vernazza (90 minutes): The hike from Corniglia (#3) to Vernazza (#4)--the wildest and greenest of the coast--is most rewarding. From the Corniglia station and beach, zig-zag up to the town. Ten minutes past Corniglia toward Vernazza you'll see the well-hung Guvano beach far below. The trail leads past a bar and picnic tables, through lots of fragrant and flowery vegetation, and scenically into Vernazza.

Vernazza-Monterosso (90 minutes): The trail from Vernazza to Monterosso (#5) is a scenic, up-and-down-a-lot 90 minutes. Trails are rough but easy to follow. Camping at the picnic tables mid-way is frowned upon. The views just out of Vernazza are spectacular.

Cinque Terre Towns

▲▲**Riomaggiore–town #1:** The most substantial non-resort town of the group, Riomaggiore is a disappointment from the train station. But walk through the tunnel next to the train tracks (or take the high road, straight up and to the right), and you land in a fascinating tangle of pastel homes leaning on each other as if someone stole their crutches. There's homemade gelati at the Bar Central. With fewer locals making the wine and more tourists visiting, the local trenino (mono-rail wine train) now carries tourists to the Madonna di Montenero sanctuary high above the town.

▲**Manarola–town #2:** Like town #1, #2 is attached to its station by a 200-yard-long tunnel. Manarola is tiny and rugged, a tumble of buildings bunny-hopping down its ravine to the tiny harbor. This is a good place to buy your picnic (stores close from 13:00-17:00) before walking to the beaches of Corniglia. The restaurants **Il Porticciolo** (closed Wednesday) near the water on the main street, or **Trattoria da Billy** (closed Thursday), with the best view in town up in the residential area, are both reasonable for the over-priced area.

▲▲**Corniglia–town #3:** A zigzag series of stairs that looks worse than it is leads up to the only town of the five not on the water. Originally settled by a Roman farmer who named it for his mother, Cornelia, its ancient residents produced a wine so famous that vases found at Pompeii touted its virtues. Today, its wine is still its lifeblood. Follow the pungent smell of ripe grapes into an alley cellar and get a local to let you dip a straw into her keg. Remote and less visited, Corniglia (pronounced kor-neel-yah) has a windy belvedere and a few restaurants. Villa Cecio serves a tasty pasta and a mean house tiramasu (just above the town across the road, tel. 812043). Past the train station is the Corniglia beach and "Albergo Europa," a bungalow village filled with Italians doing the Cinque Terre in 14 days.

▲▲▲**Vernazza**—See beginning of chapter.

▲▲**Monterosso al Mare–town #5:** This is a resort with cars, hotels, rentable beach umbrellas, and crowds. Walk east of the station through the tunnel for the old world charm (and the nearly hourly boat to Vernazza). If you want a sandy beach, this is it. Adventurers may want to rent a rowboat or paddleboat and find their own private cove. There are several coves between #4 and #5, one with its own little waterfall. (Tourist office, 10:00-12:00, 17:00-20:00, closed Sunday afternoon, tel. 817506.)

Day 16: To the Alps

We'll catch an early train to Levanto, then drive nine hours into the heart of the Swiss Alps. After a stop in Interlaken, we'll ride a gondola lift into traffic-free Gimmelwald in time for dinner at Walter's Hotel Mittaghorn (a creaky, well-worn chalet with only 3 showers and a summer-camp-style loft for your guide's 8 favorite tour buddies).

Likely activities today...
Early-morning train to Levanto*
9-hour drive into Switzerland*
Free time in Interlaken*
Drive and gondola lift to Gimmelwald*
Dinner at Walter's hotel*
Orientation for tomorrow's options*

You'll walk from 1 to 2 miles today, and sleep in Gimmelwald.

Included as an activity on BB&B tours.

SWITZERLAND (Schweiz, Suisse, Svizzera)
■ 16,000 square miles (half the size of Ireland, or 13 Rhode Islands).
■ About 6 million people (400 people per square mile, declining slightly).
■ One Swiss Franc = about US$.85, 1.2 SF = about $1.

Switzerland is Europe's richest, best-organized, and most mountainous country. Like Boy Scouts, the Swiss count cleanliness, neatness, punctuality, tolerance, independence, thrift, and hard work as virtues, and they love pocket-knives. They appreciate the awesome nature that surrounds them and are proud of their little country's many achievements.

The high average Swiss income, a great social security system, and their strong currency, not to mention the Alps, give them plenty to be thankful for.

Switzerland, 40 percent of which is uninhabitable rocks, lakes, and rugged Alps, has distinct cultural regions and customs. Two-thirds of the people speak German, 20 percent French, 10 percent Italian, and a small group of people in the southeast speak Romansch, a direct descendant of ancient Latin. Within these four language groups, there are many dialects. The sing-songy Swiss German, the spoken dialect, is quite a bit different from High German, which is Switzerland's written German. Most Swiss are multilingual, and English is widely spoken, but an interest in these regional distinctions will win the hearts of locals you meet. As you travel from one valley to the next, notice changes in architecture and customs.

Switzerland

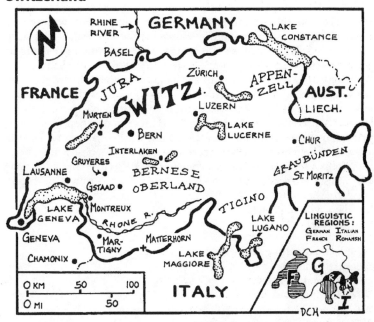

Historically, Switzerland is one of the oldest democracies (yet women didn't get the vote until 1971). Born when three states, or cantons, united in 1291, the Confederation Helvetica as it was called in Roman times (the "CH" decal on cars doesn't stand for chocolate) grew to the 23 of today. The government is decentralized, and cantonal loyalty is very strong.

Fiercely independent, Switzerland loves its neutrality and stayed out of both world wars, but it's far from lax defensively. Every fit man serves in the army and stays in the reserve. Each house has a gun and a bomb shelter. Switzerland bristles with 600,000 rifles in homes and 12,000 heavy guns in place. Swiss vacuum-packed emergency army bread, which lasts two years, is said to also function as a weapon. Airstrips hide inside mountains behind Batmobile doors. With the push of a button, all road, rail, and bridge entries to the country can be destroyed, changing Switzerland into a formidable mountain fortress. Notice the innocent-looking, but explosive, patches checkerboarding the roads at key points like tunnel entrances and mountain summits (and hope no one invades until you get past). Sentiments are changing, and in 1989, Switzerland came close to voting away its entire military. August 1 is the very festive Swiss national holiday.

New taxes have driven up prices. That, coupled with the strong franc, makes Swiss prices brutal. Hiking is free, but major Alpine lifts cost $20 to $50. Shops throughout the land tantalize tourists with carved, woven, and clanging mountain knickknacks, clocks, watches, and Swiss Army knives (Victorinox is the best brand). To figure out prices roughly in dollars, subtract 15% from the Swiss price (12F = about $10).

The Swiss eat when we do and enjoy a straightforward, no-nonsense cuisine. Specialties include delicious fondue, rich chocolates, a melted cheese dish called *raclette*, fresh dairy products (try müesli yogurt), 100 varieties of cheese, and Fendant, a good crisp local white wine, too expensive to sell well abroad but worth a taste here. The Coop and Migros grocery stores are the hungry hiker's best budget bet.

Tourist information offices abound. While Switzerland's booming big cities are cosmopolitan, the traditional culture survives in the Alpine villages. Spend most of your time getting high in the Alps. On Sundays, you're most likely to enjoy traditional sports, music, clothing, and culture.

Switzerland nitty-gritty:
Country code: 41
International access: 00
AT&T: 155-00-11
MCI: 155-0222
SPRINT: 155-9777
Emergency: 117
Ambulance: 144
Int'l telephone info. assistance: 191
Pay phones take 1 sf and 5 sf coins, and don't give change.
Senior/youth discount age: 65+
"Swiss Family Card" can save families money: for 20 SF, kids under 16 ride free on trains and lifts when accompanied by a parent.
Bank hours: 8:00-17:00 M-F. Later hour banks at train stations and larger post offices.

Interlaken
Your gateway to the wonderfully mountainous Berner Oberland is the grand old resort town of Interlaken. When the nineteenth-century Romantics redefined mountains as something more than cold and troublesome obstacles, Interlaken became the original Alpine resort. Ever since then, tourists have flocked to the Alps "because they're there." Interlaken's glory days are long gone, its elegant old hotels eclipsed by the new, more jet-setty Alpine resorts. Today, its shops are filled with chocolate bars, Swiss Army knives, and sunburned backpackers. Efficient Interlaken is a good administrative and shopping center. Take care

Interlaken

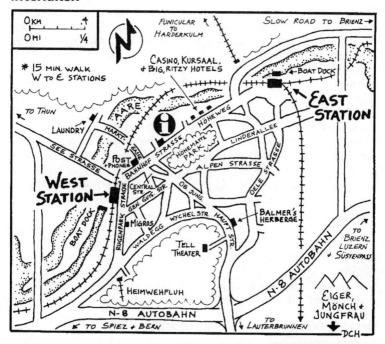

of business, give the town a quick look, view the live TV coverage of the Jungfrau and Schilthorn weather in the window of the Schilthornbahn office on the main street (Hüoheweg), and head for the hills.

Tourist Info: The tourist office (on the main street, a five minute walk from the West Station, 8:00-12:00, 14:00-18:00 daily, less on weekends and off-season; tel. 036/222121) has good information for the whole region and advice on Alpine lift discounts. (Tel. code: 036.) The train station's rail information desk has some tourist info and an exchange desk with fair rates (daily until 19:00, Sunday until 18:00). An open-late Migros supermarket is across the street (closed Sunday).

Telephone: In the center of town, next to the post office, you'll find a late-hours long-distance phone booth (7:30-12:00, 13:45-18:30 daily).

Gimmelwald and the Berner Oberland

Frolic and hike high above the stress and clouds of the real world. Take a vacation from your busy vacation. Recharge your touristic batteries up here in the Alps where distant avalanches, cowbells, the fluff of a down comforter, and the crunchy footsteps of happy hikers are the dominant sounds. If the weather's good, ride a gondola from the traffic-free village of Gimmelwald to a hearty breakfast at Schilthorn's 10,000-foot revolving Piz Gloria restaurant. Linger among Alpine whitecaps before riding, hiking, or hang gliding down (5,000 feet) to Mürren and home to Gimmelwald.

Ah, but the weather's fine and the Alps beckon. Head deep into the heart of the Alps and ride the gondola to the stop just this side of heaven—Gimmelwald.

Gimmelwald

Saved from developers by its "avalanche zone" classification, Gimmelwald (elev. 4,600 ft.) is one of the poorest places in Switzerland. Its economy is stuck in the hay, and many of the farmers, unable to make it in their disadvantaged trade, are subsidized by the Swiss government. For some travelers, there's little to see in the village. Others enjoy a fascinating day sitting on a bench and learn why they say, "If Heaven isn't what it's cracked up to be, send me back to Gimmelwald."

Take a walk through the town. This place is for real: most of the 130 residents have the same last name. They are tough and proud. Raising hay in this rugged terrain is labor-intensive. One family harvests enough to feed only 15 or 20 cows. But they'd have it no other way and, unlike absentee landlord Mürren, Gimmelwald is locally owned. (When word

Gimmelwald Side of Lauterbrunnen Valley

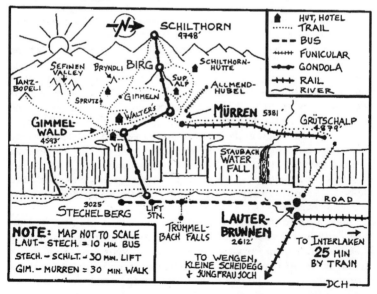

got out that urban planners had a plan to develop Gimmelwald into a town of 1,000, locals pulled some strings to secure the town's bogus "avalanche zone" building code.)

Notice the traditional log-cabin architecture and blond-braided children. The numbers on the buildings are not addresses, but fire insurance numbers. The cute little hut near the station is for storing and aging cheese, not youth hostelers. In Catholic Swiss towns, the biggest building is the church. In Protestant towns, it's the school. Protestant Gimmelwald's biggest building is the schoolhouse (one teacher, 17 students, and a room that doubles as a chapel when the pastor makes his once-a-month visit). Do not confuse obscure Gimmelwald with touristy and commercialized Grindelwald just over the Kleine Scheidegg ridge.

The **Hotel Mittaghorn**, the treasure of Gimmelwald, is run by Walter Mittler, a perfect Swiss gentleman. His hotel is a classic, creaky, Alpine-style place with memorable beds, ancient down comforters (short and fat, wear socks and drape the blanket over your feet), and a million-dollar view of the Jungfrau Alps. The hotel has two rooms with private showers and one shower for everyone else (1 SF for 5 minutes). Walter is careful not to get too hectic or big and enjoys sensitive, Back Door travelers. This is a good place to receive mail from home (mail barrel in entry hall).

To some, Hotel Mittaghorn is a fire just waiting to happen, with a kitchen that would never pass code, lumpy beds, teeny towels, and nowhere near enough plumbing, run by an eccentric grouch. These people enjoy Interlaken, Wengen, or Mürren, and that's where they should sleep.

Gimmelwald feeds its goats better than its people. There are no groceries in town. The wise and frugal buy food from the Co-ops in Mürren or Lauterbrunnen and pack it in. Walter, at Hotel Mittaghorn, is Gimmelwald's best cook (not saying much, but he is good). His salad is best eaten one leaf at a time with your fingers. There's no menu, and dinner's served at 19:30 sharp.

The only real evening fun in Gimmelwald is found at Walter's bar, on the hotel's ground floor. When the local farmers have made their hay, this is where they come to play. They look like what we'd call "hicks" (former city-slicker Walter still isn't fully accepted by the gang), but they speak some English and can be fun to get to know. Walter knows how many beers they've had according to whether they're talking, singing, fighting, or snoring. Try some good cheap beer, a strong *kaffee fertig* (coffee with schnapps), a Heidi cocoa (cocoa mit schnapps) or a Virgin Heidi. For less smoke and some powerful solitude, sit outside and watch the sun tuck the mountaintops into bed as the moon rises over the Jungfrau.

Day 17: The Alps

If the weather's good, ride the gondola up to the Schilthorn for a panoramic view at 10,000 feet (not included, about $50). Loiter around in the thin air, hike all or part way down (be careful, it's very steep and gravelly), or just stay low and play Heidi. For more Alpine thrills, the afternoon can be spent riding lifts and hiking under the Jungfrau. Back at the chalet, Walter will have fondue waiting for the pre-dinner happy hour. Bad weather options include the Ballenberg open air museum, Trummelbach falls, valley hikes, and just relaxing in Gimmelwald.

Likely activities today...
Free day for hiking, alpine lifts and train rides*
Fondue and dinner at Walter's hotel*

You'll walk anywhere from zero to 9 miles today (mostly between 5,000 and 7,000 ft. elev.), and sleep in Gimmelwald.

---

*Included as an activity on BB&B tours.

Getting Around the Berner Oberland

Rather than tackling a checklist of famous Swiss mountains and resorts, we're choosing one area to savor--the Berner Oberland. For over a hundred years this has been the target of nature-worshipping pilgrims. And the Swiss have made the most exciting Alpine perches accessible by lift or train. Part of the fun (and most of the expense) of the area is riding the many lifts. Study the "Alpine Lifts in the Berner Oberland" chart below. Lifts generally go at least twice an hour from 7:00 to 20:00 but take advantage of the time schedule to plan efficiently.

Alpine Hikes from Gimmelwald

There are days of possible hikes from Gimmelwald. Many are a fun combination of trails, mountain trains and gondola rides.
▲▲▲Hike 1: The Schilthorn, Hikes, Lifts, and a 10,000-foot panoramic view—If the weather's good, have a snack atop the Schilthorn, in the slowly revolving, mountain-capping restaurant (of James Bond movie fame). The early-bird special gondola tickets (rides before 9:00) take you from Gimmelwald to the Schilthorn and back.

In good weather the gondola ride from Gimmelwald to the Schilthorn is a thrill. Lifts go twice an hour, and the ride (including two transfers) takes 30 minutes. Watch the altitude meter in the gondola.

Linger on top of the Schilthorn. Piz Gloria has been newly renovated. There's a souvenir shop, the rocks of the region on the restaurant wall, telescopes, and a "touristorama" film room showing explosive highlights from the James Bond thriller that featured the Schilthorn and a multi-screen slide show. (It's free and self-serve. Push the button for slides or, after a long pause for the projector to rewind, push for 007.)

Watch hang gliders set up, psych up, and take off, flying 30 minutes with the birds to distant Interlaken. Walk along the ridge out back to the "No High Heels" signpost. This is a great place for a photo of the "mountain climber you." For another cheap thrill, ask the gondola attendant to crank down the window, stick your head out, and pretend you're hang gliding, ideally, over the bump going down from Gimmelwald. (For an expensive thrill, you can bungy jump from the Stechelberg-Mürren service gondola.)

Think twice before hiking down from the Schilthorn (weather can change, have good shoes). Hiking down from Birg is easier but still very steep and gravelly. Just below Birg is the Schilthorn-Hutte. Drop in for soup, cocoa, or a coffee schnapps. Youth hostelers scream down the ice fields on plastic-bag sleds from the Schilthorn. (English-speaking doctor in Mürren.)

The most interesting trail from Birg (or Mürren) to Gimmelwald is the high one via Suppenalp, Schiltalp, Gimmeln, and the Sprütz waterfall. Mürren (elev. 5,400 ft.) has plenty of shops, bakeries, banks, a TI, a modern sports complex for rainy days (see Rainy Day Options below). Ask at the Schilthorn station in Mürren for a gondola souvenir pin or sticker.

✓▲▲▲Hike 2: The Männlichen-Kleine Scheidegg Hike—This is our favorite easy Alpine hike, entertaining you all the way with glorious Jungfrau, Eiger, and Mönch views. (That's the Young Maiden being protected from the Ogre by the Monk.)

If the weather's good, descend from Gimmelwald bright and early. Catch the post bus to the Lauterbrunnen train station. Buy a ticket to Männlichen and catch the train. Ride past great valley views to Wengen, where you'll walk across town (buy a picnic, but don't waste time here if it's sunny), and catch the Männlichen lift (departing every 15 minutes) to the top of the ridge high above you.

From the tip of the Männlichen lift (elev. 7,300 ft.), hike 20 minutes north to the little peak for that king- or queen-of-the-mountain feeling. It's an easy hour's walk from there to Kleine Scheidegg (elev. 6,800 ft.) for a picnic or restaurant lunch.

If the weather's perfect and you've got an extra 100 SF burning a hole in your pocket, you might ride the train from Kleine Scheidegg through the Eiger to the towering Jungfraujoch and back. Check for discount trips up to Jungfraujoch; three trips a day (early or late, tel. 264111, weather info: tel. 551022). Jungfraujoch crowds can be frighten-

Berner Oberland

ing. The price has been jacked up to reduce the mobs, but sunny days are still a mess.

From Kleine Scheidegg, enjoy the ever-changing Alpine panorama of the North Face of the Eiger, Jungfrau, and Mönch, probably accompanied by the valley-filling mellow sound of Alp horns and distant avalanches, as you ride the train or hike downhill (30 gorgeous minutes to Wengernalp, 90 more steep minutes from there into the town of Wengen). If the weather turns bad, or you run out of steam, catch the train early at the little Wengernalp station along the way. After Wengernalp, the trail to Wengen (elev. 4,100 ft.) is steep, and while not dangerous, requires a good set of knees. Wengen is a fine shopping town. The boring final descent from Wengen to Lauterbrunnen (elev. 2,600 ft) is knee-killer-shin-splinter steep, so catch the train.

Alpine Lifts in the Berner Oberland

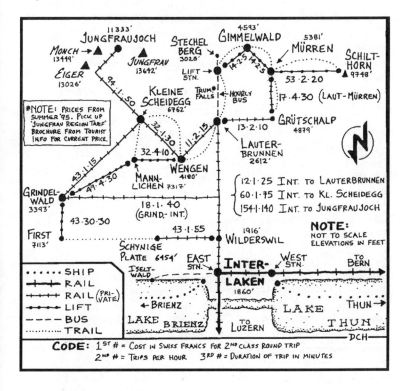

If the Männlichen lift is closed, take the train straight from Lauterbrunnen to Kleine Scheidegg. Many take the risk of slipping and enjoy the Kleine Scheidegg to Wengernalp hike even with a little snow.

▲▲**Hike 3: Cloudy Day Lauterbrunnen Valley Walk**—For a smell-the-cows-and-flowers lowland walk, ideal for a cloudy day, weary body, or tight budget, follow the riverside trail 5 kilometers from Lauterbrunnen to Stechelberg. If staying in Gimmelwald: walk up to Mürren, walk or ride the train to Grütschalp (or ride the Allmendhubel lift for a better walk down to Grütschalp), ride the funicular down to Lauterbrunnen, walk through the town, at Staubach Falls (just after the town church) follow the riverside trail to the Schilthornbahn station at Stechelberg, where you can ride the lift back up Gimmelwald. You can detour to the Trümmelbach Falls en route.

▲**Other Hikes near Gimmelwald**—For a not-too-tough 3-hour walk (there's a scary 20-minute stretch that comes with ropes) with great Jungfrau views and some mountain farm action, ride the funicular from Mürren to Allmendhübel (1,934 meters), walk to Marchegg, Saustal, and Grütschalp (a drop of about 500 meters), where you catch the panorama train back to Mürren. An easier version is the lower "Bergweg" from Allmenhübel to Grütschalp via Winteregg. For an easy family stoll with grand views, walk from Mürren just above the train tracks to either Winteregg (40 minutes, restaurant, playground, train station) or Grütschalp (60 minutes, train station) and catch the panorama train back to Mürren. An easy, go-as-far-as-you-like trail from Gimmelwald is up the Sefinen Valley. Or, you can wind from Gimmelwald down to Stechelberg (1 hour).

Walter has a "Hiking Possibilities: Schilthorn - Panoramaland" flier that describes 12 recommended hikes. For a more extensive run-down on the area (hikes, flora, fauna, culture, travel tips) get ETBD buddy Don Chmura's fine 5-SF Gimmelwald guidebook (available at Hotel Mittaghorn).

Rainy Day Options
If clouds roll in, don't despair. They can roll out just as quickly and there are some good bad-weather options. There are easy trails and pleasant walks along the floor of the Lauterbrunnen Valley. If all the waterfalls have you intrigued, sneak a behind-the-scenes look at the valley's most powerful one, **Trümmelbach Falls** (9 SF, on the Lauterbrunnen-Stechelberg road, 9:00-18:00 daily, April-October). You'll ride an elevator up through the mountain and climb through several caves to see the melt of the Eiger, Mönch, and Jungfrau grinding like God's bandsaw through the mountain at the rate of up to 20,000 liters a second (nearly double the beer consumption at Oktoberfest). The upper area, "chutes 6 to 10," are the best, so if your legs ache you can skip the lower ones and ride the lift down. Lauterbrunnen's **Heimatmuseum** (3 SF, 14:00-17:30, Tuesday, Thursday, Saturday, and Sunday, mid-June through September, just over the bridge) shows off the local folk culture.

Mürren's slick **Sports Center** (pool open only mid-June through October) offers a world of indoor activities (7 SF for use of the swimming pool and whirlpool). They'll even rent you a swimsuit.

▲▲**Ballenberg**—Near Interlaken, the Ballenberg Open Air Museum is a rich collection of traditional and historic farmhouses from every region of the country. Each house is carefully furnished, and many feature traditional craftspeople at work. The sprawling 50-acre park, laid out roughly as a huge Swiss map, is a natural preserve providing a wonderful setting for this culture-on-a-lazy-Susan look at Switzerland.

The Thurgau house (#621) has an interesting wattle-and-daub (half-timbered construction) display and house #331 has a fun bread museum. Use the 2 SF map/guide. The more expensive picture book is a better souvenir than guide. Open daily 10:00 to 17:00, April through October, 12 SF entry, half-price after 16:00 (houses close at 17:00, park stays open later), craft demonstration schedules are listed just inside the entry, tel. 036/511123. There's a reasonable outdoor cafeteria inside the west entrance, and fresh baked bread, sausage, and mountain cheese, or other cooked goodies are on sale in several houses. Picnic tables and grills with free firewood are scattered throughout the park. The little wooden village of Brienzwiller (near the east entrance) is a museum in itself with a lovely little church. Trains go regularly from Interlaken to Brienzwiller, an easy walk from the museum.

Day 18: To Beaune, France

Today we'll bid "Auf Weidersehen" to the Alps and "Bonjour" to France. Ride the gondola back down into valley floor reality, reacquaint yourself with your bus, and drive to Beaune in Burgundy for a look at provincial France. Once in Beaune you'll have time for a tour of the medieval Hotel Dieu charity hospital, and free time to stroll the pedestrian streets of the city's medieval core. We'll cap things off with a dinner featuring local specialties. After your visit here, you'll know why Burgundy is called "Profound France."

Likely activities today...
Gondola ride to meet the bus*
5 hour drive to Beaune*
Free time to tour the Hotel Dieu*
Burgundian restaurant dinner

You'll walk about 2 miles today, and sleep in Beaune.

---

* Included as an activity on BB&B tours.

FRANCE
■ 210,000 square miles—as big as Texas.
■ 58 million people (276 people per square mile, 78 percent urban).
■ US$1 = about 5 francs, 1 franc = about US$.20.
You may have heard that the French are mean and cold. Don't believe it. If anything, they're pouting because they're no longer recognized as the world's premier culture. It's tough to be crushed by the Big American Mac and keep on smiling. Be sensitive and understanding. The French are cold only if you choose to perceive them that way. Look for friendliness, give people the benefit of the doubt, develop an appetite for French-ness, and you'll remember France with a smile.

Learn some French—at least the polite words—and try to sound like Maurice Chevalier or Inspector Clouseau. The French don't speak much English, but they speak much more English than we speak French. Be patient about communication problems. Start conversations with *"Bonjour Madame/Monsieur. Parlez-vous anglais?"*

The French are experts in the art of fine living. Their cuisine, their customs, and even their vacationing habits are highly developed. Since the vacation is such a big part of the French lifestyle (nearly every worker gets 5 weeks of vacation a year), you'll find no shortage of tourist information centers, hotels, transportation facilities, and fun ways to pass free days.

France

The French munch lunch from 12:00 to 14:00 and dinner from 19:00 to 22:00 (later the farther south you go). And they eat well. A restaurant meal, never rushed, is often the day's main event. Each region has its haute cuisine specialties, and even the "low cuisine" of a picnic can be elegant, with fresh bread and an endless variety of tasty French cheeses, meats, pâtés, freshly roasted chickens, store-bought quiches, salads, rich pastries, and, of course, wine. The best approach to French food is to eat where locals eat and be adventurous. Eat ugly things with relish!

The French franc (FF or F) is divided into 100 centimes (c). A franc is worth about US$.20, and a U.S. dollar is worth about 5 francs. Divide prices by 5 to figure out the approximate cost in dollars (e.g., 65F is about $13).

France nitty-gritty:
Country code: 33
International access: 19
AT&T: 19-tone-0011
MCI: 19-tone-0019
SPRINT: 19-tone-00-87
Emergency: 17 for police, otherwise 42 60 33 22
Ambulance: 144
Telephone info. assistance to USA: 19-33-12-11
Telephone cards cost 40F and 90F
Senior/youth discount age: 60+/under age 26
Bank hours are 8:30-16:30 Tues-Fri. Later hour banks at train stations
and larger post offices. Many banks close from 12:00 to 14:00 p.m. and
all day Mondays, particularly in smaller towns.

Burgundy
Burgundy has what the rest of France wants: superior wine and
cuisine, lovely countryside, and quick access east to the Alps and south
to Provence. Only a small part of Burgundy's land is covered by vineyards, but wine-making is what they do best here. They've practiced
since Roman times. You may be surprised to find that the area is not
named after the wine but after a fifth-century barbarian tribe, the
Burgundians. Latter-day Burgundians turned Joan of Arc over to the
English. Present-day Burgundians would rather talk about wine. The
white cows you see everywhere are Charolais. They make France's best
beef and end up in *boeuf bourguignonne*.

We'll make our home base in Beaune, France's prestigious wine
capital. Beaune is Burgundy at its best.

Beaune
You'll feel comfortable right away in this hardworking but fun-loving
capital of the world's most serious wine region. Beaune has a rare wine-
soaked charm. Its tourist office gives Americans a free bottle of Burgundy on the 4th of July. Life here centers around the production and
consumption of the prestigious, expensive Côte d'Or wines. Côte d'Or
means "golden hillsides," a spectacle to enjoy in late October as the
leaves of the vineyards turn.

Beaune is a compact, thriving little city with vineyards on its door-
step. We'll limit our Beaune (pronounced "bone") ramblings to the town
center, contained within its medieval walls and circled by a one-way
ring road. All roads and activities seem to converge on the
quintessentially French place Carnot.

Tourist Info (TI): The TI, across the street from the Hôtel Dieu (Hospice de Beaune) on the place de la Halle (from place Carnot, walk toward the thin spire), has city maps, brochures on Beaune hotels and restaurants, and advice on special events. (Open April to October 9:00-20:00, otherwise 9:00-19:00; tel. 80 26 21 30.)

Sights—Beaune

▲▲▲**Hôtel Dieu**—The Hundred Years War and Black Death devastated Beaune, leaving over 90 percent of its population destitute. Nicholas Rolin, Chancellor of Burgundy and a peasant by birth, had to do something for "his people." So, in 1443, he paid to build this flamboyant Flemish-Gothic charity hospital. It was completed in only eight years. Tour it on your own; you'll find (for once) good English explanations (pick up description at ticket desk). How about those medical instruments? Yeow! The pharmacy once provided slug-slime cures for sore throats and cockroach powders for constipation. Next, shuffle into a dark room to admire Van der Weyden's dramatic *The Last Judgment* polyptych, commissioned by Rolin to give the dying something to ponder. Ask the guard to demonstrate how the huge magnifying glass works. Your visit ends with a look at Flemish tapestries. *The Story of Jacob*, woven by one person in 17 years, is magnificent. (29F, open 9:00-18:30 April through November.)

▲**Basilique Collégiale Notre Dame**—Built in the twelfth and thirteenth centuries, this is a good example of Cluny-style architecture. Enter to see the fifteenth-century tapestries (behind the altar, drop in a franc for lights), a variety of stained glass, and what's left of frescoes depicting the life of Lazarus. (Open 9:00-12:00 and 14:00-18:00.) Turn left out of the cathedral and walk into the courtyard of the Musée du Vin, located in the old residence of the Dukes of Burgundy. Stroll into the barn displaying ancient wine presses.

Musée du Vin—You don't have to like wine to appreciate this folk-wine museum. The history and culture of Burgundy and wine were fermented in the same bottle. Wander into the courtyard for a look at the Duke's Palace, antique wine presses, and a nifty model of 15th-century Beaune. Inside the museum you'll find tools, costumes, and scenes of Burgundian wine history but no tasting. There's a fine model of the wine region. Can you find the naked grape stompers? If you ever wondered how the wine bottle got its shape, you'll enjoy the last room. Buy the 3F English explanation. (20F, ticket good for other Beaune museums. Open 9:30-17:30, closed Tuesdays.)

▲▲▲**Marché aux Vins (Wine Market)**—This is Burgundy's wine smorgasbord and the best way to sample (and buy) its awesome array of wines. Large groups not admitted. Enter individually or in small, discreet groups (up to 4). You pay 50F for a souvenir traditional tasting

Beaune

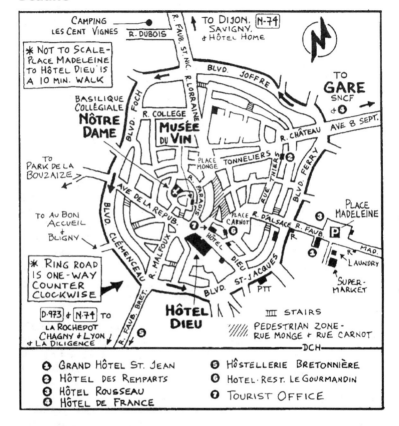

CAMPING
LES CENT VIGNES   R. DUBOIS

TO DIJON, N·74
SAVIGNY,
& HÔTEL HOME

✳ NOT TO SCALE-
PLACE MADELEINE
TO HÔTEL DIEU IS
A 10 MIN. WALK

BLVD. JOFFRE

TO
GARE
SNCF
& ❶

BASILIQUE
COLLÉGIALE
NÔTRE
DAME

R. COLLÈGE

MUSÉE
DU VIN

AVE 8 SEPT.

R. CHÂTEAU

TO
PARK DE LA
BOUZAIZE →

PLACE
MONGE

TONNELIERS

TO AU BON
ACCUEIL
&
BLIGNY

AVE DE LA REPUB.

BLVD. CLEMENCEAU

PLACE
CARNOT

R. D'ALSACE
R. FAUB.

PLACE
MADELEINE

❸

P

HÔTEL
DIEU

LAUNDRY

✳ RING ROAD
IS ONE-WAY
COUNTER
CLOCKWISE

ST-JACQUES

SUPER-
MARKET

D·973 & N·74 TO
LA ROCHEPOT
CHAGNY & LYON
& LA DILIGENCE

BLVD.

PTT

HÔTEL
DIEU

❺

⫿⫿⫿ STAIRS

//// PEDESTRIAN ZONE -
RUE MONGE & RUE CARNOT

DCH

❶ GRAND HÔTEL ST. JEAN
❷ HÔTEL DES REMPARTS
❸ HÔTEL ROUSSEAU
❹ HÔTEL DE FRANCE

❺ HÔSTELLERIE BRETONNIÈRE
❻ HOTEL·REST. LE GOURMANDIN
❼ TOURIST OFFICE

cup and get 45 minutes (though some have discreetly stretched it out to 90) to sip away at Burgundy's beloved. Plunge into the labyrinth of candlelit caves dotted with 39 wine-barrel tables, each home to a new bottle of wine to taste. You're on your own. Take your time. This is world-class stuff. The $80 reds come upstairs in the Gothic chapel at the end. (Hint: Taste better and longer by sneaking in some bread or crackers.) If you grab a little shopping basket at the beginning and at least pretend you're going to buy some bottles, the occasional time checker will leave you alone. (Open 9:00-12:00, 14:30-18:30, last entry 18:00, closes at 17:00 in winter.) Wine lovers should visit the impressive Atheneum book/wine shop across the street.

Burgundy Cuisine

Your taste buds are going to thank you for bringing them here. Considered by many to be France's best, Burgundian cuisine is peasant cooking elevated to an art. Burgundy is home to several classic dishes such as *escargots bourguignonne* (snails served sizzling hot in garlic butter), *boeuf bourguignonne* (beef simmered for hours in red wine with onions and mushrooms), *coq au vin* (chicken stewed in red wine), and the famous Dijon mustards. Look also for *jambon persillé* (cold ham layered in a garlic-parsley gelatin), *pain d'épices* (spice bread), and *gougère* (light, puffy cheese pastries). Native cheeses are Epoisses and Langres (both mushy and great) and my favorite, Montrachet (a tasty goat cheese). Crème de Cassis (a black currant liqueur) is another Burgundian specialty; you'll find it in desserts and snazzy drinks (try a *kir*).

Along with Bordeaux, Burgundy is why France is famous for wine. You'll find it all here—great reds, whites, and rosés. The key grapes are Chardonnay (producing dry white wines) and Pinot Noir (producing medium-bodied red wines). Every village produces its own distinctive wine (usually named after the village—like Chablis and Meursault). The least expensive (but still excellent) wines are the Bourgogne Aligote (white), Bourgogne ordinaire and Passetoutgrain (both red), and those from the Macon, Chalon, and Beaujolais areas. If you like rosé, try the Marsannay, considered one of the best rosés in France.

Eating in Beaune: Central Beaune's best budget restaurant is the **Relais de la Madeleine** at 44 place Madeleine (especially good lamb chops and fresh trout), tel. 80 22 07 47. The **Picboeuf** is another good bet for dinner (75 yards from place Madeleine where rue d'Alsace meets the ring road).

Gather picnics in Beaune at the *charcuterie* on rue Monge and pick up a slice of the jambon persillé (pronounced "zham-bone pehr-sill-ay"). Get your cheese at **Taste Frommage**, across the street on rue Carnot. How about that for a French stench? Gather the rest of your needs at any *épicerie* (grocery). There's a Casino supermarket just off place Madeleine, through the archway (closed Sunday).

Day 19: To Paris

You're on your way to Paris, Europe's grandest city. Your driver will give you a quick city orientation tour, drop you at your hotel and bid you "adieu" as he heads home for Belgium. Your hotel, the Castex, is in the characteristic Marais, Paris' old Jewish quarter which is now quite chic. (We hope you can stay a few days longer, but you'll need to book your hotel reservation well in advance.) Immediately upon arrival confirm any post-tour hotel reservations. After a short rest, your guide will give you a Paris orientation and a hands-on lesson with Paris' great subway system, the Metro.

You'll find Paris' sights listed in tomorrow's chapter. With dinner on your own tonight, "Eating" takes center stage.

> **Likely activities today...**
> 4-hour drive to Paris*
> Paris Metro orientation
> Walk to Ste-Chapelle and Notre Dame churches
> Evening free for dinner on your own*
>
> You'll walk about 3 miles today, and sleep in Paris.

Included as an activity on BB&B tours.

Eating in Paris
Everything goes here. Paris is France's wine and cuisine melting pot. While it lacks a distinctive style of its own, it draws from the best of all French provinces.

Paris could hold a gourmet's Olympics—and import nothing. Picnic or go to snack bars for quick lunches and linger longer over dinner. You can eat very well, restaurant-style, for 100F-130F. Ask your hotel to recommend a small nearby restaurant in the 80F–100F range. Many cafés offer fixed-price meals such as a *plat du jour* — you'll get your choice of an appetizer, entrée, and dessert at a set price. Famous places are often overpriced, overcrowded, and overrated. Find a quiet neighborhood and wander, or follow a local recommendation, but don't arrive before 19:00.

Cafeterias and Picnics
Many Parisian department stores have top-floor restaurants offering not really cheap but low-risk, low-stress, what-you-see-is-what-you-get, quick budget meals. Try **Samaritaine** (Pont-Neuf near the Louvre, 5th floor) or **Mélodine** (Métro: Rambuteau, next to the Pompidou Center, open daily 11:00-22:00).

For picnics, you'll find handy little groceries *(épiceries)* and delis *(charcuteries)* all over town (but rarely near famous sights). Good picnic fixings include roasted chicken, half-liter boxes of demi-crème (2%) milk, drinkable yogurt, fresh bakery goods, melons, and exotic pâtés and cheeses. Great take-out deli-type foods like gourmet salads and quiches abound. While in the United States wine is taboo in public places, this is *pas de problème* (no problem) in France. Most shops close from around 12:30 to 14:00.

The ultimate classy picnic shopping place is **Fauchon**, the famous "best gourmet grocery in France." It's fast and expensive but worth the detour to window shop alone. Try the new "inexpensive" bistro-cafeteria next to the bakery (26 place de la Madeleine, behind the Madeleine church, Métro: Madeleine, open 9:30-19:00, closed Sundays).

Good Picnic Spots: The pedestrian bridge, Pont des Arts, with unmatched views and plentiful benches, is great. Bring your own dinner feast and watch the riverboats light up the city for you. The Palais Royal across the street from the Louvre is a good spot for a peaceful and royal lunchtime picnic. Or try the little triangular Henry IV Park on the west tip of the Île de la Cité, people-watching at the Pompidou Center or in the elegant place des Vosges (closes at dusk), at the Rodin Museum, the Luxembourg Gardens, or after dark in the Eiffel Tower park (Champs de Mars).

Restaurants (by neighborhood)

Of course the Parisian eating scene is kept at a rolling boil, and entire books are written and lives are spent on the subject. If you are traveling outside Paris, save your splurges for the countryside, where restaurants are far less expensive and the quality of cuisine generally better. Here are a few places to consider, listed by neighborhood, to work smoothly into your busy sightseeing strategy. If you'd like to visit a district specifically to eat, consider the many romantic restuarants that line the cozy Île St. Louis' main street, the colorful, touristic, but fun string of eateries along rue Mouffetard behind the Panthéon; Montmartre, which is very touristy around the place du Tertre but hides some vampy values in the side streets (try rue Lepic); and the well-worn Latin Quarter (see below).

The Marais Neighborhood: The windows of the Marais are filled with munching sophisticates. The epicenter is the tiny square where rue Caron and rue d'Ormesson intersect, midway between the St. Paul Métro stop and the place des Vosges. We like **Le marais Ste. Catherine** at 5 rue Caron (moderate). For more conspicuous and atmospheric elegance, a coffee or dinner on the place des Vosges is good (**Ma Bourgogne** restaurant is worth the splurge). Hobos picnic on the place des Vosges itself, trying not to make the local mothers with children nervous (closes at dusk). A variety of take-away delis can be found on the rue St. Antoine, including the excellent Chinese **Delice House** (#81, open until 21:00, tables in back). Try the **Le Paradis de Fruit** (salads and organic foods mix with a young crowd on the small square at rues Turenne and St. Antoine). The couscous restaurant next door, **La Perle**, is good and cheap. **L'Énoteca** (across from Hôtel du 7ème Art at 20 rue St. Paul) has lively Italian cuisine in a relaxed, open setting. **Auberge de Jarente** (7 rue Jarente) is popular, atmospheric, and reasonable. Near the Hôtel Castex, the restaurant **La Poste** and the **Crêperie** across the street (13 rue Castex) are both inexpensive and good values.

Rue Cler Neighborhood: The rue Cler neighborhood isn't famous for its restaurants. That's why we like to eat here. **Restaurant La Serre** (29, rue de l'Exposition, 45 55 20 96) is friendly, good, and reasonable. **Au Petit Paname** (9 rue Amelie) serves a good traditional 88F menu (tel. 45 56 98 98, closed Saturday). **Au Café de Mars**, on the corner of rue Augerau and Gros-Caillou (tel. 47 05 05 91), is a contemporary Parisian café/restaurant with Franco-Californian cuisine, fair prices, and an English-speaking staff. **L'Ami de Jean** (near Hôtel Malar at 27 rue Malar) is an inexpensive and lively place to sample Basque cuisine. The **Ambassade du Sud-Ouest** is a locally popular wine store cum restaurant specializing in French Southwest cuisine. Try the *daubes de canard* and toast your own bread (46 ave. de la Bourdonnais, tel. 45 55 59 59). Two good traditional French brasseries in the area are **le Bosquet** (*plat du jour* 60F to 80F, indoor/outdoor, 46 avenue Bosquet, tel. 45 51 38 13, closed Sunday) and the dressy **Thoumieux** (79 rue St. Dominique, tel. 47 05 49 75). For a take-out meal, try **Tarte Julie's** (28 rue Cler) or classy take-out at **Flo's** (on la Motte Piquet near the École Militaire Métro stop open until 22:00).

Latin Quarter: **La Petite Bouclerie** is a cozy place with classy family cooking (moderate, 33 rue de la Harpe, center of touristy Latin Quarter). The popular **Restaurant Polidor** is an old turn-of-the-century-style place, with great *cuisine bourgeois*, a vigorous local crowd, and a historic toilet. Arrive at 19:00 to get a seat—in the restaurant, that is (60F *plat du jour*, 100F menus, 41 rue Monsieur le Prince, midway between Odéon and Luxembourg Métro stops, tel. 43 26 95 34).

Île St. Louis: Cruise the island's main street for a variety of good options. We like the **Relais de L'Îsle** (#37) and for a mini-splurge, **Le Tastevin** (#46, tel. 43 54 17 31). For crazy (but touristy and expensive) cellar atmosphere and hearty fun food, feast at **La Taverne du Sergeant Recruiter**. The "Sergeant Recruiter" used to get young Parisians drunk and stuffed here, then sign them into the army. It's all-you-can-eat, including wine and service, for 210F (41 rue St. Louis-en-Île, in the center of Île St. Louis, open Monday-Saturday from 19:00, tel. 43 54 75 42). There's a just-this-side-of-a-food-fight clone next door at **Nos Ancêtres Les Gaulois** (Our Ancestors the Gauls, 39 rue St. Louis-en-l'Île, tel. 46 33 66 07, open daily at 19:00). For a memorable picnic dinner, 10 minutes from the Marais, cross the river to Île St. Louis and find a river-level bench on the tip facing Île de la Cité.

Pompidou Center: The **Mélodine** self-service is right at the Rambuteau Métro stop. **Dame Tartine** overlooks the *Homage to Stravinsky* fountain and serves a young clientele and offers excellent, cheap, lively meals. The popular and very French **Café de la Cité** has long tables and fine lunch (44F) and dinner (65F) specials (22 rue Rambuteau, tel. 42 78 56 36).

Other locations in Paris: For an elegant splurge surrounded by lavish art nouveau decor, dine at **Julien** (200F meals with wine, 16 rue du Faubourg St. Denis, Métro: Strasbourg-St. Denis, tel. 47 70 12 06, make reservations). On Montmartre, try the excellent and cozy **Le Montagnarde** and say *bonsoir* (good evening) to Didier, two blocks down rue Lepic from the place du Tertre.

Three gourmet working-class fixtures in Paris are **Le Chartier** (7 rue du Faubourge Montmartre, Métro: Montmartre), **Le Commerce** (51 rue du Commerce, Métro: Commerce) and **Le Drouot** (103 rue de Richelieu, Métro: Richelieu-Drouot). Each wraps very cheap and basic food in a bustling, unpretentious atmosphere.

Parisian nightlife
Paris nightlife thrives in three areas: the Latin Quarter and boulevard St. Germain; the Pompidou Center-Les Halles area; and the very touristy but fun Montmartre area. Cafe lurking and sidewalk strolling are the chief pastimes.

Jazz Clubs: The Caveau de la Huchette is the handiest characteristic old jazz club for visitors, filling an ancient Latin Quarter cellar with live jazz and frenzied dancing every night (open 21:30-2:30 or later, 70F admission, 30F drinks, 5 rue de la Huchette, tel. 43 26 65 05). You'll also find several well reputed clubs bordering the Forum shopping center in Les Halles area on the rue Berger.

Day 20: Paris.

This day is a fitting finale for your tour. For his or her last act, your guide will help you find your way through the huge, newly renovated Louvre museum, and orient you to Paris' other great sights for your free afternoon.

Likely activities today...
All morning at the Louvre
Orientation to other sights
Afternoon free for sightseeing
Dinner and final evening together

You'll walk anywhere from 3 to 9 miles today, and sleep in Paris.

Note: No activities are planned for BB&B tours today.

Paris
Paris offers sweeping boulevards, sleepy parks, world-class galleries, chatty crêpe stands, Napoleon's body, sleek shopping malls, the Eiffel Tower, and people-watching from outdoor cafés. Climb the Notre Dame and the Eiffel Tower, cruise the Seine and Champs-Elysées, and master the Louvre and Orsay museums. Save some after-dark energy for one of the world's most romantic cities. Many people fall in love with Paris. Some see the essentials and flee, overwhelmed by the huge city. With the proper approach and a good orientation, you'll fall head over heels for Europe's capital city.

Orientation (tel. code: 1)
Paris is split in half by the Seine River, and circled by a ring road freeway (the *périphérique*). You'll find Paris much easier to negotiate if you know which side of the river you're on, and which subway (Métro) stop you're closest to. Remember, if you're north of the river (above on any city map), you're on the right bank (*rive droite*), and if you're south of it, you're on the left bank (*rive gauche*). The notation for the Métro stop is "Mo." In Parisian jargon, Napoleon's tomb is on la rive gauche (the left bank), Métro: Invalides. Paris Métro stops are a standard aid in giving directions.

Tourist Information (TI)
Avoid the Paris TIs—long lines and short information. This book, the *Pariscope* magazine, and one of the freebie maps available at any hotel are all you need for a short visit. The main TI is at 127 avenue des Champs-Élysées (open 9:00-20:00), but the neighborhood TIs (see Sleep-

Paris

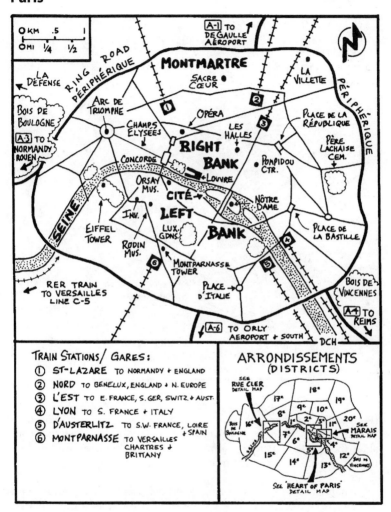

ing in Paris in Day 21 Chapter) are handier.

The *Pariscope* weekly magazine (or one of its clones, 3F at any newsstand) lists museum hours, concerts and musical festivals, plays, movies, nightclubs, and special art exhibits. For a complete list of museum
hours and scheduled English museum tours, pick up the free *Musées,
Monuments Historiques, et Expositions* booklet from any museum.

Heart of Paris

While it's easy to pick up free maps of Paris once you've arrived (your hotel has them), they don't show all the streets, and you may want the huge Michelin #10 map of Paris. For an extended stay, consider the excellent *Paris par Arrondisement* map book, as well as two fine guidebooks: *Michelin Green Guide* (somewhat scholarly) and the *Access Guide to Paris*.

There are many English-language bookstores in Paris where you can pick up guidebooks. Shakespeare and Co. (with used travel books, 47 rue de la Boucherie, across the river from Notre-Dame, 12:00-24:00), W. H. Smith (248 rue de Rivoli), and Brentano (47 avenue de L'Opéra) are three good ones.

The American Church is a nerve center for the American émigré community and publishes and distributes a handy monthly called the *Free Voice*. *France-USA Contacts*, an advertisement paper, is full of useful information for those looking for work or long-term housing.

Trains

Paris has six train stations, all connected by Métro and bus, all with luggage storage, banks and tourist information offices. Here's how they're organized: the Gare de l'Est covers destinations to the east; the Gare du Nord and Gare St. Lazare serve northern and central Europe; the gares Austerlitz and Lyon cover southern Europe and the newly revamped Montparnasse station handles western France and TGV service to France's southwest. Any station can give you schedule information, make reservations and sell tickets for any destination.

Getting Around Paris

***A word of caution: pickpockets are skilled at relieving Americans of their wallets and "fanny packs" on subways and buses. Keep valuables in your moneybelt.*

By Métro: Europe's best subway is divided into two systems; the Métro covers the city and the RER connects suburban destinations. You'll be using the Métro for almost all your trips. In Paris, you're never more than a 10-minute walk from a Métro station. One ticket takes you anywhere in the system with unlimited transfers. Save nearly 50 percent by buying a *carnet* (pronounced "car-nay") of ten tickets for about 42F at any Métro station. Métro tickets work on city buses though one ticket cannot be used as a transfer between subway and bus.

A *Formule 1* pass (30F) allows unlimited travel for a single day. If you're staying longer, the *Carte d'Orange* pass gives you free run of the bus and metro system for one week (65F, ask for the *Carte d'Orange Coupon Vert*). Be careful, the weekly pass begins Monday and ends Sunday — so mid-week purchases are generally not worthwhile. You'll also need a photo of yourself to buy a Carte d'Orange (many metro stations have self-serve photo booths). Passes can be purchased at most metro stations.

Before entering the station, find the "Mo." stop closest to your destination and which line(s) will get you there. The lines have numbers, but they're best known by their *direction* or end-of-the-line stop. (For example, the Saint-Denis/Châtillon line runs between Saint-Denis in the north and Châtillon in the south.)

Once in the Métro station, you'll see blue on white signs directing you to the train going in your direction (e.g., direction: Saint-Denis). Insert your ticket in the automatic turnstile, pass through the turnstile, reclaim and *keep your ticket until you exit the system* (fare inspectors accept no excuses from anyone). Transfers are free and can be made wherever lines cross. When you transfer, look for the orange *correspondance* (connections) signs when you exit your first train, then follow the proper "direction" sign.

Before you *sortie* (exit), check the very helpful *plan du quartier* (map of the neighborhood) to get your bearings and decide which sortie you want. At stops with several sorties, you can save lots of walking by choosing the best exit. Remember your essential Métro words: *direction* (direction), *correspondance* (connections), *sortie* (exit), *carnet* (cheap set of ten tickets), and *Donnez-moi mon porte-monnaie!* (Give me back my wallet!). Thieves thrive in the Métro.

The RER suburban train system (thick lines on your subway map identified by letters-A, B, C etc.) works like the Métro—but much speedier because it makes only a few stops within the city. One Métro ticket is all you need for RER rides within Paris. You can transfer between the Metro and RER systems with the same ticket and, unlike the Metro, you need your ticket to exit the RER system. To travel outside the city (to Versailles or the airport for example), you'll need to buy another ticket at the station window before boarding and make sure your stop is served by checking the signs over the train platform.

By City Buses: If you'll be staying in Paris for a while, the trickier bus system is worth figuring out and using. The same tickets are good on both bus and Métro, though you can't use the same ticket to transfer between the two systems, and longer rides require more than one ticket. While the Métro shuts down about 00:45, some buses continue much later. Schedules are posted at bus stops.

To ride the bus, study the big system maps at each stop to figure out which route(s) you need. Then look at the individual route diagrams, showing the exact route of the lines serving that stop to verify your route. Major stops are also painted on the side of each bus. Enter through the front doors. Punch your yellow Métro ticket(s) in the machine behind the driver, or pay the higher cash fare. Get off the bus using the rear door. Even if you're not certain you've figured it out, do some joyriding (outside of rush hour). Lines 24, 63, and 69 run Paris's most scenic routes and make a great introduction to this city.

By Taxi: Parisian taxis are nearly reasonable. A 10-minute ride costs about 50F (versus 4F to get anywhere in town on the Métro), and luggage will cost you more. You can try waving one down, but it's easier to ask for the nearest taxi stand (*"oo-ay la tet de stah-see-oh taxi"*). Sunday and night rates are higher, and if you call one from your hotel, the meter starts as soon as the call is received. Taxis are tough to find on Friday and Saturday nights, especially after the Métro closes.

Helpful Hints

Museums: Most museums are closed Mondays or Tuesdays. Most offer reduced prices and shorter hours on Sundays. Many begin closing rooms 30 minutes before the actual closing time. For the fewest crowds, visit very early, at lunch, or very late. Most museums have shorter hours

from October through March, and holidays are usually January 1, May
1, May 8, July 14, November 1, November 11, and December 25.
Youth and Senior Discounts: Those under 26 and over 60 get big dis-
counts on some sights.
Restaurants: Check price lists before ordering at any café or restaurant.
Prices should include tax and tip. And remember, you pay more to sit.
Rude surprises await sloppy tourists.
Toilets: Carry small change for pay toilets, or walk into any café with
outdoor tables like you own the place and find the toilet in the back.
Walking: Pedestrians don't have the right of way—drivers do and they
know it.
Theft Alert: Use your moneybelt, and never carry a wallet in your back
pocket or a purse over your shoulder. Don't wear a fanny/waist pack
in the Métro.
Telephone Cards: Pick up the essential French phone card (*telecarte*) at
any tobacco shop (*tabac*), post office, or tourist office (*une petite carte* is
40F; *une grande* is 90F). You'll need it for most calls.
Useful Telephone Numbers: American Express, 47 70 77 07; American
Hospital, 46 41 25 25; American pharmacy at 47 42 49 40 (Opéra); Police, 17; U.S. Embassy, 43 12 22 22; Paris and France directory assistance, 12; AT&T operator 19 00 11; MCI operator 19 00 19; Sprint 19 00
87.

Sights—Paris

The price of Parisian sights continues to climb. To control these costs,
know if you qualify for an age discount (under 18, 26 or over 60), visit
the more expensive museums on Sundays when they're half off for all,
and consider purchasing the *Carte Musees et Monuments* (museum/
monuments pass) if you plan to do some serious sightseeing and don't
qualify for age discounts. It's sold at museums, main Metro stations,
and tourist offices and gets you into all major sights including Versailles
with no lining up (which can save you an hour at Versailles). One day -
70F, three consecutive days - 140F, five consecutive days - 200F. With
average sights running at 35F or more this card pays for itself quickly if
you plan to see more than two museums/sights in one day, or more
than four in a three-day period.
▲▲▲Sainte-Chapelle—The triumph of Gothic church architecture, a
cathedral of glass, like none other. It was built in just five years to house
the supposed Crown of Thorns (which cost the king more than the
church). Downstairs was for commoners, upstairs for royal Christians.
Hang out at the top of the spiral stairs and watch the room's beauty
suck the breath from emerging tourists. There's a good little book with
color photos on sale that explains the stained glass in English. There are
concerts almost every summer evening (120F). Even a beginning violin

class would sound lovely here. (Open daily 9:30-18:00, off-season 10:00-16:30, 27F. Stop at the ticket booth outside the church, or call 43 54 30 09 for concert information. Handy free public toilets just outside.)

▲▲**Notre-Dame Cathedral**—The cathedral is 700 years old and packed with history and tourists. Climb to the top for a great gargoyle's-eye view of the city (entrance on outside left, open 9:30-17:30, closed at lunch and earlier in off-season; you get over 400 stairs for only 27F). Study its sculpture (Notre-Dame's forte) and windows, take in a mass, eavesdrop on guides, walk all around the outside. (Open 8:00-18:45, treasury open 9:30-18:00, admission 15F for treasury. Ask about the free English tours, normally Wednesdays at noon June-September. Sunday mass at 8:00, 8:45, 10:00, 11:30, 12:30, and 18:30. Tel. 43 26 07 39). Clean 2.50F toilets are in front of the church near Charlemagne's statue.

Back outside, the archaeological crypt offers a fascinating look at the remains of the earlier city and church (enter 100 yards in front of church, 27F, daily 10:00-18:00). Drop into Hôtel Dieu, on the square opposite the river, for a pleasant courtyard and a look at a modern hospice, offering many a pleasant last stop before heaven. If you're hungry near Notre-Dame, the only grocery store on the Île de la Cité is tucked away on a small street running parallel to the church, one block north.

▲▲**Deportation Memorial**—The architecture of this memorial to the French victims of the Nazi concentration camps is a powerful blend of water, sky, bars, confinement, concrete, eternal flame, the names of many concentration camps, and a crystal for each of the 200,000 victims. (Open 10:00-12:00 and 14:00-19:00, closes at 17:00 in off-season, east tip of the island near Île St. Louis, behind Notre-Dame, free.)

▲▲**Latin Quarter**—This area, which gets its name from the language used here when it was an exclusive medieval university district, lies between the Luxembourg Gardens and the Seine, centering around the Sorbonne University and boulevards St. Germain and St. Michel. This is the core of the Left Bank—the artsy, liberal, hippy, Bohemian district of poets, philosophers, and winos. It's full of international eateries, far-out bookshops, street singers, pale girls in black berets, and jazz clubs. For colorful wandering and café-sitting, afternoons and evenings are best.

▲▲▲**The Louvre**—This is Europe's oldest, biggest, greatest, and second-most-crowded museum (remember the Vatican?). The newly renovated Richelieu wing and underground shopping mall extension add the finishing touches to *Le Grand Louvre Project* (that started in 1989 with the pyramid entrance) and are extremely helpful and dazzling additions to the museum. You can enter the pyramid for free until 21:30. (Go at night to see it glow.) Once inside, walk toward the inverted pyramid and uncover a post office, a Virgin Megastore, a dizzying assortment of eateries (up the escalators) and the Palais Royal Metro entrance.

A new pricing policy allows you to save 50% by entering the musuem after 15:00. The Louvre is open 9:00-18:00 and closed Tuesdays. On Mondays and Wednesdays, the Richelieu wing is open until 21:30 and 21:45 respectively. (40F until 15:00, 20F after 15:00, on Sundays and for the younger and older, and free if you're under 18. Use the handy ticket dispensing machines to save time if lines are long. Tel. 40 20 53 17 or 40 20 51 51 for recorded information. Métro: Palais-Royale/Musée du Louvre—not the Louvre stop.)

Don't try to cover the museum thoroughly. The 90-minute English-language tours leave nearly hourly except Sundays and Mondays and are the best way to enjoy this huge museum (find Accueil des Groupes desk at entry, information tel. 40 20 50 50, 33F). *Mona Winks* includes a self-guided tour of the Louvre as well as of the Orsay, the Pompidou, and Versailles.

A good do-it-yourself tour of the museum's highlights would include (in this order, starting in the Denon wing): Ancient Greek (Parthenon frieze, Venus de Milo, Nike of Samothrace); Apollo Gallery (jewels); French and Italian paintings in the Grande Galerie (a quarter-mile long and worth the hike); the Mona Lisa and her Italian Renaissance roommates; the nearby Neoclassical collection (*Coronation of Napoleon*); and the Romantic collection with works by Delacroix and Gericault.

Best Impressionist Art Museums: The following three museums offer the best look at Impressionist art in Paris:

▲▲▲**Orsay Museum**—This is Paris's long-awaited nineteenth-century art museum (actually, art from 1848-1914), including Europe's greatest collection of Impressionist works (call for 35F English tour schedule). Start on the ground floor. The conservative establishment "pretty" art is on the right, then cross left into the brutally truthful, and at the time, very shocking art of the realist rebels and Manet. Then go way up the escalator at the far end to the series of Impressionist rooms (Monet, Renoir, Degas, et al) and van Gogh. Don't miss the Art Nouveau on the mezzanine level. The museum is housed in a former train station (Gare d'Orsay) across the river and 10 minutes downstream from the Louvre. (Open 9:00-18:00 in July and August and all Sundays, 10:00-18:00 other days, Thursdays until 21:45, closed Mondays, most crowded around 11:00 and 14:00. 36F, 24F for the young and the old, tel. 40 49 48 14.) 1, rue Bellechasse, Metro: Solferino, RER: Musee d'Orsay.

▲**L'Orangerie**—This small, quiet, and often overlooked museum houses Monet's water lilies, many famous Renoirs, and a scattering of other Impressionist works. (27F, closed Tuesdays, located in the Tuileries Gardens near the place de la Concorde.)

▲**The Marmottan**—In this intimate, lesser visited museum you'll find more than 100 paintings by Claude Monet (thanks to his son Michel) and a variety of other famous Impressionist works. (36F, open 10:00-17:30, closed Mondays, 2 rue Louis Boilly, Métro: La Muette. Tel. 42 24 07 02.)

▲▲**Napoleon's Tomb and the Army Museum**—The emperor lies majestically dead inside several coffins under a grand dome—a goose-bumping pilgrimage for historians—surrounded by the tombs of other French war heroes and Europe's greatest military museum, in the Hôtel des Invalides. Follow signs to the "crypt" where you'll find Roman Empire-style reliefs listing the accomplishments of Napolean's administration. The dome is newly restored and glitters with 26 pounds of gold. (Open daily 10:00-18:00, 35F, tel. 44 42 37 67. Métro: La Tour Maubourg.)

▲▲**Rodin Museum**—This user-friendly museum is filled with surprisingly entertaining work by the greatest sculptor since Michelangelo. See *The Kiss, The Thinker*, and many more. Near Napoleon's Tomb. (Open 9:30-17:45, closed Mondays and at 17:00 in off-season. 27F, 17F on Sunday, 5F for gardens only—Paris's best deal as many works are well displayed in the gardens, tel. 47 05 01 34. 77 rue de Varennes, Métro: Varennes. Good self serve cafeteria and idyllic picnic spots in back garden.)

▲▲**Pompidou Center**—Europe's greatest collection of far-out modern art, the Musée National d'Art Moderne, is housed in this colorfully exoskeletal building. After so many Madonnas and Children, a piano smashed to bits and glued to the wall is refreshing. It's a social center with lots of people, street theater, and activity inside and out—a perpetual street fair. Ride the escalator for a free city view from the café terrace on top and don't miss the free exhibits on the ground floor. (Open Monday-Friday 12:00-22:00, Saturdays, Sundays, and most holidays 10:00-22:00, closed Tuesdays; 35F, 24F for the younger and older, free Sundays from 10:00-14:00; tel. 44 78 12 33, Métro: Rambuteau.)

▲**Jeu de Paume**—Modern art fans should not miss this one time home to the impressionist art collection now located in the Musee d'Orsay. Completely renovated, this museum hosts rotating exhibits of top contemporary artists, brilliantly displaying their works. 35F, open 12:00-19:00, 10:00-19:00 weekends, closed Mondays. Located on the place de la Concorde, just inside the Tuileries gardens on the rue de Rivoli side. Métro: Concorde.

▲**Beaubourg**—This was a separate village until the twelfth century, and today it includes the area from the Pompidou Center to the Forum des Halles shopping center. Most of Paris's hip renovation energy over the past 20 years seems to have been directed here—before then it was a slum. Don't miss the new wave fountains (the *Homage to Stravinsky*) on the river side of the Pompidou Center or the eerie clock you'll find through the *Quartier d'Horloge* passage on the other side of the Pompidou Center. A colorful stroll down rue Rambuteau takes you to the space age Forum des Halles, Paris's largest shopping mall, on the site of what was once an outdoor food market. As you tour this shopping mecca, peek into the huge 350-year-old St. Eustache Church. The striking round building at the end of the esplanade is Paris's old Bourse, or Commercial Exchange. For an oasis of peace, continue to the interior gardens of the Palais-Royal. (Métro: Les Halles or Rambuteau.)

▲▲**Eiffel Tower**—Crowded and expensive but worth the trouble. The higher you go, the more you pay. We think the view from the 400-foot-high second level is plenty. Pilier Nord (the north pillar) has the biggest elevator—with the fastest moving line. The Restaurant Belle France serves decent 90F meals (first level). Don't miss the entertaining free movie on the history of the tower on the first level. Heck of a view. (Open daily 9:00-23:00; 20F to the first level, 38F to the second, 55F to go all the way for the 1,000-foot view. On a budget? You can climb the stairs to the second level for only 12F. Arrive early for fewer crowds. Tel. 45 50 34 56. Métro: Trocadero. RER: Champs de Mars.) For another great view, especially at night, cross the river and enjoy the tower from Trocadero. Or have a picnic in front of the tower after the grass guards have left.

▲**Montparnasse Tower**—A 59-floor superscraper, cheaper and easier to get to the top of than the Eiffel Tower. Possibly Paris's best view, since the Eiffel Tower is in it and the Montparnasse tower isn't. Buy the photo-guide to the city, go to the rooftop and orient yourself. This is a fine way to understand the lay of this magnificent land. It's a good place to be as the sun goes down on your first day in Paris. Find your hotel, retrace your day's steps, locate the famous buildings. (Open summer 9:30-23:00, off-season 10:00-22:00, 42F. Métro: Montparnasse.)

▲**Samaritaine Department Store View Point**—Enter the store, go to the rooftop (ride the elevator from near the Pont Neuf entrance, then find the spiral staircase; watch your head). Quiz yourself. Working counterclockwise, find the Eiffel Tower, Invalides/Napoleon's Tomb, Montparnasse Tower, Henry IV statue on the tip of the island, Sorbonne University, the dome of the Panthéon, Sainte-Chapelle, Hôtel de Ville (city hall), the wild and colorful Pompidou Center, Sacré-Coeur, Opéra, and Louvre. You'll find light but costly meals on the breezy terrace and a moderately priced restaurant on the fifth floor with fine views and dull food. (Rooftop view is free. Métro: Pont Neuf, tel. 40 41 20 20.)

▲▲**Sacré-Coeur and Montmartre**—This Byzantine-looking church is only 100 years old, but it's very impressive. It was built as a praise-the-

Lord-anyway gesture after the French were humiliated by the Germans in a brief war in 1871. The place du Tertre was the haunt of Toulouse-Lautrec and the original Bohemians. Today it's mobbed by tourists and unoriginal Bohemians—but still fun. Watch the artists, tip the street singers, have a dessert crêpe and wander down the rue Lepic to the two remaining windmills (there were once thirty) and down the rue des Saules to see Paris' only vineyard. The church is open daily and evenings. (Plaster of Paris comes from the gypsum found on this *mont*. Place Blanche is the white place nearby where they used to load it, sloppily.) Métros: Anvers (use the funicular to avoid stairs, one Metro ticket) or closer, but less scenic Abbesses.

Pigalle—Paris's red-light district, the infamous "Pig Alley," is at the foot of Butte Montmartre. Oo la la. More shocking than dangerous. Stick to the bigger streets, hang onto your wallet, and exercise good judgment. Can-can can cost a fortune as can con artists in topless bars. Métro: Pigalle.

▲▲▲**Place de la Concorde and the Champs-Élysées**—Here is Paris's backbone and greatest concentration of traffic. All of France seems to converge on the place de la Concorde, Paris's largest square. It was here that the guillotine made hundreds "a foot shorter at the top"—including King Louis XVI. Back then it was called the place de la Revolution.

Catherine de Medici wanted a place to drive her carriage, so she started draining the swamp that would become the Champs-Élysées. Napoleon put on the final touches, and ever since it's been the place to be seen. The Tour de France bicycle race ends here, as do all French parades of any significance (Métro: FDR, Etoile, or George V).

▲▲▲**Arc de Triomphe**—Napoleon had the magnificent Arc de Triomphe constructed to commemorate his victory at the Battle of Austerlitz. There's no arch bigger in the world—and no more crazy traffic circle. Eleven major boulevards feed into the place Charles de Gaulle (Étoile) that surrounds the arch. Watch the traffic tangle and pray you don't end up here in a car. Take the underpass to visit the eternal flame and tomb of the unknown soldier. There's a cute museum of the arch (open daily 10:00-18:30, 32F) and a great view from the top.

▲▲**Luxembourg Gardens**—Paris's most beautiful, interesting, and enjoyable garden-park-recreational area is a great place to watch Parisians at rest and play. Check out the card players (near the tennis courts), find a free chair near the main pond, and take a breather. Notice any pigeons? A poor Ernest Hemingway used to hand-hunt (strangle) them here. The grand Neoclassical domed Panthéon is a block away. (Park open until dusk, Métro: Odéon.)

▲**Other Parisian Parks**—If you enjoy the Luxembourg Gardens and want to see more, try these central parks: **Parc Monceau** (Métro:

Monceau), **Le Buttes Chaumont** (Métro: Buttes Chaumont), and the **Jardin des Plantes** (Métro: Jussieu).

▲**Le Marais**—This once smelly swamp (*marais*) was drained in the twelfth century and soon became a fashionable place to live, at least until the Revolution. It's Paris at its medieval best. This is how much of the city looked until, in the mid-1800s, Napoleon III had Baron Haussmann blast through the boulevards (open and wide enough for the guns and marching ranks of the army, too wide for revolutionary barricades), creating modern Paris. Here you'll find a tiny but thriving Jewish neighborhood; Paris's most striking and oldest square, place des Vosges; a monument to the revolutionary storming of the Bastille at place de la Bastille (nothing but memorial marks on the street is left of the actual Bastille prison); the new controversial Opera House; the largest collection of Picassos in the world; Paris's great history museum (see below); and endless interesting streets to wander. (Métro: St. Paul.)

Carnavalet (History of Paris) Museum—Inside this fine example of a Marais mansion, complete with classy courtyards and statues, are paintings of Parisian scenes, French Revolution paraphernalia, old Parisian store signs, a guillotine, a superb model of sixteenth-century Île de la Cité (notice the bridge houses) and rooms full of fifteenth-century Parisian furniture. (Open 10:00-17:30, closed Mondays; 27F, 23 rue du Sévigné, tel. 42 72 21 13. Métro: St. Paul.)

▲**Picasso Museum (Hôtel de Sale)**—The largest collection in the world of Pablo Picasso's paintings, sculpture, sketches, and ceramics as well as his personal collection of Impressionist art. It's well explained in English and worth ▲▲▲ if you're a fan. (Open daily except Tuesdays 9:30-18:00, and until 22:00 on Wednesdays; 27F; 5 rue Thorigny, tel. 42 71 25 21. Métro: St. Paul or Rambuteau.)

▲**Père Lachaise Cemetery**—Littered with the tombstones of many of the city's most illustrious dead, this is your best one-stop look at the fascinating and romantic world of the "permanent Parisians." The place is confusing, but maps (from the guardhouse or the cemetery flower shops) will direct you to the graves of Chopin, Molière, and even Jim Morrison. In section 92, a series of statues memorializing the war makes the French war experience a bit more real. (10F maps at flower store near entry, closes at dusk.)

St.-Germain-des-Prés—A church was first built on this site in A.D. 452. The church you see today was constructed in 1163 and has been recently restored. The area around the church hops at night, with fire eaters, mimes, and scads of artists. (Métro: St.-Germain-des-Prés.)

Grande Arche, La Defense—A new Paris attraction is a modern architectural wonder and the pride of modern Paris. Built to celebrate the 200th anniversary of the 1789 French Revolution, the place is big — 38 floors on more than 200 acres, holding offices for 30,000 people. Notre

Dame Cathedral could fit under its arch. Take the Métro or RER to La
Defense, then follow signs to Grande Arche. Great city views from the
Arche elevator (40F includes a film on its construction) and a huge shop-
ping mall for comparison shoppers (open daily, weekends 9:00-20:00).
Best Shopping—Forum des Halles is a grand new subterranean center,
a sight in itself. Fun, mod, colorful, and very Parisian (Métro: Halles).
The Lafayette Galleries behind the Opera House is your best elegant,
Old World, one-stop, Parisian department store-shopping center. Also,
visit the Printemps store and the historic Samaritaine department store
near Pont Neuf.

Good Browsing: Rue Rambuteau from the Halles to the Pompidou
Center, the Marais/Jewish Quarter/place des Vosges area, the Champs-
Élysées, and the Latin Quarter. Window-shop along the rue de Rivoli,
which borders the Louvre. The rue de Rivoli is also the city's souvenir
row, especially for fun T-shirts. Ritzy shops are around the Ritz Hotel at
place Vendôme (Métro: Tuileries).

Paris walks
These are listed in order of importance. Your guide may have already
covered some of this territory with your group. But if not, grab a map
and discover more of Paris!

Walk 1: St. Germain Blvd, Luxembourg Gardens
Start with a Métro ride to the Louvre-Rivoli stop (not to be confused
with the museum stop which is called Palais Royal-Musée du Louvre).
Exit the station, walk to the river, jog right, and cross the pedestrian-
only bridge (Pont des Arts). Take your time and lots of photos here, and
grab a bench. On the Left Bank, find your way around to the right side
of the Palais de l'Institut de France (that domed semi-circular building
in front of you), part of which is Académie Français, then angle left up
the rue de Seine. Consider a stop at the very Parisian La Palette café,
then take a brief right on rue de Buci. Take a left onto the famous boulevard St. Germain, the heart and soul of Paris cafés and shopping. Look
for Paris's most expensive café, Au Deux Magots, as soon as you enter
St. Germain. (Hemingway hung out here while writing *The Sun Also
Rises*, back when they didn't charge $9 for a glass of champagne.) Check
out Paris's oldest church, St. Germain des Pres, then cruise the boulevard St. Germain, making a right at the place de l'Odéon. Meander
around the temple-like Theatre de l'Odéon into Paris's most beautiful
park, the Luxembourg Gardens. Grab a chair by the center fountain
and contemplate where you are—as Hemingway loved to do, right here.
(The handiest Métro stop from here is Luxembourg or Odéon, back on
boulevard St. Germain.) To make this a longer walk, combine it with
Walk 4.

Walk 2: Latin Quarter, Louvre, Champs-Élysées, Arc de Triomphe

Start at the St. Michel Métro stop, where you'll find the heart of an uncharacteristically sleepy Latin Quarter. This is a street-hoppin' place at night. It uses mornings to recover. Walk down rue de la Huchette (past the popular jazz cellar at #5—check the schedule) and over the bridge to Notre-Dame cathedral. It took 200 years to build this church. Walk around to its impressive back side and visit the moving memorial to the 200,000 French people deported by Hitler in World War II. Across the bridge is the Île, or island, of St. Louis (we'll tour it later). Walking back through the center of the Île de la Cité, you'll come to the Ste-Chapelle church, a Gothic gem. After touring it, continue to the tip of the island (lovely park) through the peaceful, triangular place Dauphine. Next, cross the oldest bridge in town, the Pont Neuf, to the Right Bank. Drop into the Samaritaine department store across the bridge—don't miss the remarkable interior of this French JC Penney. Lunch on the fifth floor (cafeteria open 11:30-15:00, 15:30-18:30). Then tackle the Louvre, at one time Europe's grandest palace and today its most grueling and overwhelming museum. The new Louvre entry is a magnificent glass pyramid in the central courtyard. After mastering the Louvre, unwind with a stroll through the Tuilleries to the place de la Concorde, where over 1,300 heads rolled during the French Revolution, and bop up the world's most famous street, the Champs-Élysées. From the majestic Arc de Triomphe, you can take the Métro home.

Walk 3: Eiffel Tower, Rodin and Orsay Museums

Take the métro to Trocadéro. Exit the subway, following the Sortie Tour Eiffel signs to one of Europe's great views (come back at night for a real thrill). From here, the tower seems to straddle the military school (École Militaire). Napoleon lies powerfully dead under the golden dome of Les Invalides to the left. Take the elevator up to the second level of the tower, then walk away from the river through the park. Follow the third cross street left into the classy area around rue de Grenelle. Turn right on rue Cler for a rare bit of village Paris (shops closed 13:00-16:00 and on Mondays). Assemble a picnic and follow avenue de la Motte Piquet left to the grand esplanade des Invalides, a fine picnic spot. The Hôtel des Invalides, with Napoleon's tomb and the Army Museum, is on your right. Cross the square, turn right on avenue des Invalides, and look for the Rodin Museum (Hôtel Biron) on the left. Tour the great sculpture museum. You can picnic or eat in the cafeteria surrounded by Rodin's works in the elegant backyard.

Now it's on to the dazzling Musée d'Orsay. Make a right when you come out of the Rodin Museum and a quick left on rue de Bourgogne, follow it to the Assemblée Nationale, where you'll turn right on rue de l'Université, cross boulevard St. Germain, and follow signs to the Musée

d'Orsay. If you still have energy after this museum, walk away from
the river and hook up with Paris's best people-watching, shopping, and
café street, the boulevard St. Germain.

Walk 4: Marais, Île St. Louis, Picasso Museum, Pompidou Center
Start in front of the Hôtel de Ville, the old city hall (Métro: Hôtel de
Ville). Admire the superb restoration, then follow the river down to the
Pont Louis Phillipe. Cross it into the charm and tranquility of the Île St.
Louis. Bisect the island along rue St. Louis (good place for dinner tonight), admiring the doorway at #51 and the minuscule travel book-
store at #35, then take the last left across the Pont de Sully and angle up
the rue du Petit Musc to the rue St Antoine. A left on the rue St. Antoine
and a right on the rue Biraque takes you into the most beautiful square
in Paris, the place des Vosges. Now it's decision time: Are you a Picasso
fan or more curious about Parisian history? Tour either the Picasso
Museum or the Carnavalet Museum, then drop down to the rue Rosiers
(the heart of Paris' Jewish community) for some character and lunch or
grab a falafel sandwich to go. Resume your stroll down rue Rosiers and
turn right when it ends. A left on rue des Francs Bourgeois brings you
back to the twentieth century with the bizarre architecture of the
Pompidou Center. Join the fray around the center and take in a street
show or two. Ride the escalators through the Star Wars tubes of the
Pompidou to the top for the view and consider seeing its excellent modern art collection on the fourth floor. (See Beaubourg, listed under Sights,
for more information and ideas on the Beaubourg area.)

Sidetrips from Paris
▲▲▲Versailles—Every king's dream, Versailles, was the residence of
the French king and the cultural heartbeat of Europe for about 100
years—until the Revolution of 1789 ended the notion that God depu-
tized some people to rule for Him on earth. Louis XIV spent half a year's
income of Europe's richest country to build this palace fit for the ultimate divine monarch. Europe's next best palaces are, to a certain de-
gree, Versailles wanna-be's.
   Versailles is 12 miles from downtown Paris. Subway to any RER-C
station (the RER paralleling the Seine River) and follow the RER signs
to the train bound for *Versailles R.G.* (Rive Gauche station). Do not ride
Versailles C.H. trains; they stop at a different Versailles station, farther
from the palace. (30F round-trip, 25 minutes each way; trains run every
15 minutes, most but not all trains go to Versailles. Check the stops
listed on signs over the platform, or ask a local for help. From the
Versailles R.G. station, it's a 10-minute walk to the palace.)
   There's a helpful tourist information office across the street from
Versaille's R.G. station, and two info-desks on the approach to the pal-

ace. Ask questions and read the useful brochure, *Versaille Orientation Guide*, to help you understand your sightseeing options.

The base price of 42F gets you into the main palace for a self-guided tour. (The base price is only 28F for those under 26, over 60, and anyone visiting on Sunday or arriving 1.5 hours before closing time on other days.) To the base price, add 25F for a guided tour, 25F for a Walkman-cassette tour, or 22F for admission to both Trianon châteaus in the garden. Read on before purchasing your ticket.

The main palace is open Tuesday through Sunday from 9:00-18:00, and October through April from 9:00-17:30 (last entry 30 minutes before closing, closed Mondays, information tel. 30 84 76 18 and 30 84 74 00). Peak visitation is from 9:00 to 15:00; Tuesdays and Sundays are most crowded. If you dislike crowds, arrive at 16:00 (and pay a reduced admission charge), tour the main palace and then the gardens after the palace closes.

If you are interested only in the base-price self-guided tour, join the line at entrance A (to the right as you face the palace). Enter the palace and take a one-way walk through the state apartments and the magnificent Hall of Mirrors. Before going downstairs at the end, take a historic stroll clockwise around the long room filled with the great battles of France murals. If you don't have *Mona Winks*, the guidebook called *The Châteaux, The Gardens, and Trianon* gives a room-by-room rundown.

If you are interested in a private tour, pay the base-price admission at the same time you pay for your tour (entrance D). The tours, led by an English-speaking art historian, take you through sections of Versailles not included in the base-price visit. Tours last 60 minutes, and groups are limited to less than 30. There are six different English-speaking tours possible; each costs 25F. If you've never been to Versailles, I strongly recommend the tour of the Opera and church or the tour of Louis XV apartments (some people do both). Register for your tour(s) and times at entrance D (to the left and front as you face the palace). The tours leave from entrance F, straight across the courtyard from entrance D. Another option is the self-guided Walkman-cassette tour of the King's Chamber (25F, entrance C, to the left and front as you face the palace, 30 yards from entrance D). If the guided-tour line pushes your patience, this is a good option.

Many enjoy the gardens as much if not more than the palace. This is a divine picnic spot. Food is not allowed into the palace, but you can check your bag (and picnic) at the palace entrance, pick up your bag after your tour, and head off for your picnic. Or try the decent restaurant on the canal in the gardens. Every Sunday from May through October, when music fills the king's backyard and the garden's fountains are in full squirt (at 11:15 and 15:30), there's a 21F admission charge for

Versailles

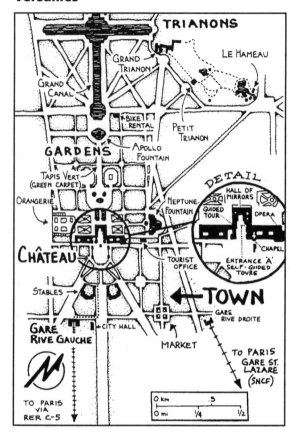

the gardens—well worth it. (Free except Sundays from May-October, open 7:00 until sunset.)

In the gardens, you'll find the Grand Trianon and the more intimate Petit Trianon, châteaus built for the king as private refuges from the palace. (10:00-18:00 May through September; off-season 10:00-17:00 with lunch break, except Saturdays and Sundays, open all day; closed Monday; Grand Trianon-23F, Petit Trianon-13F. For 60F, payable at the main palace, you can get a combination ticket to the palace and both Trianons.)

Walk 45 minutes from the palace, take the 30F tourist train, or pedal a bike (rented in the garden) to visit the Little Hamlet where Marie Antoinette played peasant girl, tending her perfumed sheep and mani-

Paris Area

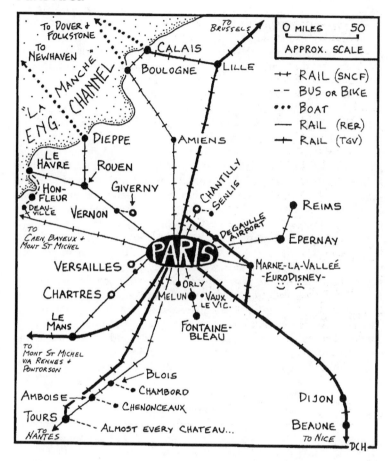

cured garden, in her almost understandable retreat from reality.

The town of Versailles is quiet and pleasant. The central market is a great place to pick up a picnic, and the cozy crêperie on rue de la Deux Portes has a crêpe selection that would impress Louis himself.

▲▲Chartres—This is one of Europe's most important Gothic cathedrals. Malcolm Miller, or his impressive assistant, gives great "Appreciation of Gothic" tours daily (except Sundays and off-season) normally at noon and 14:45. Verify in advance, call the TI at: (16) 37 21 50 00. Each tour is different, and costs 30F. Just show up at the church, open 7:00-19:00. Find time to explore Chartres's pleasant center city and discover

the picnic perfect park behind the cathedral. The TI is next to the cathe-
dral and has a map with a self guided tour of Chartres, open 9:30-18:45).
Chartres is a one-hour train trip from Paris, hourly departures from the
Gare Montparnasse, about 140F round-trip.

▲▲Château of Chantilly (pronounced "shan-tee-yee")—One of
France's best château experiences is just 30 minutes and 40 francs by
RER train from Paris's Gare du Nord station and then a 20-minute walk.
This château has it all: moat, drawbridge, sculpted gardens, little hamlet (the prototype for the more famous *hameau* at Versailles), lavish interior that rivals Versailles, world-class art collection (including two
Raphaels), and reasonable crowds. (Open daily except Tuesdays, 10:00-
18:00, off-season 10:30-12:45 and 14:00-17:00, required French language
tour included in admission price of 35F; 15F for gardens only.) Horse
lovers will enjoy the nearby stables (expensive) built for a prince who
believed he'd be reincarnated as a horse. The quaint and impressively
preserved medieval town of Senlis is a 30-minute bus ride from the
Chantilly station.

▲Giverny—Monet's gardens and home are very popular with his fans,
so popular that you should count on a long wait to get in and serious
crowds once in. Still, the ponds, water lilies and lovely gardens are pleasant and provide a more personal look at this very popular artist's life.
The new American Impressionist Art Museum in Giverny, devoted to
American artists who followed Claude to Giverny (worth the time if
you've made the effort to get here, same price and hours as Monet's
home), and the growing popularity of Monet's garden have made this
sight a headache, even to devout fans. (Open 10:00-18:00, April 1-Octo-
ber 31, closed off-season and Mondays; 35F, 25F for gardens only; tel.
32 51 28 21. Nice restaurant next door has pricey but good lunches.)
Take the Rouen train from the Paris's Gare St. Lazare station to Vernon,
a pleasant Normandy city (erratic schedule, very little service between
8:00 and noon, check ahead). To get from the Vernon train station to
Monet's garden 4 km away, take the Vernon-Giverny bus (summer only),
walk, hitch, taxi, or rent a bike at the station (55F, busy road). Or take an
organized, painless day trip ("Paris Vision" is one company offering
them) for not much more than the cost of doing it on your own. Ask for
details at your hotel.

▲▲Vaux-le-Vicomte—This château is considered the prototype for
Versailles. In fact, when its owner, Nicolas Fouquet, gave a grand party,
Louis XIV was so jealous that he arrested the host and proceeded with
the construction of the bigger and costlier, but not necessarily more splendid, palace of Versailles. Vaux-le-Vicomte is a joy to tour, elegantly furnished, and surrounded by royal gardens. It's not crowded, but it's difficult to get to without a car. Take the 75F (1-way) train ride from Paris'
Gare de Lyon to Melun. Rent a bike (crummy ride on a busy road) or

taxi (about 70F) the 6 km to the château. (Open daily 10:00-18:00, a steep 56F; gardens only, 30F. Special candle-lit visits cost 68F and are on Saturdays 20:30-23:00, May through September, and Fridays and Saturdays in July and August. The fountains run from April through October on the second and last Saturdays of each month from 15:00–18:00. Tel. 64 14 41 90.)

▲▲Disneyland Paris—Europe's Disneyland is basically a modern remake of the one in California—with most of the same rides, smiles, and a French-speaking Mickey Mouse. Locals love it, except for the fact that the weather is gray and wine is hard to find. It's worth a day if Paris is handier than Florida or California. Crowds are a problem. Avoid Saturdays, Sundays, Wednesdays, school holidays, July and August if possible. The park is occasionally so crowded that they close the gates at 60,000 people (tel. 64 74 30 00 for the latest). After dinner the crowds are gone. Food service is fun but expensive. Save money with a picnic. (Disney brochures are in every Paris hotel. Ride the RER, about 33F each way, for 30 minutes direct from downtown Paris to Station Marne-la-Vallee, which takes you right to the park's gate. The last train to Paris leaves shortly after midnight. Open daily 9:00-23:00 in summer and off-season Saturdays and Sundays, 9:00-19:00 off-season weekdays, 195F adults, 150F for kids 3 to 11, 25F less in spring and fall, tel. 60 30 60 30 for park and hotel information.)

See tomorrow for Paris hotels and airport connections.

Day 21: Post-tour Tips

Paris has much more to offer, and you'll be fully oriented to enjoy a few more days here if your travel plans allow. "Bonne chance," and thanks for traveling with us!

This chapter contains information on:
- Paris hotels (for those staying after the tour)
- Sample train connections out of Paris (p. 196)
- Getting to Paris's airports (p. 197)

Sleeping in Paris (about 5F = $1)
If you're planning to stay longer in Paris after the tour is over, reserve a room a couple of months in advance. To call or fax Paris from the USA, dial 011-33-1-local number. For more information, see "Telephoning" (p. 27) and "Faxing your hotel reservation" (p. 30).

Paris is a huge city with a huge selection of hotels for your post-tour stay here. To keep things manageable, we've focused on three safe, handy, and colorful neighborhoods, listing good hotels and helpful hints for each neighborhood to help make you a temporary resident.

Carefully choose your price range and your neighborhood. French hotels come with a star classification. One star is simple, two has most of the basic comforts, and three is, for this book, plush. (Stars are indicated here by an *.) Old, characteristic, budget Parisian hotels have always been cramped. Now they've added elevators, W.C.'s, and private showers and are even more cramped. Almost every hotel accepts Visa and Mastercard.

While you can save up to 100F by finding the increasingly rare room without a shower, these rooms are often smaller, and many places charge around 20F for each shower you take down the hall. Rooms with a double bed (*grand lit*) are cheaper than rooms with twin beds (*deux petits lits*). Showers (*douches*) are cheaper than baths (*bain*). And a toilet in the room costs even more. Breakfasts are usually optional and 20F to 40F (prices listed are without breakfast). You can save about 10F each by eating in a nearby café, more by picnicking. Singles, unless the hotel has a few closet-type rooms that fit only one twin bed, are simply doubles inhabited by one person, renting for only a little, if any, less than a double.

Assume Paris will be tight. Have a reservation. Conventions clog the city in September (worst), October, May, and June. July and August are easier. Most require prepayment for a reservation far in advance (call or fax first, and if they won't take a credit card number, follow up with a $50 traveler's check or a bank check in francs for the first night).

Sleep code: **S**=Single, **D**=Double/twin, **T**=Triple, **Q**=Quad, **B**=Bath/

shower, **WC**=Toilet, **CC**=Credit Card (**V**isa, **M**astercard, **A**mex). Note: Quad rooms will almost always be 2 double beds.

Sleeping in the Marais Neighborhood (4th district, Métro: St. Paul, zip code 75004): Those interested in a Soho/Greenwich, gentrified, urban jungle locale will enjoy making the Marais/Jewish Quarter/St. Paul/ Vosges area their Parisian home. The Marais is a cheaper and definitely a more happening locale than rue Cler (see below). Narrow medieval Paris at its finest, only 15 years ago it was a forgotten Parisian backwater. Now the Marais is one of Paris's most popular residential areas. It's a short walk to Notre-Dame, Île St. Louis, and the Latin Quarter. The Métro stop St. Paul puts you right in the heart of the Marais.

Paris, Marais Neighborhood

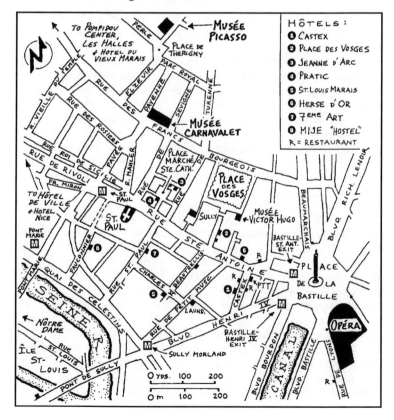

Castex Hôtel** (SB-215F, SBWC-235F to 265F, DB-280F to 310F, DBWC-300F to 340F, TBWC-440F, extra bed 75F, 25F breakfast, CC:VM, 5 rue Castex, just off place de la Bastille and rue Saint Antoine, tel. 42 72 31 52, fax 42 72 57 91, Métro: Bastille) is pleasant, clean, cheery, quiet, and run by the very friendly Bouchand family (son Blaise, pronounced "blaze," speaks English). This place is a great value, with the distinctly un-Parisian characteristic of seeming like it wants your business. Because our tour groups keep the Castex filled much of the year, you'll need to reserve well in advance (by phone or fax and leave your Visa number).

Hôtel de la Place des Vosges** (DBWC-420F to 440F, 40F breakfast, CC:VMA, 12 rue de Biraque, just off the elegant place des Vosges, and just as snooty, tel. 42 72 60 46, fax 42 72 02 64, English spoken), quasi-classy with a freshly made, antique feel, rents 16 rooms on a quiet street.

Grand Hôtel Jeanne d'Arc** (DBWC-380F to 450F, TBWC-550F, QBWC-570F, extra bed 75F, 35F breakfast, 3 rue Jarente, tel. 48 87 62 11, fax 48 87 37 31) is a cozy and friendly place with an elegant breakfast room. On a quiet street, this is one of the best options in the Marais.

For the Marais' most central (this means a busy street), hotel, slip into the turn-of-the-century **Hôtel de Nice** **, and be warmly greeted and well-treated for a very fair price (SBWC-350F, DBWC-400F, TBWC-500F, 42 bis rue de Rivoli, tel. 42 78 55 29, fax 42 78 36 07).

You'll get three stars for the price of two at the exceptionally comfortable **Hotel de Vieux Marais****; it's quiet, friendly, and has a breakfast room you'll melt into (SBWC-385F, DBWC-465F to 505F, TBWC-550F to 665F, tucked away on a small street near the Pompidou Center and the rue du Temple at 8 rue du Platre, tel. 42 78 47 22, fax 42 78 34 32).

Hôtel St. Louis Marais** (SBWC-500F, DBWC-600F to 720F, 40F breakfast, CC:VM) offers a wood-beamed ceiling and antiques-everywhere lobby, but overrated rooms, 1, rue Charles V, tel. 48 87 87 04, fax 48 87 33 26.

Hôtel Pratic* (S-150F, D-230F, DB-275F, DBWC-340F, showers 10F, 25F breakfast, 9 rue d'Ormesson, 75004 Paris, tel. 48 87 80 47, fax 48 87 40 04) has a slightly Arabic feel in its cramped lobby. The rooms are clean and bright, stairs are many, and it's right on a great people-friendly square.

The bare bones and dumpy **Hôtel Moderne** (D-160F, DB-220F, 3 rue Caron, tel. 48 87 97 05), next to Hôtel Pratic, might be better than a youth hostel if you need privacy.

Hôtel de 7ème Art** (DWBC-410F to 470F, 35F breakfast, all with shower, WC, TV, 20 rue St. Paul, tel. 42 77 04 03, fax 42 77 69 10) is a

Hollywood nostalgia place (run by young, hip Marais types) with dull rooms, a full service café/bar and Charlie Chaplin murals.

MIJE "Youth Hostels": The Maison Internationale de la Jeunesse des Etudiants (MIJE) runs three classy old residences in the Marais for travelers under age 30. Each offers simple, clean, single sex, mostly two- and four-bed rooms for 120F per bed, including shower and breakfast. Rooms are locked 12:00 to 16:00 and at 1:00 a.m.. MIJE Forcy (6 rue de Fourcy, just south of the rue Rivoli), MIJE Fauconnier (11 rue Fauconnier), and the best, MIJE Maubisson (12 rue des Barres) share one telephone number (42 74 23 45) and Métro stop (St. Paul). Takes reservations only a few days ahead. MIJE Fourcy offers good 52F dinners.

Marais Helpful Hints: Place des Vosges is Paris's oldest square, and is the heart of the Marais. Victor Hugo lived at #6 (small museum). Rue des Rosiers is the teeming main-street Paris for the Orthodox Jewish community. The new opera house is to the east, and a short wander west takes you into the hopping Beaubourg/Les Halles area. Paris's biggest and best budget department store is BHV, next to the Hôtel de Ville. Marais post offices are on rue Castex, and on the corner of rue Pavée and Franc Bourgois.

The nearest TI is in the Gare de Lyon (arrival level open 8:00-20:00, tel. 43 43 33 24). Neighborhood laundromats are at 40 rue de Roi de Sicile and at 23 rue de Petit Musc. Most banks, shops, and other services are on the rue St. Antoine between Métro stops St. Paul and Bastille.

Sleeping in the Rue Cler Neighborhood (7th district, Métro: École Militaire, zip code 75007): Rue Cler, a village-like pedestrian street, is safe, tidy, and makes you feel like you must have been a poodle in a previous life. How such coziness lodged itself between the high-powered government/business district and the expensive Eiffel Tower and Invalides areas, is a mystery. This is the ideal place to call home in Paris. Living here ranks with the top museums as one of the city's great experiences.

On rue Cler, you can eat and browse your way through a street full of tart shops, colorful outdoor produce stalls, cheeseries, and fish vendors. Plus it's an easy walk to the Eiffel Tower, Les Invalides, and the Seine, as well as the Orsay and Rodin museums.

Hôtel Leveque* (S/D-195F to 225F, DB-290F, DBWC-315F to 360F, TBWC-425F, CC:VM, 29 rue Cler, tel. 47 05 49 15, fax 45 50 49 36 for reservation confirmations, English normally spoken, except by friendly Michele, who is very creative at communicating) is simple, clean, and well run, with a helpful staff, a singing maid, and the cheapest breakfast (25F) on the block. Reserve by phone: leave Visa number. No elevator, right in the traffic-free thick of things.

Paris, Rue Cler Neighborhood

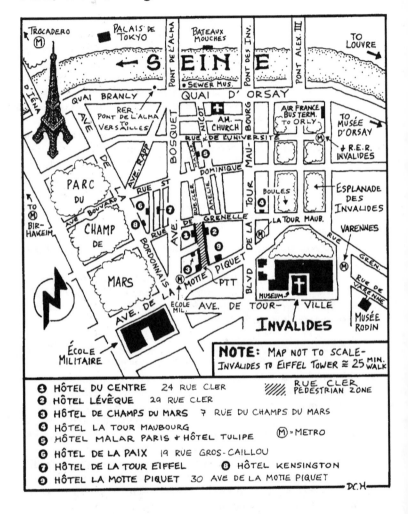

The **Hôtel du Centre*** (D-225F to 250F, DBWC-360F to 390F, TBWC-460F, 30F breakfast, TV, showers 10F, CC:VMA, 24 rue Cler, tel. 47 05 52 33, fax 40 62 95 66), across the street from Leveque, is strange, Edith Bunker-esque, and less welcoming.

The **Hôtel du Champs de Mars**** (DBWC-370F to 425F, TBWC-510F, 35F breakfast, CC:VM, 7 rue du Champs de Mars, tel. 45 51 52 30), with its fine rooms and helpful English-speaking owners, Francoise and Stephane, is a top rue Cler option.

Hôtel la Motte Piquet** (DBWC-330F to 430F, third person-100F, 33F breakfast, CC:VM, 30 avenue de la Motte Piquet, on the corner of rue Cler, tel. 47 05 09 57, fax 47 05 74 36), with a plush lobby and basic, comfortable rooms, is high on gadgets and low on charm.

Hôtel de la Paix** (S-155F, DB-285F to 360F, TBWC-400F, 19 rue du Gros-Caillou, tel. 45 51 86 17) is a well-worn, spartan place, with new beds, bright bed lights, easy telephone reservations, and no elevator. It's run very agreeably by English-speaking Noël.

The best normal three-star hotel in the area is the **Hotel Relais Bosquet**, very sharp and very hotelesque (DBWC-575F to 810F, 53F breakfast, 19 rue de Champs de Mars, just renovated, tel. 47 05 25 45, fax 45 55 08 24).

Hôtel de la Tour Eiffel** (SBWC-320F, DBWC-370F, 25F breakfast, CC:VM, 17 rue de l'Exposition, tel. 47 05 14 75, fax 47 53 99 46), with petite but wicker-pleasant rooms, all with private facilities and TVs, is like a small salad with lots of dressing.

Hôtel Eiffel Rive Gauche** (DWC-F250, DBWC-350F, 410F, and 465F, 35F breakfast, CC:VMA, with TV and phone, 6 rue du Gros-Caillou, tel. 45 51 24 56, fax 45 51 11 77) is an impersonal but decent value on a quiet street, with a tiny leafy courtyard giving the place a little more brightness than average.

Hôtel Malar Paris* (DB-300F, DBWC-370F to 400F, TBWC-430F to 520F, QBWC-600F, 25F breakfast, CC:VM, 29 rue Malar, tel. 45 51 38 46, fax 45 55 20 19), run by friendly Mylene Caill and her husband, is cozy, quiet, and a great value if you don't mind stairs.

If you're willing to pay a smidgen more for quiet, romantic wood-beamed comfort and a pleasant leafy courtyard, try the unusually charming (for Paris) **Hôtel de la Tulipe**** (DBWC-430F to 530F, CC:VM, next to the Hôtel Malar, 33 rue Malar, tel. 45 51 67 21, fax 47 53 96 37), and if you're feeling regal, stay at the *trés* elegant manor-house-like **Hôtel La Tour Maubourg*****(SBWC-450F to 600F, DBWC-650F to 750F, suites for up to four-850F to 1,240F, prices include breakfast featuring freshly squeezed orange juice, tel. 47 05 16 16, fax 47 05 16 14, next to the Invalides, 150 rue de Grenelle).

Hôtel Kensington** (SWC-310F, DBWC-385f-490F, 28F breakfast, extra bed 80F, CC:VMA, 79 Avenue de La Bourdonnais, tel. 47 05 74 00, fax 47 05 25 81), on a stately street closer to the Eiffel Tower, is bigger, more professional, and a fair value. The nearby **Hôtel Royal Phare**** offers small but cheery rooms (DBWC-300F to 380F, 40 avenue de la Motte Piquet, tel. 47 05 57 30, fax 45 51 64 41) and often has rooms when others don't.

Rue Cler Helpful Hints: Become a local at a rue Cler café for breakfast, or join the afternoon crowd for *une bière pression* (a draft beer). Cute shops and bakeries line the rue Cler, and there's a self-serve laundry at 16 rue Cler. The Métro station and a post office with phone booths are at the end of rue Cler, on avenue de la Motte Piquet. Your neighborhood TI is at the Eiffel Tower (open May-September 11:00-18:00, tel. 45 51 22 15). There's a small late-night grocery on rue de Grenelle near the Champ de Mars. You can change money on the rue Cler at the Bank Populaire (across from the Hôtel Leveque).

At 65 quai d'Orsay, you'll find the **American Church and College**, the community center for Americans living in Paris. The interdenominational service at 11:00 on Sunday and the free Sunday concerts (18:00) are a great way to make some friends and get a taste of émigré life in Paris. Stop by and pick up copies of the *Free Voice* and *France-U.S.A. Contacts* newspapers (tel. 47 05 07 99). Information is available for those in need of housing or work through the community of 30,000 Americans living in Paris.

Afternoon *boules* (lawn bowling) on the esplanade des Invalides is competitive and a relaxing spectator sport. Look for the dirt area to the upper right as you face the Invalides.

For a magical picnic dinner, assemble it in no fewer than six shops on rue Cler and lounge on the best grass in Paris (the police don't mind after dark) with the dogs, frisbees, a floodlit Eiffel Tower, and a cool breeze in the Parc du Champs de Mars.

For an after-dinner cruise on the Seine, it's just a short walk across the river over the bridge (Pont d'Alma) to the Bâteaux Mouches. For corn flakes, baked beans, and Cracker Jacks, The Real McCoy (194 rue de Grenelle) is an "authentic" American grocery store. Also, don't miss the chocolate Eiffel Towers at La Maison du Petit Four on 187 rue de Grenelle.

Traveling in France after the tour?

If you plan to reserve hotel rooms in other French cities, remember that from Paris you must first dial 16, followed by the eight-digit number. Once you're outside Paris, just dial the eight-digit number for any other town in France. To call back into Paris from anywhere else in France, dial 16-1, then the eight-digit number.

Train Connections out of Paris

France's rail system radiates from Paris making almost any destination easily accessible.

Paris to Mont St. Michel: 4.5 hrs. via Rennes (2 daily) from Montparnasse station.

Paris to Amboise (Loire Valley): 2½ hrs. direct from Austerlitz station (8 daily).
Paris to London: 3 hours by Chunnel (5 daily). 7½ hrs. by train/boat, 4 times per day.
Paris to Amsterdam: 6 hours, 10 daily (some require a transfer in Brussels). Works well as a night train (11:20 p.m. to 8:00 a.m.) with couchette reservations.

Airport Connections

Taxis are the most convenient (and expensive) way to get to the airport. For two or more people, they can be a good value. Your hotel will call a taxi for you. The meter starts ticking when the taxi heads to your hotel. Rates are higher during the night. Most taxis take three people. Four people need a pricier "grand taxi," which can be reserved by your hotel the night before you leave. We've included approximate prices below. Your guide or escort will give you an update.

The RER (suburban metro) is economical, though more complicated. If you're traveling light, alone, and to Charles de Gaulle airport, it's a good way to go.

The airport bus is most convenient for those staying in the rue Cler neighborhood after the tour and flying out of Orly.

Getting to Charles de Gaulle Airport (tel. 48 62 22 80)

The airport is about 14 miles from Paris. There are two terminals. You'll most likely fly out of terminal 1. (The terminals are connected every few minutes by a free shuttle bus, called a *navette*.)

Taxi: A taxi from your hotel to the airport will cost roughly 230F. Add an extra 50F for night-time (or pre-dawn) travel or for a grand taxi. Allow at least 40 minutes.

RER: Take the métro to the Gare du Nord. Buy a ticket at the RER ticket office (around 45F) to the airport. At the airport stop (Roissy, the end of the line), catch a free shuttle bus (*navette*) to the airport terminal. Allow at least an hour for the entire trip.

Airport bus: Take the métro to the Opera stop. The Air France airport bus leaves from 11 rue Scribe (in front of American Express) every 15 minutes. Allow at least 40 minutes for the bus ride (around 48F).

Getting to Orly Airport (tel. 49 75 15 15)

The airport is 8 miles from Paris. You'll most likely fly out of Terminal Sud.

Taxi: A taxi from your hotel to the airport will cost roughly 175F. Add about 50F for night-time (or pre-dawn) travel or for a grand taxi.

Allow at least 40 minutes.

RER: Because it's complicated (involving metro, RER, and rail transfers), we don't recommend taking the RER to Orly.

Airport bus: Take the métro to Invalides. The Air France airport bus leaves every 15 minutes for the 30-minute ride (around 32F). If your post-tour hotel is in the rue Cler neighborhood (close to the Invalides metro stop), this is a convenient, economical way to get to Orly.

Sleeping at the airports

If you have an early flight, you might want to cuddle up to your plane.

Charles de Gaulle: If you have an early flight, consider sleeping in Terminal 1 at **Cocoon,** 60 "cabins," single 250F, double 300F. Take the elevator down to "boutique level"; it's near the Burger King, tel: 48 62 06 16, fax 48 62 03 21. You get 16 hours of silence buried under the check-in level with TV and WC. The **Hotel IBIS** (at the Roissy Rail station; free shuttle bus to either terminal takes 2 minutes) offers more normal accommodations (400F double with full bath, tel: 48 62 49 49, fax 48 62 54 22).

Sleeping at Orly Airport: The only reasonable hotel is the **IBIS Hotel** (400F double, tel: 46 87 33 50, fax 46 87 29 92), with free frequent shuttle service to the terminal.

If you're enjoying this trip, we haven't finished with you yet...

Our Best of Europe tour is designed to give you a memorable taste of the best that each country has to offer. When your appetite tells you it's time to dig into a fulfilling regional delicacy, remember that ETBD offers a fresh new assortment of in-depth regional tours every year. As a Very Important Back Door Tour Survivor, every summer you'll receive early information on our next year's tours. So if you've enjoyed your taste of the Best of Europe, keep our menu handy. The next course may be even better.

Here's a sampling of regional tours we offer from time to time...

✓ **The Best of France in 21 Days,** fully guided, BB&B, and fully guided "Slow Dance" tours.

✓ **The Best of France & Italy in 21 Days,** fully guided tours from Paris to Rome (and Rome to Paris).

✓ **The Best of Italy in 21 Days,** fully guided and BB&B tours.

✓ **The Best of Germany/Austria/Switzerland in 21 Days,** fully guided and BB&B tours.

✓ **The Best of Turkey in 14 Days,** fully guided tours.

✓ **The Best of Britain in 21 Days,** fully guided and BB&B tours.

✓ **The Best of Ireland in 21 Days,** fully guided tours.

✓ **The Best of Scandinavia in 16 Days,** fully guided and BB&B tours.

✓ **The Best of Spain & Portugal in 21 Days,** fully guided and BB&B tours.

See the latest issue of our free quarterly newsletter for specifics, or call our Tour Desk at 206/771-8303 ext. 17.

Bon appétit!